THE
DEMOGRAPHIC
INVESTOR

FINANCIAL TIMES
MANAGEMENT

About our books

We work with leading authors to develop the strongest ideas in business and finance, bringing cutting-edge thinking and best practice to a global market.

Under the Financial Times Pitman Publishing imprint we craft high quality books which help readers to understand and apply their content, whether studying or at work.

To find out more please visit our website:

www.ftmanagement.com

THE
DEMOGRAPHIC
INVESTOR

Strategies for Surviving
the Pensions Crisis

RICHARD CRAGG

FINANCIAL TIMES
PITMAN PUBLISHING

FINANCIAL TIMES
MANAGEMENT

LONDON · SAN FRANCISCO
KUALA LUMPUR · JOHANNESBURG

*Financial Times Management delivers the knowledge,
skills and understanding that enable students,
managers and organisations to achieve their ambitions,
whatever their needs, wherever they are.*

London Office:
128 Long Acre, London WC2E 9AN
Tel: +44 (0)171 447 2000
Fax: +44 (0)171 240 5771
Website: www.ftmanagement.com

A Division of Financial Times Professional Limited

First published in Great Britain in 1998

© Financial Times Professional Limited 1998

The right of Richard Cragg to be identified as
Author of this Work has been asserted by him in accordance
with the Copyright, Designs and Patents Act 1988.

ISBN 0 273 63736 3

British Library Cataloguing in Publication Data
A CIP catalogue record for this book can be obtained
from the British Library.

1 3 5 7 9 10 8 6 4 2

Typeset by M Rules
Printed and bound in Great Britain by
Biddles Ltd, Guildford and King's Lynn

*The Publishers' policy is to use paper manufactured
from sustainable forests.*

ABOUT THE AUTHOR

Richard Cragg has over 30 years' experience in investment, spanning financial centres in three continents, and has consistently been at the forefront of opening up new and emerging markets to investors. Most recently Senior Executive, Investment Banking Division at Deutsche Morgan Grenfell, his career as a Fund Manager, Analyst and Head of Research has included spells at James Capel & Co, Lyall & Evatt in Singapore and Confederation Life Inc in Toronto. He is the author of two investment books and has been a regular speaker at international finance conferences. He does not ride a motorbike.

For Sandy, Robin,
Carrie and Tim

ACKNOWLEDGEMENTS

This book would have had far rougher edges but for the help of Dr David Coleman. Besides reviewing the demographics sections in great detail and making many important suggestions for their improvement, he also brought to my attention a key research paper that greatly improved my understanding of the immigration debate. Thanks are also due to Andrew Sinclair, Dr John Ermisch and Georges Mathews for supplying research material, Dr David Miles for his encouragement and timely research papers, and to David and Helen Osman, Geoffrey Dennis and Martin Braune for their meticulous proof reading. The errors that remain are my own.

I wish to thank a number of organisations that have allowed me to reproduce their data with their permission. They include: the Council of Europe, DRI/McGraw-Hill, Eurostat, IIASA, IMD World Competitiveness Yearbook, The Institute of Actuaries, InterSec Research Corp., Merrill Lynch, OECD, The Office of National Statistics, Salomon Smith Barney, Oxford University Press, Inc., Transparency International and UBS Asset Management. Crown copyright is reproduced with the permission of the Controller of Her Majesty's Stationery Office.

CONTENTS

Part II
THE ECONOMIC CONSEQUENCES OF DECLINE

Part III
AUSTERITY OR STATE BANKRUPTCY?

FOREWORD

The dominant factor for business in the next two decades . . . is not going to be economics or technology. It will be demographics.

The key factor for business will not be the over*population of the world, which we have been warned of these last 40 years. It will be the increasing* under*population of the developed countries – Japan and the nations of Europe and North America.*

Peter F. Drucker[1]

These two observations lie right at the heart of this book. Within their lifetimes most of its readers will find themselves victims of a demographic juggernaut that has been gathering momentum for decades and will take decades more to stop – if it can be stopped at all. Over the next half century, the populations of Europe, Russia and Japan will fall steeply in the absence of immigration. Birth rates remain stubbornly below replacement levels, despite the best efforts of pronatalist governments to reverse their long-term decline. Moreover, their workforces are falling even faster than the overall population, while the armies of pensioners continue to grow.

I hope to persuade you that these trends are highly damaging not only to the very fabric of European society, *but to your own wealth and health.* Levels of production, consumption and investment will decline, and in the most seriously affected countries, there will be insufficient manpower both to keep the wheels of industry turning – even at lower production levels – and to maintain services for the growing number of sick and elderly at today's standards . . . unless there is a sharp rise in the level of immigration, beginning early next century. *Despite currently high levels of unemployment, Germany may have to contemplate a workforce that is up to 40% immigrant by 2050. The public debate should start now.*

Population decline also makes the cost to governments and workers of paying State pensions progressively more expensive, as fewer workers have to finance the growing army of pensioners. Assuming the same levels of benefits, social security contribution rates could rise by over 100% for countries such as Germany by 2050, encouraging employees to avoid this mounting burden by joining the informal economy, bringing forward the day when the whole State pension system goes bankrupt throughout Europe.

The same factors apply with even greater force to the State health system throughout Europe. The annual cost of treating a person aged 85+ in the UK is around *11 times* that for a child aged 5–15, and the number of the very elderly is rising rapidly. More of the cost of pensions, health care and of looking after the fragile elderly will be borne directly by individuals rather than the State, leading to decades of personal austerity.

By this stage, you may be ready to slash your wrists or seek a sufficiently high building to jump off. Please don't. There is another way, based on the best tradition of self-help, and using the demographic tools that predicted this looming crisis to chart a course for individuals wishing to provide for their future. One of the prime objectives of this book is to supply these tools, and explain how they can be used to create long-term investment portfolios that ideally should deliver their best returns just when they are needed most, when you retire in 20–30 years' time.

How to read this book

The book is divided into four distinct parts. Part I opens by explaining why demography is such a powerful tool in predicting a range of social and economic trends and how demographers do their sums. It then focuses on the factors affecting birth rates, to show why it is possible to make projections so far into the future, why birth rates in the EU will continue to decline and why pronatalist policies have largely failed. Finally it shows that declining birth rates are a worldwide – although not a universal – phenomenon, and that countries as different as China, Thailand and Brazil are already close to, or even below, replacement rate.

Part II explains the economic consequences of population decline, for example, the likely fall in output and consumption and the sectors of the economy most at risk, and it opens up the debate on immigration policy. It predicts a general economic slowdown in the EU and Japan, with consequences for the stockmarket.

Part III projects the soaring costs of pensions, healthcare and the care of the elderly, as population ages. It predicts the likely collapse of the State pension system and national health services throughout Europe, and possibly the accompanying collapse of the single currency. Different countries will encounter very different demographic pressures, and react by imposing very different tax and social security regimes on their populations. For the most demographically challenged, this could mean decades of austerity. Investors, industrialists and workers may logically be expected to vote with their feet and move from high to low tax areas, until the strain in the former becomes intolerable and the system breaks down.

Part IV uses screening techniques that are heavily based on demographics to narrow down an investment universe that should enable investors to construct long-term investment portfolios to provide for the services the State will increasingly be unable to supply. To add some flesh to the bones, this section also reviews the prospects of the major equity markets, both from the standpoint of current competitiveness and their long-term demographic potential, before suggesting a final shortlist of countries for the demographic investor.

Reference

1 Drucker, P. F. (1997) 'Looking ahead: implications of the present', *Harvard Business Review*, Sept.–Oct.

INTRODUCTION

Two futures?

This is a book about the future – yours and your children's. It is therefore a book about possible scenarios. Historians take the fabric of the past and tease out the threads or themes, to find how they are woven together in patterns which explain, say, the causes of war or the Industrial Revolution. This is different – it takes existing trends and tries to extrapolate 20–50 years ahead.

Futurology is a dangerous game, and – some would say – not worth playing. Victorian fears that London would sink into a swamp of horse manure because of the growth of the carriage trade, or that the world would run out of coal now seem absurd. Even The Club of Rome's[1] interactive computer models using the best available data predicted a world of pollution, overpopulation and famine that has been wide of the mark, or at least premature.

Some of these earlier predictions were invalidated by new technologies or discoveries – the automobile and Texan oilfields – but more recent predictions have been sufficiently influential to help bring about their own invalidation, like subatomic particles whose behaviour depends on whether or not they are observed. Their message is 'this is the way things could turn out if nothing is done'. But if the consequences of inaction are so far-reaching that even the most *laissez-faire* government is stung into action, or if entrepreneurs see a new niche to exploit, the predicted crisis point may never be reached.

The AIDS crisis is a case in point. Western governments have sufficiently publicised the risks to cause a change in sexual behaviour that has cut the spread of the disease – although not yet in Africa or Asia – while prospects of reward have spurred the world's drug companies to develop a number of promising treatments. The Club of Rome helped increase awareness of both population and pollution problems and spurred government action on car emissions, CFCs and global warming.

In a way, my position is similar to Pascal's justification for his belief in God; if one is wrong, nothing is lost, but if there *is* a God, the rewards are beyond price. In the case of this book, if enough people believe the key arguments, then it is likely that some measures will be taken to avert their outcome. There are no prizes for being a latter-day Cassandra – making accurate, if gloomy predictions which nobody believes, and hence being powerless to prevent their fulfilment. If this sometimes means writing with more passion and fewer caveats than is considered acceptable by full-time academic demographers, then so be it.

Ideally, therefore, this book will paint a future that you certainly won't like, and which I hope will be proven wrong. But because it does not deal with sudden catastrophe, but with the slow relentless tick of demography, and because it will involve substantial financial sacrifice by almost everyone alive in the West today, it is likely that many politicians, trade unions and pensioners will continue to duck the issues raised. In Douglas Adams' phrase, they become 's.e.p.'s' – somebody else's problems – things you don't see if you don't really want to.[2] Hopefully it will provide the tools for individuals to take charge of their own financial futures, and they will need to as State health and pension schemes crumble throughout Europe.

The book will cover a range of issues, but they are all ultimately linked in to population growth or decline. This gives a certain measure of comfort in that, barring wars or pestilence, for the next 16 (and probably the next 20) years, we know pretty exactly the population of working age and that of the population in retirement. These comprise the main building blocks in my argument. (The key uncertainty arises over predictions about birth rates, but this will affect the argument only later on, say, after 2015.) Many people take on major financial commitments stretching 20–25 years into the future in the form of mortgages. There is no reason why they should not also adopt similarly long-term investment strategies for their retirement.

To persuade you that this is important, before getting into the meat of the argument, I would like to fix your minds on two possible, if highly caricatured, futures which we Europeans could be entering next century. I hope they will convince you that doing nothing is not an option. Over the next 20 years there is an inevitability about the demographics. How you and your political leaders make use of the implications could be the most important factors influencing your family's future.

Scenario I: The death of Europe (ca. AD 2100)

Although he recognised the importance of the task he had been set by the National Museum of the Philippines – that of preserving for posterity some record of the declining civilisation of Europe – Carlos Martinez nevertheless felt depressed as he boarded the plane from Manila to London. He thought about the boneshaking ride he would have to endure to get from the only terminal still operational into the crumbling capital. Throughout Africa, Indonesia and the Philippines, high speed trains made journeys between city centres easy. Not much point for Europe, though. With a population which had halved since the end of the millennium, there was no longer a workforce large enough to maintain the track. Besides, when the Board of Eurotunnel had paid the IRA to blow a hole in the Channel Tunnel to claim the insurance and pay off their massive arrears of debt, the tunnel had been flooded for 20 miles. The contractors and the owners were locked in legal battles specifically designed to prevent decisive action being taken. 'Flood in Channel tunnel – Continent cut off'. Who cares? Few Europeans travelled anyway, these days. Eurotunnel's banks had gone bankrupt, and their only satisfaction had been to have the entire Eurotunnel Board executed for economic sabotage.

This book will cover a range of issues . . . all ultimately linked in to population growth or decline.

Martinez was a cultured man. He had read widely and knew of the huge contribution that Europe had made to the world. How had it fallen to this level only 250 years after the Great Exhibition proclaimed to the world Britain's confidence in its manifest destiny? Throughout the Continent, buildings were abandoned and decaying for want of people to occupy and tend them. The young had emigrated to a better life in Ireland, whose booming economy now boasted a population of 10 million of the brightest and the best. Of those that remained, the largest single source of employment was tending the aged and infirm. Continental Europe had become God's waiting room, although the collapse of the health services meant that the wait was getting shorter. Life expectancy had been declining for a decade. Euthanasia, voluntary or otherwise, was one of the few growth industries.

The population high-water mark had lapped the shores of Europe during the last decade of the 20th century and had receded – gradually at first, but with increasing momentum over the next century. Russia had led the way – a nation of almost 150 million at its peak had given up and died of chronic depression and alcoholism. Those with talent were now in Ireland, Israel or the USA. The Siberian oil and coal cities had been abandoned, as successive Presidents had failed to come to their aid, their unpaid workers fleeing South to scratch a living on the black soils not poisoned by radio-activity from ancient reactors.

Throughout Western Europe, villages and then whole towns had shrunk below viability. Land and property had lost all value. Italy these days just meant Milan, and Spain was just Madrid, their hinterlands reclaimed by forest. The classical south was extinct. In time, he thought, the whole of Europe will become a series of Piranesi tableaux – ragged beggars on the steps of the ruined Notre Dame or St. Paul's – and all because governments failed to take decisive action when there was still time . . .

Scenario II: Switzerland writ large

As he looked out of the window of his panelled office in the heart of the city, Hilmar Kopper III had a problem. How could he invest profitably the 10 billion euro per month that poured relentlessly through the doors of his bank's investment division from the country's booming biotech companies, the Internet providers and hotel chains, and their thrifty employees. At least, he reflected, it was a problem worth having. How different it had been for his grandfather 50 years ago as he had battled to rescue the bank from the worst crisis it had known since the 1930s. The strikes of protest at the collapse of the German welfare state had engulfed the nation. Daimler-Benz had been brought to its knees, and bankruptcies amongst the Mittelstand had rekindled the neo-Nazi movement.

Thank goodness the German people had recoiled from the edge of the abyss. They had rediscovered frugality. Saving for a future denied them by the State, they had poured their pension contributions first into bonds, then as interest rates fell, into German equities. Freed from the bureaucratic shackles and crippling taxes of recent years, entrepreneurs began to flourish. Risk-taking became acceptable. Encouraged by their success in their own market, German investors moved overseas, slowly at first but soon in such volumes that at long last the euro declined from its absurd peak, and like the first swallows of spring, tourists from the Far East began to appear, attracted by Europe's cultural heritage now accessible at reasonable cost.

Throughout Western Europe, villages and then whole towns had shrunk below viability.

Faced with a population decline that could within a century lead to national extinction, the government had finally reacted. Taking money from the budgets for healthcare and from the sale of public sector utilities, Germany had embarked on the most generous pronatalist policy the world had yet seen. You couldn't afford not to have a family. Birth rates had risen above replacement rate and, remarkably, were staying there. No longer did the country need to rely on *Gastarbeiter* to man their factories, thanks to the growing number of young Germans entering the workforce, and the days when the homes of immigrant Turkish workers were targeted by the unemployed were a distant memory. Major capital investments were coming

> *. . . Europe . . . had become a larger version of Switzerland, living rather well off a mix of high technology industries, tourism and investment income.*

from abroad, encouraged by prospects of rising consumption and a sensible exchange rate. Germany was reviving, and the rest of Europe was beginning to follow.

True, all the protected coal mines and much of the industrial base were no more; in particular the producers of consumer goods were unable to cope with previous high wage costs and falling demand as spending declined while savings increased. But exports of investment goods were booming as Asian countries, hit by the steep declines in their own workforces, sought to maximise productivity. Outside the main cities, biotech companies were flourishing, and their royalties from overseas were rising strongly.

All in all, there didn't seem much wrong with a Europe that had become a larger version of Switzerland, living rather well off a mix of high technology industries, tourism and investment income, and whose people, having grown increasingly self-reliant, could look forward to a future free from destitution in their old age.

References

1 The Club of Rome comprises a loose grouping of businessmen, intellectuals and non-elected government officials from a number of countries. It was founded in 1968 with the twin aims of promoting greater understanding of the world's problems, seen as highly interconnected, and stimulating the adoption of new attitudes, policies and institutions to deal with them. Three world models were developed, the first two by Jay Forrester of MIT, and the most sophisticated model, World 3, developed under the direction of Dennis Meadows was presented in the book, *The Limits to Growth* (1972), Potomac Associates.
2 Douglas Adams (1982) *Life, the universe and everything*. Pan Books.

Part I

TOOLS OF THE TRADE

DEMOGRAPHY FOR BEGINNERS

The scope of demography

Demographers are a cautious breed, but they deal with an exciting field for which they are justified in making far larger claims than might be expected from the dictionary definition of their profession:

> **Demography.** n. That branch of anthropology which deals with the life-conditions of communities of people, as shown by statistics of births, deaths, disease, etc. (*Source*: OED.)

Their subject forms a main sinew of the 'hidden hand' that guides economies, and, by extension, the policies of their governments. Its influence pervades every aspect of economic life. Under the bureaucratic heading of 'planning' it may be called upon by government to project demand for new housing or school places, while the private sector may use it to forecast demand for anything from babygrows to Zimmer frames. We are looking at an altogether larger canvas, however, since demographic trends can influence the course of civilisation itself. For past evidence of this, we can look as far back as the expansion of the Greek empire through setting up colonies throughout the Peloponnese, or the major movement of peoples between AD 400 and AD 700 from the steppes of Russia down to the Mediterranean, that brought about the sack of Rome in 410. Both processes had a demographic component – population growth outstripping local food supply, triggering migration into new areas.

Towards the end of the eighteenth century, this concept was seized upon by Malthus, who foresaw that if population continued to increase geometrically – without prudential restraint – while food supply grew only arithmetically, in time countries would be brought to famine and death, possibly leading to civil disorder and even the overthrow of the existing society. The simplicity of the mathematics which underlined the awful inevitability of their conclusions was clear to anyone, and his book, *Essay on Population*, published in 1798, has been a major influence on political thought up to the present day.

Malthus recognised that the ability to support a family was greatly influenced by income, and that while the middle classes might need only a modest adjustment to their lifestyles to provide for larger families the same was not true for the working classes. He campaigned against the operation of the Poor Law, as interpreted by the Speenhamland magistrates, which seemed to him to give the poor a licence to be irresponsible in the size of their families in the sure knowledge that they would be supported by the parish. He believed that a family should be made to feel the effect of a new child financially. Echoes of this can be found in the former UK Conservative government whose ministers railed against unmarried mothers 'sponging' off the State, and in the policies of the present Labour government.

Demography has developed the mathematical tools to create more accurate long-term forecasts of births and deaths, thanks to the statistical work pioneered by Kuczynski in the 1920s. These, computerised and leavened with a number of other variables relating to economic growth, energy consumption, productivity and pollution (all population-dependent), eventually culminated in *The Limits to Growth*. This seminal work of the 1960s, redolent with Malthusian metaphor, heightened public awareness of the problems of untrammelled population growth and became the icon of the Green parties and the steady-state economists, who believed that it was possible to create a flourishing society without the need to increase GDP.

If these examples have helped to establish the historical credentials of demography, what will be its contribution in years to come? It is at its most effective when combined with an economic overlay. This leads to some very thought-provoking conclusions that should influence the strategies of industrialists, fund managers, politicians and workers alike. Central to this book is the projected decline of the European workforce and its consequences.

- In the national sphere, these include:
  - the choice between economic decline or rising immigration, with all its political and social ramifications;
  - the bankruptcy of the State pension system throughout Europe;
  - the soaring cost of healthcare and homecare;
  - the trickle down of inherited property (and the growth of euthanasia?)
- In the private sector it will affect everything from the viability of department stores to the structure of domestic industry, especially the balance between the domestic market and exports, and between consumer and capital goods.
- In *Realpolitik* it will influence the way the rest of the world deals with a Europe that is too diminished to act as world policeman, and is no longer an important market for Asian goods – in short a backwater.

As we shall also see, Europe is likely to become increasingly dependent on Asian – especially Mainland Chinese – savings to fund government debt. We may need long spoons to sup with Chinese dragons, let alone Korean tigers.

Nursery slopes

To get to grips with the book's arguments you must familiarise yourselves with some of the basic ideas in demography and some of the most frequently used terms, starting with babies. This won't hurt.

Any large population will contain women in a whole range of age groups who differ widely from each other in their attitude to families, their social and economic circumstances and their physiological ability to bear children. To make sense of patterns of births, demographers may sort women into age groups, and follow the fertility of each age group over time, calculated as the number of births per 1000 women in each cohort. This is known as the 'age-specific fertility rate' (ASFR). For example, in Table 1.1, which shows the changes in the UK since 1960, the ASFR of 173.5 for the 25–29 age group in 1960 means that, on average, 1000 women in *each* year of age from 24 to 29 would give birth to 173.5 babies.

Table 1.1 Age-specific fertility rates and total fertility rates (TFRs), UK, 1960–93

Year	Live births per 1000 females at specific ages							TFR
	15–19	20–24	25–29	30–34	35–39	40–44	45–49	
1960	33.5	166.7	173.5	104.0	48.9	14.6	0.9	2.71
1965	44.5	178.9	181.6	105.1	50.4	13.3	1.0	2.87
1970	49.1	156.7	155.3	82.2	36.3	9.2	0.6	2.45
1975	36.7	116.1	123.7	59.4	20.9	5.1	0.4	1.81
1980	30.5	113.5	134.9	71.4	23.1	4.5	0.4	1.89
1985	29.5	95.5	122.9	86.5	31.0	5.0	0.3	1.83
1993	30.9	81.8	114.2	86.8	33.8	6.1	0.3	1.76

Source: Office of Population Censuses and Surveys.

It is worth noting at this stage how births in the younger age groups have fallen far more rapidly than those in the 30–34 age group. We will be looking in more detail at the factors influencing this, and how it has affected overall birth rates.

We can look at this data in two distinct ways – taking an instantaneous snapshot of fertility in a given year, known as the 'total fertility rate', or

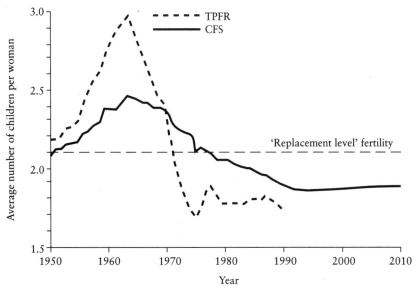

Figure 1.1 1994-based national population projections
Source: Central Statistics Office © Crown copyright 1996.

TFR, or following the fertility of a given cohort across time. (A cohort is a group with a common demographic factor, for example women born in 1945, that is observed over time.) By tracking the fertilities of women born in different years through their reproductive lives, taken as 15–49, we can measure changes in completed family size (CFS) over time, and also in the number of children born to women by a given age.

The TFR for, say 1997, is effectively the number of children that would theoretically be born to a woman throughout her reproductive life, if her fertility rate at all times between the ages of 15 and 49 corresponded exactly to the 1997 fertility rates of women in these age groups. For example, in Table 1.1, it is derived by adding up all the cohort fertility rates per 1000 women, multiplying by 5 (since the ASFR is the average rate for women in a five-year cohort), then dividing by 1000. It is a rough and ready figure and can fluctuate wildly from year to year under the influence of economic conditions, wars and civil unrest. (As we will see later, these mainly affect the decision to start a family in a given year, and the decline in births in one year may be offset later on. Couples with existing children do not face the same decline in living standards and are less sensitive to the timing of a further birth.)

For this reason demographers have tended until recently to prefer CFS as a more stable indicator for predicting future birth rates. It is however a lagging indicator, like a sort of 28-year moving average, as the chart in Figure 1.1 illustrates (28 years corresponds to the average age of motherhood in the UK).

For example, the 1995 number for CFS relates to women who have reached the age of 45 in 1995, that is, the cohort born in the period 1945–50. These women have experienced entirely different social and economic conditions, educational and career opportunities and peer group pressures from those born 20–30 years later. In practice, this has led to TFRs consistently below those predicted from CFS since 1970, and hence to the overestimates of births which have been a feature of demographic projections for a decade or more.

How does population grow?

In general, demographers couldn't care less about boys – it's girls who reproduce. So, from the TFR they first strip out the births of boys to arrive at a figure known as the 'gross reproduction rate', or GRR. This represents the number of girls that would be born to a woman during her lifetime on the basis of that year's birth statistics. (In practically every society, roughly 5% more boys are born than girls, but despite the rigours of motherhood, girls live longer. Taking the 15 countries of the EU, the ratio of females to males rises to 1:1 around age 50, 1.2:1 by 65–69 and 2.7:1 by 85+.)

Not all girls survive to the end of their period of fertility, even in the West. By deducting those deaths (around 1–2% of those born) from the GRR we get the net reproduction rate, or NRR. In concrete terms, an NRR of 1.0 means that a woman will exactly replace herself through the birth of a daughter, and that if NRR remains at that level over time the population will reach stability. In countries in the West, where mortality rates are low, this would equate to a TFR of around 2.10.

An NRR persistently below 1.0 implies a long-term population decline, even if in the short run it is actually increasing. This is not as contradictory as it sounds. Indeed it is actually happening through much of Europe and parts of Asia. An above-average number of women is currently in age groups likely to show the highest birth rates, while rising life expectancies and a relatively small number of elderly is keeping deaths below births.

Of pyramids, pillars and the perils of going pear-shaped

A good way to illustrate visually how populations develop their own momentum is to draw age pyramids, separately showing the number of males and females in successive five-year age groups. The stylised pyramids in Figure 1.2 represent population changes as countries move from high to low fertility – the so-called demographic transition. Since the introduction of mass inoculation of infants against smallpox, and the mass spraying of DDT to combat malaria began in the 1940s, death rates in developing countries have fallen sharply, particularly for women in childbirth. Birth rates themselves have also fallen, but not as steeply and after a lag. NRRs have risen above 1.0 (up to 2.25 in West Africa), resulting in a steady increase in the number of children born in successive

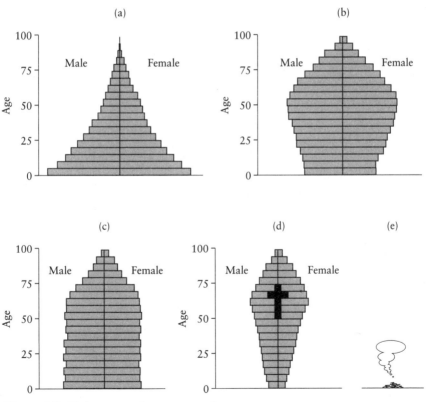

Figure 1.2 Going . . . going . . . gone?

years (*see* Figure 1.2a). The broad base of females below the age of 16 who will shortly enter their reproductive lives ensures that even a drastic decline in fertility rates cannot prevent a strong increase in new births over at least the next 20 years. These births themselves will generate secondary ripples in a further 20 years. By 2025 there will be more females than today below the age of 16 available to start families, although these will be offset by an increasing number in their thirties who will experience far lower birth rates. The pyramid has become truncated, but the relatively low proportion of elderly means that, overall, the total population will continue to grow for many years thereafter.

By contrast, the picture for high-income countries is more of a Chinese lantern (*see* Figure 1.2b), with a prominent thickening between the ages of 20 and 39. (In more detailed age pyramids for European countries and the former USSR, it is possible to detect not only the post-war baby boom of 1946–8 but secondary and tertiary ripples, peaking in 1963 and 1983.) The fact that the large grouping of females in the peak childbearing years (25–29) has singularly failed to arrest the decline in births is our first sign of trouble ahead. By 2000 this cohort will be replaced by ever smaller-sized cohorts, making the job of preventing population decline even harder.

This bulge, travelling slowly through the Chinese lantern like a meal through a snake, will in time disappear out of the top of the chart. Unlike low-income countries, however, there is already a large number of the very old, and this number will rise significantly over the next 30 years. This will have major implications for health and long-term care costs (*see* Chapter 9).

Finally, it should be noted that the World Bank[1] has drawn up its projections on the basis of NRR in all high-income countries recovering to a level of 1.0 by 2035. Should this happen, the bulge eventually disappears, our Chinese lantern becomes a pillar (*see* Figure 1.2c), with almost equal numbers in each cohort and a stable population thereafter. If this fails to happen, as I will be arguing in Chapters 2 and 3 birth rates will be a lot lower. Our pyramid goes pear-shaped, or should I say, 'coffin-shaped' (*see* Figure 1.2d) – and with it, our future (*see* Figure 1.2e).

Reference

1 World Bank, *World Population Projections 1994–95*, p. 14.

MAKING SENSE
OF FERTILITY

Factors affecting birth rates

In the course of this book, we will examine a number of factors thought to influence birth rates. For convenience, although not necessarily in order of importance, they can be set out as follows:

- cultural traditions – e.g., what family size is the norm in a given society;
- availability of State funding or a social framework to support the sick and elderly – and hence the need for descendants;
- the general availability and usage of contraceptive techniques, including abortion;
- factors moulding public opinion and aspirations (e.g., the spread of television);
- episodes of war or civil unrest;
- episodes of steep economic downturn (e.g., the 1930s Depression or the collapse of communism in the USSR and Eastern Europe);
- the impact of large economic burdens on spending power (high mortgages, student loans or saving for retirement);
- extent of cohabitation (regarded as a less stable relationship than marriage);
- impact of government policies designed to encourage or discourage families of a particular size (e.g., Romania and Singapore respectively);
- overall level of education, especially of women;
- changes in the wage differential between men and women;
- change in contraceptive practice due to the AIDS pandemic (e.g., South Africa);
- fall in male fertility attributed to environmental factors;
- homeostasis – an almost mystical belief that somehow human populations, irrespective of culture, religion or economic system, will ultimately return to replacement rate.

These factors do not apply with equal force across all countries. For example, Western countries have long since had the power to determine the size of their families; indeed the fertility rate in the UK began to decline around 1870 – well before the development of reliable contraceptive devices. With the spread of prosperity, education and television, many countries in both Asia and Latin America have undergone a far more rapid and extreme demographic transition from high to low birth rates than has been experienced anywhere in Europe before the collapse of communism. On the other hand, the same cannot be said of much of Africa. Even in Europe, conditions differ markedly between countries, with the pronounced difference in TFRs between Italy and Sweden being ascribed to differences in the level of government support for the family.

An intellectually persuasive theory derived by Easterlin[1] linked birth rates with the family size and economic well-being of the parents in order to explain the way birth rates seemed to follow cycles that oscillated on either side of a long-term trend. It takes as its starting point the view that future economic expectations are conditioned by childhood experiences, and that when they themselves become adults, couples try to reproduce the same relative standard of living. Their prospects of doing so will be influenced not only by the overall level of economic prosperity, but also their wage levels relative to the general workforce. Since competition for jobs is most intense within a given cohort, the larger the relative size of the cohort, the greater the competition, the lower the earnings and ultimately the smaller the family that a couple can afford to raise. On this theory, average family size should oscillate around a trend between generations.

During the 1930s, for example, birth rates fell steeply under the impact of economic conditions, leading to a reduction in the number of school leavers joining the workforce some 15–16 years later. This gradually led to reduced competition for jobs and hence higher real wages than would have been the case if birth rates had been maintained at pre-1930 levels, and ultimately enabled couples to have earlier and larger families than would have been economically prudent in their parents' generation. At some stage in the future, greater competition between members of cohorts born in the boom years will depress family incomes and ultimately, family size – i.e., the cycle starts again.

Such a model nicely explains the post-War UK baby boom when manpower shortages due to low birth rates in the 1930s were aggravated by wartime casualties, enabling a unionised workforce to achieve significant increases in real income, and hence to afford more children. On the other hand, it failed to predict the downturn in birth rates in the UK and West Germany in the 1970s, and there are clearly other factors at work. The most obvious differences in social conditions between the 1930s and the 1970s are:

- the rise of the working woman

- the growing importance of tertiary education as work demands higher skills
- the growth of home ownership.

These factors will be examined in detail later in this chapter.

A more damaging criticism is that one of its fundamental premises – that children from large families tend to produce large families in their turn – is not supported by the evidence. Nor does Easterlin's model explain satisfactorily the steep decline in fertility in, say, Asia, where three decades of strong economic growth have greatly boosted real family incomes, logically enabling them to support ever-increasing numbers of children. The reverse, in fact, has been the case, with TFRs tumbling at an unprecedented rate over the period. Nevertheless aspects of the model have been incorporated in later theories.

It is clear that the factors affecting fertility are complex, *but the view that will be expressed in this book is that a number of those cited above combine to operate as a one-way ratchet that has over time edged fertility rates down to progressively lower levels in a considerable part of the world population, and continues to do so.* (The principal exceptions to this would seem to be the white nations of North America and Australasia; both are currently on plateaux, the one at the higher, the other at a lower level, but in this context, it is worth pointing out that the same could also have been said of the UK, until a further slide began in the 1990s. The assertion that their fertility has stabilised or is actually in a gentle uptrend is not proven.)

The story so far

Until the Industrial Revolution, predicting overall trends in marriages and births seemed a relatively straightforward affair – they followed changes in real wages, admittedly after a decided lag. Since a worker's major item of expenditure was food, specifically bread and beer, a succession of bad harvests which cut availability and raised the price of grain was a key determinant in his ability to support a wife and family.

With new sources of employment opening up, as textile mills and railways spread across the country, this relationship became more complex. UK birth rates peaked around the 1870s, some 20 years after the British empire reached the height of its power, before beginning a long decline. The link between spending power and birth rates reasserted

14

itself with a vengeance during the 1930s. During the Depression, birth rates plummeted because of the lack of a social security net to save families of the unemployed from hardship. Throughout Europe, NRRs fell below 1.0, even in Germany, although British eugenicists may have drawn grim comfort from birth rates of the 'lower orders' having fallen faster than those of the 'ruling classes,' vindicating both Malthus and Darwin in one. Table 2.1 gives a breakdown of births per 1000 for 1911, 1921 and 1931.

Table 2.1 Births per 1000 husbands under 55; wives under 45

Class	1911	1921	1931
Professional/higher business ranks	119	98	94
Lower professional/business ranks	132	104	90
Skilled workers	153	141	120
Semi-skilled workers	158	162	133
Unskilled workers	213	178	153

Source: The Royal Commission on Population.

Perversely, birth rates picked up before the 1939–45 War, as re-armament brought back employment, and persisted at high levels from 1943 onwards. It was felt at the time that once the flurry of marriages with returning soldiers had run its course, they would resume their decline. The Report of the League of Nations on *The Future Population of Europe and the Soviet Union* gloomily concluded that 'In some countries of Western and Northern Europe, the population may never again reach its pre-War size.'

Projections for the population of England and Wales made immediately post-war were heavily influenced by the impact of the 1930s on birth rates. While they correctly concluded that birth rates would subside from the 1947 peak, they failed to factor in the post-war recovery, the scarcity of labour resulting from wartime losses and the depressed birth rates of the 1930s and the success of the newly formed Welfare State which provided some protection from unemployment. As a result, their expectations for birth rates and hence population turned out to be too pessimistic. Indeed, births, which had declined from the 1947 level of 1 million, resumed their uptrend by the mid-1950s, breaching the 1 million level again in 1964, when TFR reached a remarkable 2.95. By that stage it looked as if the UK population could be heading towards 70 million by the end of the century, but as mysteriously as it had begun to rise, birth rate began to decline again, reaching a record low TFR of 1.63 in March 1977.

A key feature during this period was the abrupt, and so far permanent, decline in the number of fourth and higher order births. Between 1965 and 1975, the number of births in that category fell by a staggering 66%. Their proportion of live births fell from 16.6% to 8.2%. That of third children fell by 45%, although the proportion of third children has stabilised at a somewhat higher level (15.7% *vs* the low point of 13.5% in 1975). The era of the two-child family had begun.

For over 20 years, UK births have been running below replacement rate, and after stabilising in a narrow range for around a decade, NRR now seems poised to fall to new lows. What grounds are there for this view, given that even full-time demographers failed to predict both the 1960s boom and the subsequent collapse, and that household surveys held between 1982 and 1989 still pointed to women of all ages between 18 and 29 regarding the 'ideal' family size as being just over two children on average?[2] Indeed, why should birth rates not return to at least replacement levels, as they did after the 1930s?

My argument centres around factors influencing *the age at which a woman has her first child, since this is regarded as the greatest single determinant of final family size.*[3] For example, women in the 1946 birth cohort who had their first child while in the 15–19 age group produced on average 2.8 children by the age of 36, against 1.9 children for those who produced their first child at 28–30.

Table 1.1 shows that over a 33-year period, births to women over the age of 34 comprise a minor part of the total. The reason is partly physiological – the age of peak physiological fecundity is around 23, and it becomes progressively harder to conceive for women over the age of 30. While, therefore women may choose to defer starting a family, for reasons discussed below, in some cases, postponement can become cancellation. Indeed, there has been a steady rise in the number of women who have never had a child (*see* Table 2.2).

Whereas only 15% of women born in 1949 were still childless by the age of 35, over one-quarter of those born in 1964 were still childless at that age. By the age of 45, regarded as the end of a woman's reproductive life, 13% of women born in 1949 were still childless, but it is now projected that around 22% of all women born in 1964 or later will be childless at that age. This implies that those women who do decide to have children will have to produce, on average, 2.7 per

Table 2.2 Percentage of women without any live-born children, UK, 1969–94

Women born in	Age 25	Age 35	Age 45	Approx. end of childbearing
1924	45	18	16	1969
1929	45	17	15	1974
1934	39	12	11	1979
1939	35	12	11	1984
1944	34	12	10	1989
1949	40	15	13	1994
1954	48	20	*17	1999
1959	55	23	*19	2004
1964	60	*28	*22	2009
1969	61	*29	*22	2014

* Projections (see Table 2.3)
Source: Population Trends No. 85, Autumn 1996, Office for National Statistics © Crown Copyright.

woman in order to achieve overall replacement rate – a prospect now looking increasingly unlikely.

The figures are considerably higher than their equivalent in other European countries. For example, the family inquiry associated with the 1990 French census established that 12% of the 1960 generation and 14% of the 1965 generation were childless.[4] The table is also further confirmation that one shouldn't believe everything one is told. The same GHS enquiry about 'ideal' family size revealed that over the six-year period 1982–4 to 1988–9, a maximum of 8% of women interviewed expected to have no children.

The fact that the average age of women at the birth of their first child has risen steadily throughout Europe for at least 25 years clearly contributes to the problem (see Table 2.3).

Table 2.3 Mean age of women at birth of first child

Country	1970	1980	1993
France	23.8	24.9	*27.4
Former W.Germany	24.3	25.2	27.6
Ireland	25.3	24.9	27.6
Italy	25.1	25.1	27.4
UK	23.5	24.4	26.2

*1992
Source: Recent Demographic Developments in Europe, Council of Europe, 1995.

The trend shows no sign of halting: indeed in 1996, the average age of a woman at the birth of her first child in the UK *within marriage* had reached 28.8 – the highest recorded since 1938.

As mentioned earlier, the large cohort of women now in the peak fertility 25–29 age group will be replaced by substantially smaller cohorts over the next decade, implying a significant fall in births, other factors being equal.

No kids please – I'm feeling insecure

Of course, saying that birth rate has been depressed because of a steady rise in the age at which women start their families is more descriptive than explanatory. The question is why this trend has taken place at all. Attempts to correlate birth rates with, say, levels of unemployment, changes in real disposable income or overall consumer confidence have met with little success over the past few decades. The themes I wish to advance below take into account the growing feeling of job insecurity throughout the Continent, the high cost of home ownership, which forces a trade-off between work and motherhood, and the perceived need of women to secure a degree of financial independence to insulate themselves from the growing risk of marriage breakdown – principally through higher educational attainment.

To set the scene, it is worth quoting from the 1997 *Survey of Employment Satisfaction in Europe* conducted by International Survey Research (ISR) Ltd, comparing 1997 responses to those of its 1990 survey. Whereas the proportion of favourable responses remains high, particularly for job satisfaction, working relationships, operation efficiency, company identification, safety and working conditions:

. . . feelings of employment security are in free fall throughout Europe. This trend is particularly significant in Germany, Belgium, Italy, France and the UK. However concerns about their future security are now endemic amongst employees in all the major economies of Europe.[5]

Are these fears exaggerated? According to a UK government-supported study by Business Strategies on the future of work, by far the majority of workers will still be in full-time employment by 2005 (*see* Table 2.4).

At the same time there is increasing evidence of the use of short-term contract labour in businesses subject to strong swings in demand – for example, chocolates in the run up to Christmas, lawn mowers in spring or ice cream in summer. Besides getting the flexibility to meet demand,

Table 2.4 UK employment by tenure, 1985–2005

Type of employment	1985 %	1995 %	2005 %
Permanent	84	82	79
Part-time	21	24	25
Self-employed	11	13	13.5
Temporary	5	6	8

the employer benefits from lower stock levels, lower overheads and in most cases is not required to contribute to pensions. As we shall see, with growing recognition that the UK State pension will become increasingly inadequate over the next half century, the lack of occupational pensions in such jobs will only add to a feeling of insecurity.

The major restructuring that took place in the UK in the 1980s and 1990s and was responsible for the sharp improvement in labour productivity is now forcing its way into Europe. A sign of the times is the huge upsurge in management buyouts (MBOs) takeovers and mergers in Germany, adding to job uncertainty.

In Spain, labour laws have been so restrictive that employers refuse to hire permanent workers they cannot dismiss if business conditions deteriorate. As a result, unemployment remains high at over 20%, and the only work available is on the basis of short-term contracts which employers are not obliged to renew on expiry. This inability to secure a stable long-term source of income hardly gives couples confidence to set up home and start a family. *It is not surprising that TFR hit a low of 1.15 in 1996, implying that, if maintained, the population could halve in little more than a generation.*

The growing feeling of job insecurity seems likely to continue throughout the Continent for several years to come, despite the efforts of governments to force companies to preserve jobs.

We shall now examine how economic pressures, the revolution in higher education and changes in employment patterns can affect birth rates.

Economic pressures: are mortgages bad for babies?

The reason for focusing specifically on this particular component of household expenditure is that it is the one on which it is impossible to economise, once committed. If times are hard, one can stop eating out, buy cheaper food, postpone buying a new suit or replacing the car or washing machine, but monthly mortgage payments must be made at all costs.*

In the UK a number of financial factors have enabled young adults to buy their own homes at a comparatively early age, and it is precisely the age group that up to now has been the most likely to start a family that has taken the major commitment of a house and mortgage. Thanks to the availability of cheap long-term finance from mortgage companies, tax credit on mortgage interest, low transaction costs and government moves to widen home ownership, the British have taken to homebuying in droves. A strong additional reason has been the fear of not having a foot on the ladder during a period when high inflation resulted in negative borrowing costs in real terms.

Older households have higher incomes and are also more likely to have repaid their mortgage and own their property outright (*see* Table 2.5).

Table 2.5 Financing of owner-occupied property, 1994–5 by age of head of household

	<25	25–29	30–44	45–59	60–64	65–69	80+
Owned outright	1	1	4	21	49	57	54
Owned with mortgage	24	55	65	56	27	7	2
Rented	75	44	31	23	24	36	44
	100	100	100	100	100	100	100

Source: Living in Britain, Table 11.9(a), 1994, Office for National Statistics © Crown Copyright.

The move into homebuying has resulted in a steady increase in the share of household income spent on housing – up from around 12.5% in 1971 to 16% in 1982, a level since broadly maintained. Between 1985 and 1989, the price of an average dwelling more than doubled, and the combination of rising house prices and rising mortgage rates pushed

* It might be argued that, even if currently two-thirds of British homes are being bought, I am ignoring the importance of the one-third who rent. The point is that those males who rent are far more likely to be single, widowed or divorced rather than married; according to the 1994 GHS Survey, 79% of households headed by a married male owned their property, with only 21% renting, *vs* 33% for the general population.

home-buyers into an increasingly onerous position. As a percentage of average income, annual mortgage repayments for both first-time buyers and moving owner-occupiers rose steadily from 12% and 14% respectively in 1971 to 25% and 35% at the 1990 peak, admittedly with wide fluctuations along the way. Over the same period, tax relief on mortgages (MIRAS) has been steadily cut back by successive governments, thereby raising the net cost to borrowers.

Financial pressures caused by the ballooning of repayments after 1989 led to a sharp increase in mortgage arrears and in the number of homes being repossessed. The number of net new mortgages taken out each year has also slowed down sharply since 1991. The 1993–4 *Survey of English Housing* found that 6% of homeowners buying through a mortgage were in arrears with a further 14% experiencing difficulty, although not actually in arrears. Altogether, some 1.5 million households were having problems in this area, with problems being greatest for those who bought in 1989 and 1990; around 25% of these were either in arrears or in financial difficulty. Even though employment prospects have improved substantially since then, it could have taken some years to eliminate accumulated arrears, leading to postponement or even cancellation of a family. By 1996/7, the proportion of mortgagees in arrears was still 3%.

Since by far the majority of mortgages is in joint names, the scope for trading employment for motherhood might be expected to decline sharply during such periods, and this has been confirmed by studies. For example, a report for the Rowntree Foundation[6] noted a strong negative correlation between housing costs and the number of first births, but not for births of second children, reflecting the fact that the decline in living standards resulting from starting a family is far more pronounced than in the case of a couple with an existing child increasing the size of their family.

This ties in also with the fact that the major decline in births to women in the 20–29 cohort was offset by a rise in birth rates of the 30–39 cohort. It could reasonably suggest that the former were finding growing financial difficulties as a result of mortgages recently acquired, while older houseowners had escaped from that position. Certainly *Family Spending Surveys* show that households whose heads are under 30 devote a significantly higher portion of household expenditure to housing than do households headed by older people. In 1995–6 housing represented around 19.6% of expenditure in households headed by persons under 30, *vs* 18.2% for those headed by 30–49-year-olds and only 13.5% for those headed by 50–64-year-olds. In the early 1990s, the contrast was even more extreme (*see* Table 2.6).

Table 2.6 Net housing expenditure as % of average weekly expenditure by age of head of household

	<30	*30–49*	*50–64*	*65–74*	*75+*	*All*
1996–7	18.4	17.2	12.8	13.4	16.0	15.9
1995–6	19.6	18.2	13.5	14.1	14.0	16.7
1994–5	20.4	17.7	13.0	13.4	15.0	16.4
1993	20.3	17.5	13.1	12.3	16.0	16.2
1992	22.0	18.7	14.2	13.3	15.8	17.4

Sources: Family Spending 1992 to 1996–7, Office for National Statistics © Crown Copyright.

Over the period 1991–5 the ratio of average house prices to average wages has experienced a dramatic decline to levels last seen 20 years ago, but this has been offset by rises in other housing costs, keeping the ratio of housing to total expenditure close to its recent peak. The combination of low wage inflation, negative equity, persistent arrears to be repaid and lingering feelings of job insecurity kept the housing market subdued until mid-1996. House prices recovered by some 8% in 1996, a further 7.7% in 1997 and mortgage lenders expect a 5% rise this year.[7] (The rise in prices has been strongest in the south, where demand has been buoyed by sharply rising salaries and bonuses in the City. Elsewhere, prices have risen by far less. Even so, the rises are above the rate of wage inflation, and this, combined with rises in mortgage rates and council taxes will again raise the proportion of household income spent on housing, which may hinder a recovery in birth rates.)

If it is accepted that birth rate is sensitive to major identifiable costs such as housing, then might it also be affected by other such items? Later on we will see just such a long-term burden looming over the horizon in the form of soaring State pension and health care costs.

Margaret Thatcher and the working woman

The election of a Conservative government in 1979 opened up a period of traumatic and fundamental change within British industry, both public and private. The power of the unions was greatly curtailed, enabling managers to rationalise manning levels and introduce new technologies previously denied them. The coal industry was run down amid increasingly ineffective protests from the miners; British Steel and British Airways were privatised and began the transformation that made them bywords for efficiency and service. What Thatcher didn't do, a strong currency did. Productivity soared, but at the cost of employment, especially in the more highly paid male-dominated industries. The government had promoted home ownership, on the view that a property-owning nation was more likely to vote Tory, but it left a growing number of homes at risk, because an unemployed husband couldn't pay the mortgage.

The same government steadily tightened the conditions to be fulfilled to qualify for unemployment benefit, while the actual benefit levels also fell in real terms. Industry closures have borne down most heavily on manual workers, and it is at least plausible to believe that the combination of unemployment – either actual or anticipated – and the depression of real incomes have contributed to the sharp decline in working class fertility. As we shall see, women are becoming less keen to marry or cohabit with, and start a family with, a male who is unemployed or whose job prospects are uncertain.

The combination of rising male unemployment, reduced benefits and the need to service mortgages has made household income increasingly dependent on that of the wife. Fortunately, as male manual jobs were swept away, so opportunities were created in industries requiring dexterity rather than strength, or in services where women would not be at a competitive disadvantage. Throughout Europe, women have been entering the workforce in increasing numbers, a trend we can measure through participation rates. This represents the proportion of the population in particular age groups that is either employed or actively seeking work (*see* Table 2.7). Table 2.7 shows that the USA, which has been one of the most successful countries in arresting the fall in male participation rates, has also recorded one of the best trends in female participation rates, over the period.

While there is a nice symmetry about participation rates for many countries – the fall in male participation being roughly balanced by the rise in female rates – this does not necessarily represent a direct substitution. Blastfurnacemen are not losing their jobs to women. On the other hand, women are occupying a growing number of professional and managerial positions. In October 1996 the glass ceiling to the boardroom was shattered when Pearson became the first of the FTSE-100 Companies to

Table 2.7 Participation rates (all age groups) by country, 1975–94

Country	Males					Females				
	1975	1980	1985	1990	1994	1975	1980	1985	1990	1994
Canada	87.2	87.5	86.2	86.5	83.7	50.5	58.4	63.8	69.2	68.5
USA	88.7	88.5	87.8	88.3	87.5	55.0	61.5	65.6	69.8	70.5
Japan	89.7	89.0	87.8	88.1	90.5	51.7	54.9	57.2	60.4	62.1
Australia	89.9	87.6	85.0	85.6	84.1	49.7	52.5	54.1	61.9	62.4
France	84.9	83.0	78.1	75.6	74.5	53.0	56.0	56.1	57.6	59.6
Germany	87.3	84.3	82.3	80.8	78.0	50.8	52.8	52.9	57.0	60.8
Ireland	91.1	88.7*	85.5	80.4	78.5	34.8	35.8*	36.7	43.3	46.1
Italy	79.2	80.6	77.2	76.0	73.5	29.8	38.9	40.5	44.4	42.5
Spain	91.0	88.8	83.0	79.3	78.0	33.8	33.8	34.8	42.2	45.8
Sweden	91.0	89.8	87.5	87.6	82.2	68.9	75.8	79.7	82.7	76.6
UK	na	na	75.7	75.4	72.7	na	na	49.4	53.1	52.8

*1981

Source: © OECD 1973–93 Labour Force Statistics. Reproduced by permission of the OECD.

appoint a female CEO. The new Labour government contains 120 women MPs. It is too soon to say whether this latter might have any impact on measures that could benefit families – there seems no correlation between the number of women MPs and TFRs in Western Europe, unless the position of the UK is considered anomalous (see Table 2.8).

Table 2.8 Women MPs and fertility rates by country

Country	% women MPs (1997)	TFRs	
		1991–4	1995
UK	18 (up from 9)	1.78	1.71
Germany	26	1.32	1.24
Netherlands	32	1.59	1.53
Sweden	40	2.04	1.74

In view of what has been said about the economic pressures bringing British women into the workplace, it may seem surprising that overall participation rates, though rising, are still below those in many other countries. In fact, it represents the results of two opposing trends – a sharp rise in participation by women in the 25–29 age group offsetting a decline in that of the 15–19 age group, the result of a marked swing to higher education over the past five years. Similar trends for 16–19-year-olds are evident throughout Europe, though not in the USA. (Don't take the figures in Table 2.9 too literally when comparing differences between countries; the classification is not uniform, but the *trends* are significant.)

Table 2.9 Female participation rates 1984–93 by country and age group

Country	Year	16–19	20–24	25–34	35–44
UK	1984	66.0	71.6	60.9	70.5
	1990	67.9	75.5	70.0	76.2
	1993	58.0	71.2	70.7	76.8
France	1984	13.7	67.0	72.1	69.3
	1990	8.1	57.6	76.1	74.3
	1993	5.9	49.7	77.7	77.7
Germany	1984	39.6	71.1	62.0	60.3
	1990	34.8	72.7	66.3	66.4
	1993	32.8	72.0	71.7	73.5
Spain	1984	34.3	55.9	45.1	30.8
	1990	31.2	61.4	60.8	45.1
	1993	25.8	57.7	65.1	52.4
USA	1984	51.8	70.4	69.8	70.1
	1990	51.8	71.6	73.6	76.5
	1993	49.8	71.3	73.6	76.7

Source: © OECD, 1973–93 Labour Force Statistics. Reproduced by permission of the OECD.

These trends are expected to persist well into the next century. The continuing trend to further and higher education will produce a corresponding decline in participation rates in the 16–24 age group, which will be offset as these newly qualified graduates join the workforce to put their studies into practice, enjoy the rising pay differential over less qualified workers and, perhaps, repay their accumulated student loans. They will be helped in this by the fact that the size of the 25–44 age group will show little growth for the foreseeable future.

These forecasts show the UK in a favourable light with a modest growth in the workforce over the next decade. As we move towards the middle of the next century, we will see a growing gap opening up between the size of the UK workforce and those of its European neighbours which if properly appreciated could be an increasingly important competitive advantage.

The growing participation of women whilst that of men declines means that by 2006, women will represent 46% of the civilian workforce against 37% in 1971 and 44% in 1993. The crucial role played by

Table 2.10 Projections for labour force and participation rates

	16–24	25–44	45–59	60–64	65+	Total
	Labour force – Great Britain (000)					
1984(E)	6214	12 201	7077	1252	429	27 172
1994(E)	4710	14 301	7922	1051	437	28 421
1996(F)	4404	14 609	8227	1049	429	28 717
2001(F)	4313	14 893	8748	1105	409	29 469
2006(F)	4519	14 609	9252	1295	416	30 092
	Participation rates – UK (percentages)					
Males						
1984(E)	81.8	96.1	90.0	57.5	8.7	75.9
1994(E)	75.1	94.1	86.1	51.0	7.6	72.6
1996(F)	72.4	94.2	86.4	50.4	7.5	72.2
2001(F)	70.3	94.4	85.3	49.7	7.0	71.5
2006(F)	69.3	94.2	83.7	49.1	6.8	70.0
Females						
1984(E)	69.1	65.6	63.3	21.8	3.1	49.2
1994(E)	64.6	73.5	69.3	25.3	3.2	53.0
1996(F)	63.6	74.8	70.4	26.6	3.0	53.7
2001(F)	63.3	77.8	71.9	29.0	2.8	55.5
2006(F)	63.2	81.3	72.6	31.9	2.9	56.7

(E) = Estimate   (F) = Forecast
Source: New Earnings Survey, Office for National Statistics © Crown Copyright 1998.

women throughout Europe in providing household income was high-lighted by a recent Mori[8] survey conducted on behalf of a US charity, Whirlpool Foundation, in France, Germany, Britain, Italy and Spain. This revealed that 59% of employed women polled provided 50% or more of their household income. In France and Germany, more than one in three women supplied all the household income.

Women's independence: you can't trust a man

Up to now, we have looked at rising female participation as responding to the need to preserve household incomes in the face of rising mortgage costs, but there is another aspect to work – security. Awareness of the growing frequency of marital breakdown, with the attendant risk of being left in poverty, is one of the factors driving women to plan their own futures financially independent from men. (This is somewhat ironic, since there is a strong correlation across Europe between the percentage of women in employment and their divorce rate; by getting a job, a woman is more likely to risk the divorce she fears.)*

As an example of this wish for financial independence, the proportion of new mortgages advanced by building societies to women under their own names has risen from 10% in 1983 to 18% in 1994 and has remained at high levels ever since. The corollary to this is that the need to remain in employment to service the mortgage becomes paramount. In other words, it is very much more difficult for a single woman to service a mortgage and start a family, a factor which may help explain growing childlessness in the under-thirties. (By contrast, mortgages in joint names normally take only a portion of the wife's earnings into account in calculating the size of the advance.)

The passport to achieving this independence is *education*.

The revolution in education

Until comparatively recently, many countries in the West paid relatively little attention to some very basic questions about the education they provided. Up to what standard and age should the State provide education? Should it be made relevant to the needs of employers? How can standards be raised? Within Europe, it was mainly the Germans who gave education a practical relevance through the apprenticeship system. The British, who had built an industrial revolution through the labours of untrained amateurs, thought this an all-too-earnest approach; education

---

* The option of cohabitation seems even less satisfactory for stability, since the relationships are less permanent and break up more frequently, but this has not impeded their growth. Between 1979 and 1994, the percentage of women aged 18–49 who were married fell from 74% to 57%, while those remaining single rose from 18% to 29%. Roughly one in three single women aged 25–34, the age group in which most births take place, is cohabiting. By 1996, 35.5% of all births were outside marriage, and there was a marked difference in the mean age of motherhood, 25.8 *vs* 29.6 for births within marriage. Despite the strong rise in the proportion of births outside marriage, however, it seems unlikely that the overall fertility rate will be driven up by this. For a start, the mean age of mothers giving birth outside marriage has been rising at the same rate as for those who are married. Moreover, the determination of the present government to target single mothers by tightening the benefit system may act as a deterrent to early births.

was to teach people how to think, not to equip them for the workplace. Besides the employers were not prepared to spend money to provide training.

Globalisation and the growing economic strength of the countries of the Far East changed the views of Western governments who increasingly began to see a correlation between economic success and the academic achievements of their children. Both overseas and domestic capital investors made it clear that availability of a skilled educated workforce was a high priority for any company seeking to establish a new factory. From the 1960s onwards, international league tables were compiled to pinpoint the deficiencies in the existing system and to find ways of narrowing the impressive lead of such countries as Japan, Singapore and South Korea in mathematics and the sciences.

To the chagrin of teachers, the data so far suggests that there is little correlation between achievement in these subjects and spending per pupil (on a purchasing power parity basis), class size or the amount of time devoted to teaching a particular subject – which leaves the methods and quality of teaching itself. In the UK at least, the system is being shaken up, with pass rates improving at both GCSE and A-levels, courses being made more relevant to future employers and the number of places in further and higher education expanded substantially. Indeed, the latest survey of 13-year-olds in 41 countries, the *Third International Maths and Science Study* (TIMSS), puts England close behind Germany and above the USA in maths, and substantially above both in science scores.

Better teaching, leading to success in GCSEs, may encourage pupils to remain at school for A-levels and possibly to progress to university. The publication of school league tables clearly gives teachers an incentive to raise pass rates. Could this, unwittingly, reduce the nation's fertility rates?

Education and family size

Women's education is as bad for babies, or at least for family size, as mortgages are, since it not only defers the start of a family, but leads to smaller families. Table 2.11 suggests that whereas, for the earlier cohort, higher educational achievements led only to a deferment of births (and, indeed, a catch-up with less qualified mothers by the end of fertility), a widening gap has developed for the younger cohort which is unlikely to be made up over the remaining 15 years.

Further and higher education: more pressure on birth rates?

At school, female students have steadily closed the gap in qualifications received compared to those of males. By 1980/1 they had surpassed boys in their GCSE grades and in A-levels by 1990/1 (*see* Table 2.12).

In Scotland, where educational standards are higher, the gap has become even wider (*see* Table 2.13). *Is it just a coincidence that Scotland's TFR, which was higher than England's until 1980 has since fallen well below it – or do exam results hold the key? If so, will England's TFR fall in time to Scotland's level of 1.52?*

Table 2.11 Mean number of children born by specific ages of women by women's year of birth and highest qualifications attained

| Women's year of birth | Highest qualification attained | | | | |
	A-level	GCSE grades A–C	Other	None	Total
Mean number of children born by age 20					
1940–4	0.04	0.19	0.12	0.24	0.16
1950–4	0.05	0.14	0.15	0.39	0.21
Mean number of children born by age 25					
1940–4	0.56	0.78	0.98	1.24	1.01
1950–4	0.34	0.71	0.82	1.29	0.82
Mean number of children born by age 30					
1940–4	1.41	1.58	1.77	2.02	1.80
1950–4	0.98	1.37	1.50	1.92	1.47
Mean number of children born by age 45					
1940–4	2.05	2.03	2.19	2.46	2.28

Source: 1991 General Household Survey, p. 231, Table 11.11, Office for National Statistics © Crown Copyright 1991.

Table 2.12 Qualifications attained in England

| | Males | | | Females | | |
	1980/1	1990/1	1993/4	1980/1	1990/1	1993/4
3 or more A-levels	10	13	14	8	14	15
1 or more A-level	16	21	21	15	23	23
5 or more GCSE grade A–C	24	36	39	26	44	48
1 or more GCSE grade A–C	50	63	64	55	73	75
1 or more GCSE grade A–G	87	95	91	90	95	93

Source: ibid.

These achievements have provided the springboard to further and higher education, particularly to females (*see* Table 2.14).

Table 2.13 Qualifications attained by region 1993/4

	2 or more A-levels		5 or more GCSE grades A–C	
	Males	*Females*	*Males*	*Females*
England	18	20	39	48
Wales	20	19	35	44
Scotland	24	31	45	56

Source: Office for National Statistics © Crown Copyright 1991.

Table 2.14 Female participation rates in further and higher education

	1980/1		1985/6		1990/1		1994/5	
	F	*P*	*F*	*P*	*F*	*P*	*F*	*P*
Further education								
Age 16–18	11.1	12.0	13.6	18.6	17.0	14.8	27.3	11.5
19–20	1.3	11.2	1.6	12.4	2.2	13.1	3.8	12.5
21–24	0.5	14.9	0.5	15.6	0.7	17.1	1.4	16.6
Higher education								
Age 16–18	3.0	0.2	3.2	0.2	4.9	0.3	8.0	0.2
19–20	9.8	0.9	11.4	1.0	14.9	1.2	26.6	1.0
21–24	2.9	1.0	3.4	1.1	4.5	1.5	8.4	1.8

*F = full time; P = part time
Source: UK Education Statistics 1995. Crown Copyright is reproduced with the permission of Her Majesty's Stationery Office.

Between 1980 and 1995, the number of university students doubled from 827 000 to 1.659 million, but most of the growth has been telescoped into a fraction of that time. In the three years to 1993/4 the number of full-time students in higher education rose by 40% and of those in further education by 50% – a rate of growth greater than that of the preceding decade, and from a higher base. The report of the Dearing committee released in July 1997 envisages participation rates increasing further to 45% of school leavers, permitting a further 300 000 undergraduates to enter higher education by 2015.

To finance this expansion undergraduates will be required to repay tuition fees of £1000 per annum in addition to maintainance grants, and they are likely to graduate with debts of £8–10 000 to be repaid out of income when their annual salary exceeds a threshold level. While it is too early to assess the impact of the upsurge in female enrolment in further and higher education since 1990, we can argue by analogy from what has been experienced by women with qualifications up to A-level. Even though graduates earn 11–14% more than non-graduates, such a burden could well discourage women from starting a family within a short time of graduation – the outstanding loan continues to compound at a real rate of interest. *Research shows that the fertility rate of US graduates is roughly 25% below the US national average[9]: as the UK reaches its target of 45% participation rate in higher education, and student debts accumulate, the pressure on birth rates could intensify.*

The rewards of education, better jobs . . .

Qualifications improve chances in the job market for both men and women (*see* Table 2.15). They also lead to higher pay (*see* Table 2.16).

Table 2.15 Highest qualification level attained

	Higher education	A-level or equivalent	Other	No qualifications
	%	%	%	%
Men 16–64				
Working	87	87	79	64
Unemployed	6	8	10	12
Inactive	7	5	10	23
Women 16–59				
Working	82	76	70	56
Unemployed	3	8	6	5
Inactive	14	16	24	39

Source: General Household Survey 1994, p. 226, Table 10.6(a) and (b) © Crown Copyright 1996.

There seems to be a trend developing of more qualified women gaining ground, less qualified women losing ground. Clearly the incentives to succeed through gaining higher qualifications are increasing. Thanks to their rising qualifications, women have improved their position in the market, and have moved steadily up from semi-skilled status to that of employers, managers and professionals (*see* Table 2.17).

Between 1981 and 1993, the number of women employed in managerial and administrative positions rose by over 100%, while those in professional categories rose by 40.5%. According to studies carried out

Table 2.16 Usual gross weekly earnings by highest qualification attained (Median income, £, of persons in full-time employment)

	Degree or Equivalent		Higher education below degree level		A-level or equivalent		GCSE grades D–G or equivalent*		No qualifications	
	1995	1994	1995	1994	1995	1994	1995	1994	1995	1994
Men	473	464	363	346	318	302	285	240	250	240
Women	363	355	312	297	229	225	206	185	167	161
Women % Men	76.7	76.5	86.0	85.8	72.0	74.5	72.3	77.1	66.8	67.1

* Also commercial qualifications including apprenticeships
Source: General Household Surveys 1994/5, Office for National Statistics © Crown Copyright 1996.

Table 2.17 Breakdown of employment by sex and socio-economic class, 1975–94

	Men			Women		
	1975	1985	1994	1975	1985	1994
Professional	5	6	7	1	1	2
Employers/managers	15	19	21	4	7	11
Intermediate/junior non-manual	17	17	17	46	48	48
Skilled non-manual and own account non-professional	41	37	35	9	9	8
Semi-skilled manual and personal service	17	16	14	31	27	22
Unskilled manual	5	5	5	9	7	9

Source: General Household Surveys 1994/5, p. 39, Table 2.32, Office for National Statistics © Crown Copyright 1996.

by the University of Warwick,[10] the trend will continue until at least the end of the century. There will be a further pronounced increase in the number of women in the above categories between 1993 and 2001 – by 38.5% and 33.1% respectively – while the number in clerical and secretarial positions is expected to remain stable. The proportion of all jobs in the managerial/administrative and professional categories held by women is projected to rise from 34.3% to 39.9% and from 40.7% to 43.9% respectively over the period.

Accordingly, the steady improvement in the ratio of women's weekly earnings relative to those of men, which has taken place since the Equal Pay Act of 1976, seems set to continue (*see* Table 2.18).

Table 2.18 Ratio of women's to men's gross hourly wages (%)

	Median		Highest decile	
	1987	1997	1987	1997
Manual	70.1	70.6	68.0	70.4
Non-manual	61.5	70.2	61.4	69.1

Source: New Earnings Survey, Tables A29.1, A29.2, 1997, Office for National Statistics © Crown Copyright 1997.

. . . fewer births

This turns out to be a very important trend when it comes to explaining a couple's decision to start a family. To understand why, you must forget love of children and think of the decision in purely commercial terms. Your family is simply another form of consumer durable, with high maintenance costs. Each partner in the couple contributes human capital to the child in the form of goods or time, financed by income from employment. The father's income is unaffected by the birth of a first child, since he will only rarely be required to trade his time at work (and hence his income), for minding a child. Furthermore, the higher his earning power, the greater amount of goods he can bestow on the children, or – the more children he can support for a given minimum standard of living.

On the other hand, the higher the mother's income, the greater the loss in purchasing power as she leaves employment to have children and becomes a housewife. Research which correlates births with relative pay (women's hourly pay divided by men's) for the period 1952–85 confirms this: the higher the woman's net relative wages, the lower the likelihood of birth.[11] This applies almost irrespective of age group or birth order, and this factor has been primarily responsible for the decline in British fertility during this period. Specifically, the analysis shows that *a 10% increase in women's pay relative to men's would reduce average family size by about 0.1 children.*

(Another spin-off from the increasing participation in higher education is that investment in children no longer ends at 16 but is likely to continue into their early twenties, raising the opportunity cost of children even more.)

Data from the New Earnings Survey (April 1996) shows women's hourly rates as a percentage of men's (*see* Table 2.19).

Table 2.19 Women's hourly wage rates* as % of men's

Age group	%
21–24	93.8
30–39	89.0
40–49	74.5
50–59	77.1

* in full-time employment
Source: New Earnings Survey April 1996, Table 12.6. Office for National Statistics © Crown Copyright 1996.

The widening of the pay gap above the age of 40 may reflect disparities in place before the enactment of the Equal Opportunities Act in 1975. As more qualified women move through the system, the discount in older cohorts will decline, bringing down the average differential. Combining this data with the University of Warwick projections and further rises in female participation rates points to an on-going decline in family size.

Can I see your degree?

In magnetism, and sometimes in love, opposites attract. But while this may be true for personality, it certainly does not apply in the matter of educational qualifications. When choosing a mate, the British select from those with a similar educational background, with women being rather more picky than men. The 1995 GHS revealed that 61% of women degree holders married men with degrees, the same proportion as in 1994, whereas only 33% of men returned the compliment, down from 36% in 1994. Bright women also went upmarket. Only 21% of women with higher education below degree level married men of similar rank (*vs* 23% in 1994), but a further 30% married degree holders, a sharp rise from the 24% of 1994. For men in this category, the figures are 16% and 20% respectively, *vs* 17% and 18% in 1994.

Those with no qualifications also tended to marry each other – in 1995, 66% of such men married women in this category, and 52% of unqualified women married unqualified men, *vs* 65% and 53% in 1994. This may not affect birth rates too much (although as wage differentials for qualifications continue to widen, opportunity and wealth could become more concentrated), since the higher income forgone when a well-qualified woman trades employment for motherhood will offset her partner's ability to support a larger family.

Work, sweet work

A curious thing has happened in the workplace over the past few years. Because companies are making real efforts to make their workforce feel more valued through 'empowerment' and 'teamwork,' the office is actually becoming enjoyable. Indeed, it may be becoming more attractive than home for some. After all, home life largely consists of doing uninteresting chores such as cleaning, washing and shopping for the family at the end of a full day's work. If this is indeed the case, what is to stop women, who are anyway being increasingly involved in the workforce, and increasingly well-paid, from backing out of family life completely?

References

1 Easterlin, R. A. (1961) 'The American baby boom in historical perspective', *American Economic Review*, 51: 869–911.
   (1968) *Population, Labour Force and the Long Swings in Economic Growth*, New York, NBER.
2 *Population Trends No 71*, Spring 1993, OPCS.
3 Kiernan, K. (1987) 'Demographic experiences in early adulthood: a longitudinal study.' PhD Thesis, University of London.
4 Prioux, F. (1996) *Population*, May/June No. 3, Institut National d'Etudes Demographiques.
5 International Survey Research Ltd. (1997) *Tracking Trends*, p. 12.
6 Ermisch, J. (July 1990) *Fewer babies, longer lives*, Joseph Rowntree Foundation.
7 *Financial Times*, 6 January 1998.
8 *Women: Setting New Priorities* (Jan. 1996) Whirlpool Foundation.
9 Rindfuss, R. R., Morgan, S. P. and Offut, K. (Aug. 1996) 'Education and the Changing Age Pattern of American Fertility, 1963–1989, *Demography*, Vol. 33, No. 3.
10 Institute for Employment Research, University of Warwick, *Review of the Economy and Employment*.
11 *See* Ref. 6.

DECLINE AND FALL

Although so far I have focused mainly on the UK, the phenomenon of declining birth rates is worldwide – although not universal. The current chapter presents fertility trends across a range of countries to illustrate this fact, to examine some of the causal factors – e.g., economic collapse in Eastern Europe, AIDS in South Africa and education in Asia – and in some cases, to give the first hints of the broad population changes to be expected in the years ahead.

Fertility declines in Western Europe

With the exception of the USA, all major Western countries are below replacement levels and most have been for decades. Eurostat's latest TFRs for Europe, together with those for the USA, Japan, India and China for comparison are shown in Table 3.1.

Table 3.1 Total fertility rates 1990–4 and 1995

Country	TFR		Country	TFR	
	1990–4	*1995*		*1990–4*	*1995*
EUR 15	1.50	1.43	EEA	1.51	1.44
Germany	1.32	1.24	Switzerland	1.55	1.48
Spain	1.28	1.18	USA	2.10	2.06
France	1.72	1.70	Japan	1.50	1.48
Ireland	2.00	1.87	India	3.50	3.27
Italy	1.29	1.17	China	1.90	1.82
UK	1.78	1.71	Other LDCs	4.30	4.06

Sources: Eurostat, *Statistics in Focus*, 1996.

As a result, with the exception of Ireland, populations are static or facing decline, unless propped up by immigration, as in the case of Germany or Italy (*see* Table 3.2).

These declines may appear unimportant when spread over 50 years, but as we probe more deeply, we will see that they will have a major impact on everything from State pensions to immigration policy, and even the very ability of countries in Europe to function at all: *see* Part II.

Fertility declines in Eastern Europe

The fall of the Soviet Union has had a dramatic impact on both fertility and emigration in the countries of Eastern Europe. Russian GDP fell by

Table 3.2 Population projections 1995–2050 (millions)

Country	1995 m	2020 m	2050 m	1995–2020 Change %	2020–50 Change %
Germany	81.1	76.4	65.8	−5.8	−13.8
Italy	57.9	55.1	47.8	−4.7	−13.3
Spain	39.1	38.5	34.9	−1.5	−9.5
UK	58.3	60.3	59.4	+3.5	−1.5
Ireland	3.6	4.3	4.7	+19.0	−1.3
France	58.1	62.1	61.6	+6.9	−0.8

Source: World Population Projections 1994–5, IBRD/The World Bank, Washington, DC, 1994.

43% between 1991 and 1996, and not surprisingly, birth rates have fallen. What is more surprising is that even in Poland, whose economy is booming after two years of steep decline, birth rates have continued to fall. It is possible that households find it difficult to adjust to the high levels of inflation seen since 1990, or that the Consumer Price Index fails to capture expenditure on goods and services provided free under communism but now supplied by the private sector. In real terms they may now be worse off, despite economic growth in recent years. If the trends highlighted in Table 3.3 persist, they could have a profound effect on capital investment by, and trading relationships with, their Western neighbours.

For example, Hungary, whose TFR has remained below replacement rate since 1977, lost 5% of its population since 1981, and projections based on 1992 data (when TFR was 20% higher than in 1996), point to a further 8% fall by 2020. Similarly, Bulgarian fertility has been below replacement since 1980, and population has fallen by 7% since then, due to a rise in the number of elderly, tumbling birth rates and massive emigration to escape falling living standards and soaring unemployment. Even Romania, where birth rates were kept high during the Ceaucescu regime, is forecast to lose 6% of its numbers by 2020, a projection that could prove optimistic since it is based on low levels of emigration. We shall look in more detail at the plight of two countries, East Germany and Russia.

East Germany

The potential for economic and political uncertainty to disrupt family life is nowhere better illustrated than in the case of East Germany following

Table 3.3 Fertility, GDP growth rates and inflation rates in Eastern Europe, 1990–6

Country		1990	1991	1992	1993	1994	1995	1996
Bulgaria	TFR	1.81	1.65	1.54	1.46	1.37	1.23	1.24
	GDP	−9.9	−11.7	−7.3	−2.4	1.4	2.6	−3.0
	CPI	19.3	333.5	82.0	72.8	96.2	62.0	125.0
Czech. Rep.	TFR	1.89	1.86	1.72	1.67	1.44	1.28	1.18
	GDP	−1.6	−14.2	−6.4	−0.9	2.6	4.8	4.4
	CPI	10.0	56.7	11.1	20.8	10.0	9.1	8.9
Hungary	TFR	1.86	1.87	1.77	1.69	1.64	1.57	1.46
	GDP	−3.5	−11.9	−4.3	−0.6	2.9	1.5	1.0
	CPI	28.9	35.0	23.0	22.5	18.8	28.2	23.6
Poland	TFR	2.04	2.05	1.93	1.85	1.80	1.61	1.60
	GDP	−12.0	−8.6	1.5	3.8	5.2	7.0	6.1
	CPI	585.8	70.3	43.0	36.9	33.3	26.8	19.9
Romania	TFR	1.83	1.56	1.51	1.44	1.41	1.34	1.30
	GDP	−5.6	−12.9	−8.8	1.5	3.9	6.9	4.1
	CPI	5.1	174.5	210.9	290.3	136.8	32.3	56.9
Russia	TFR	1.89	1.73	1.55	1.39	1.40	1.34	na
	GDP	−3.0	−5.0	−14.5	−8.7	−12.7	−3.9	−5.0
	CPI	5.0	93.0	2509	896	302	198	48

Sources: Council of Europe, Recent Demographic Developments in Europe 1997, EIU World Outlook, 1995 and 1997. © The Economist Intelligence Unit. Reproduced by permission of the Economist Intelligence Unit.

reunification. In the period 1991–3, the number of marriages, divorces, births and abortions collapsed. TFR continued to decline in 1994, and has remained depressed in 1995. Indeed, NRR is running at roughly 40% of replacement levels. The real pressure has been felt on first order births. Presumably the combination of sharply increased financial commitments and a marked fall in household income on starting a family could not be justified during such a period; the fall in living standards for couples with an existing child would be much less. A 1992 survey of German women aged 20–39 (Table 3.4) revealed a strong divergence between the reasons given for the decline in fertility by residents in East and West Germany.

While this might suggest that these postponed births could be made up in subsequent years, economic uncertainty remains high, Unemployment continues to rise, despite heavy construction expenditure, and with unit

Table 3.4 1992 Survey of public opinion in Germany

East Germany		West Germany	
Unfavourable economic situation	78%	Hedonism	53%
High cost of raising children	61%	Housing market	51%
Fear of the future	49%	Economic problems	51%

labour costs 20% higher than West Germany, this trend is unlikely to reverse. Prospects for the weak 1996 recovery in birth rates to gather momentum seem bleak, although some demographers believe that the convergence with West German birth rates could take place by 2008. Between 1988 and 1995 the country lost 1 million people, 6% of the total. Half went through emigration, half through the collapse in births. Some of the more industrial and mining regions have been badly affected, but the funds from the West for rebuilding their infrastructure may be drying up. Even allowing for this convergence, the population of the eastern Länder could continue to decline.

The Russian Federation and the FSU

Reliable economic data since 1990 is sparse and has been subject to substantial revision but the fall in living standards has been far more severe than for its western neighbours. Real GDP in 1996 was estimated at only 55% of the 1989 level. During this period of severe economic crisis, the number of marriages dropped from 9.5 per 1000 population (‰) in 1988 to a mere 5.9‰ in 1996, while divorces rose from 3.9‰ in 1988 to a peak of 4.6‰ in 1994, before declining to 3.8‰ in 1996. After decades in which fertility remained at or above replacement rate, the TFR crashed from 2.13 in 1988 to 1.34 in 1995. Second order births fell by 57% and third order births by 63% over the period.

The combination of falling births and a five-year decline in life expectancy for men led to a natural decrease in population of 3.5 million between 1992 and 1996, offset by a net inflow, largely of Russian nationals (including the Armed Forces) returning from the newly independent states of Georgia, the Ukraine, Kazakhstan, Kyrgyzstan, Uzbekistan and the Baltic Republics. Even so, *net population fell by 1.2 million between 1992 and 1996 and is predicted to fall from 147 million to 123 million within three decades,*[1] *some 30 million less than projected by the World Bank in 1994/5.*

Russia and its neighbours, Belarus and Ukraine, face a growing demo-graphic problem on their southern flank; while their combined population fell by 1.1 million in 1995 (births minus deaths), that of their Muslim former satellites, Azerbaijan, Kazakhstan, Kirghizstan, Tadjikistan, Turkmenistan and Uzbekistan, rose by 1 million. The latest projections from the International Institute for Applied Systems (IIASA) for the European FSU (comprising Azerbaijan, Armenia, Belarus, Georgia, the Russian Federation, Ukraine and the Baltic Republics), which do not use the World Bank methodology, show combined population falling steeply in all but two of nine possible scenarios. Table 3.5 shows the mid-range and the worst-case scenarios, both of which take mid-range assumptions for life expectancy and migration.

Table 3.5 Population projections for European FSU (1995–2095)

Period	Fertility (TFR)		Year	Population (millions)	
	Central	Low		Central	Low
1995–2000	1.50	1.35	1995	238	238
2010–15	1.58	1.24	2010	231	223
2020–5	1.64	1.27	2020	224	207
2050–5	1.84	1.40	2050	187	139
2095	2.05	1.55	2100	135	51

Source: IIASA, The Future Population of the World, p. 452.

Japan: setting sun

The first country in the Far East to transform its economy, Japan is now pointing the way to demographic decline in the rest of the region, and in other developing countries. In the immediate post-war period, population rose sharply, adding some 40 million between 1945 and 1975. Ever since then, however, the medium variant population projec-tions made by the Ministry of Health and Welfare (MHW) after every five-year census have been consistently too high, and the outturn has gen-erally been closer to the pessimistic variant. The 1992 projections made by the MHW[2] are based on two TFR scenarios. The medium variant projects TFR to fall to 1.49 in 1994, before recovering to 1.80 by 2025 and to replacement rate by 2090. On this basis, population falls from a 1995 level of 125.5 million to 123.0 million by 2030 and 95.7 million by 2090. *On the pessimistic variant, which assumes TFR falling to 1.36 in 1998, recovering to 1.45 in 2025 and 1.68 in 2090, population halves to 61.6 million by 2090.*

Even on the medium variant the population will decline because of the downward momentum that has built up over 50 years. The population of working age has already passed its peak, and the continuing rise in the overall population reflects increasing life expectancy for the elderly. For comparison, the World Bank projects a population of around 115 million by 2050, similar to the medium variant. The two other main Japanese studies (Japan Center for Economic Research, 1991, and Sumitomo Life Insurance Institute, 1994) are closer to the pessimistic variant. The actual 1995 TFR of 1.46 was already below the low point assumed in the medium variant, and fell further to 1.41 in 1996, and 1.39 in 1997.

Interestingly enough, the blame for this state of affairs has, as in the UK, been laid at the door of sky-high property prices, the result of cheap credit, capital gains taxes and death duties that made land sales prohibitively expensive while other tax loopholes restrict supply. Because 5% of land in Tokyo is still zoned as farmland and tax breaks are given to 'urban farmers', there are still some 89 000 acres of farmland and 56 000 acres of vacant land in the Greater Tokyo area.

In theory, this has created massive paper profits for the fortunate 62% who own their own homes. By the early 1990s it was said that 1 million people living within a 36-mile radius of central Tokyo owned property worth over Y500 million (US$4 million), and a further 3.5 million owning property worth Y100 million. While the boom has been short-lived, starting in 1985 and ending in 1990, it has put intolerable pressure on new owners. Condominium prices within a 12-mile radius of Tokyo rose to more than 10 times average salary, forcing would-be buyers into distant hinterlands where they can be obtained at a still onerous five times salary. By 1997, prices of new condominiums had eased significantly, but by that stage, the banks were not prepared to lend.

South Africa – surprise!

An odd footnote, this, but worth mentioning. The latest (1996) South African census has revealed that the total population is some 4 million, or almost 10%, lower than the 42.1 million that had been estimated from the 1991 census. Indeed, some semi-official publications had set the figure as high as 44.6 million, before the latest number was released. It will be interesting to see whether further analysis confirms that this is due to an unexpected and previously unrecorded fall in the birth rate. It appears that after falling from 3% per annum in the 1980s to around 2.2%, there has been a further decline to 1.9%.

The other possibility is, of course, AIDS; some 2.4 million South Africans now have the disease, and, since 1991, the proportion of pregnant women infected has risen from 1% to 16% by the end of 1997,[3] and could rise further because of the failure of the government to institute a coherent awareness campaign, and the reluctance of black South Africans to use condoms. One in three pregnant women in Zimbabwe was infected by 1996. If the disease is unchecked, life expectancy in South Africa could fall from 63 to 40 by 2010 on some estimates. The 1994 World Bank projections of a population of 69 million by 2025 no longer seem feasible.

Fertility declines in developing countries

These present a more extreme pattern of fertility decline than that of the West, perhaps in part due to the growing use of contraception. The International Conference on Population and Development (Cairo 1994) estimated that 57% of couples in developing countries were using contraception (admittedly only 38%, excluding China) *vs* only 14% in 1960–5. There is still some way to go before they reach the 70% achieved in developed countries, however, and in the countries of sub-Saharan Africa, where birth rate is highest, usage is below 10%.

Not only did TFRs peak at levels well above those in Europe, but the decline has been compressed into a far shorter period. TFRs in Japan have fallen from a comparatively modest 4.0 in 1949 to the present 1.46 over 48 years: as we shall see, Brazil's TFR has dropped from 6.0 to 2.5 in only 40 years, and Turkey's from 6.40 to 2.55 in 36 years. So, while Japan will have one of the oldest populations in the world by 2050 (one-third of the population will be over the age of 65 by that date on the pessimistic scenario), the *rate* of ageing will be much faster in countries as different as Brazil, China and Thailand, with the result that the proportion of their populations over the age of 65 will reach Japanese levels by 2100.

The same countries are all now below replacement levels, although the momentum from previous years of high fertility will ensure that their populations continue to grow for some time to come. What is remarkable is that neither the politics of the government (whether socialist, communist or capitalist), nor the stance of government or religious leaders on birth control have greatly changed the trend. (This does not augur well for those countries that need to restore fertility to replacement levels.)

Brazil

The experience of Brazil typifies that of other developing countries. The 59% decline in TFRs from 6.00 in 1960–5 to 2.48 by 1990–5 has been sufficient to produce an absolute decline in the number of annual births since the 1980s, even though the age of marriage has fallen rather than risen. The age pyramid is becoming lantern-shaped. NRR is now below 1.0 and the population is set to stabilise by 2030. The decline affected all regions and social strata. Even the impoverished North-East is closing the gap with the rest of the country; over the same period the region's TFRs fell by 53% to 3.50. The corollary is that the more prosperous states are significantly below replacement rate.

The government was officially pronatalist in the past, and passed laws against the dissemination of birth control information about devices. It was only in 1974 that the right of couples to plan their families and have access to contraceptive techniques was conceded. The states and municipal authorities in the poor North-East initiated local family planning in the 1970s but the Federal Government programme (PAISM) begun in 1986 has had little impact.

The Catholic church was and remains implacably opposed to all forms of birth control other than so-called 'natural' methods, but by retarding access to modern methods has compelled women to rely on abortion and sterilisation.[4] Sterilisation in now the most frequent form of birth control. In the North-East, the proportion of married women aged 15–44 who had been sterilised rose from 25% in 1986 to 37% in 1991. Furthermore there has been a sharp drop in the median age of sterilisation – down from 36.6 in the North-East and 38.2 in São Paulo in 1986 to 29.7 and 31 respectively by the early 1990s.

(Part of the reason for this is that doctors push patients into caesarean operations for financial reasons. While caesarean operations are covered by the State, tubal ligations are not, but surgically speaking it is convenient to combine the two. The doctor therefore arranges for a patient to be classified as high-risk and in need of caesarean delivery. The tubal ligation is carried out at the same time with the woman paying the cost privately.)

In a country where literacy rate is low and newspapers hard to obtain, television is ubiquitous and could have a significant role in moulding aspirations for the good life, but studies reveal a high correlation between level of education, income and socioeconomic class on the one hand and fertility on the other. The results of the August 1996 census confirm that the slowdown in birth rate is continuing. Prospects here remain encouraging since the level of education is rising significantly. According to the Brazilian Institute of Geography and Statistics (IBGE), 90% of children aged between seven and 14 now attend school, and 66.8% of those aged 15–17 do so – up from 55.3% five years ago. For women aged 20 or over, education was found to be the most important determinant of current fertility – an observation that has echoes in our next example, Thailand.

Thailand

While the population has risen from 26.2 million in 1960 to 56 million by 1990, fertility rate has fallen sharply, reaching replacement rate by the end of the 1980s. The decline, as in Brazil, has reached most social groups, and fertility differentials by occupation and education have been almost eliminated. The number of infants had begun to decline in the late 1970s, and the number entering primary schools also fell by the early 1980s. By the mid-1980s, the total size of the primary school population had peaked, helping the Thai government to fulfil its goal of universal primary education. By 1990, the number of children of high school age had begun to decline, and by 1995, so had the number in the 15–24 age group and entering the labour force.

The Seventh National Five-Year Plan (1992–6) estimates that under median variant fertility assumptions, the population will reach 74 million by 2015 and peak at below 80 million (NES DP 1991). Later projections[5] which recognise that TFR in Bangkok is already down to 1.5 and that urbanisation and the spread of secondary and higher education will diffuse lower fertility to other regions, suggest a peak of only 70 million by 2025. (AIDS is not considered to make a serious impact on total population – 700–800 000 cumulative deaths are forecast to 2005.)

(This raises an important point about the World Bank forecast, which is based on an NRR of 1.0 persisting from 1995 onwards, and shows a figure of 75.2 million in 2015 and equilibrium at 104 million by 2150. It may well be that the demographic transition towards low fertility is stronger and more persistant than generally accepted. If so, the same may also be true of other fast-growing economies in Asia.)

Sayonara, Baby . . .

Up to now, I have only covered economic factors affecting family size. It is time to add an eerie postscript. Not all infertility is through choice and there is growing evidence that unknown factors are at work which may actually make it harder to conceive. Although some studies in the early 1970s seemed to suggest a decline in men's ability to produce sperm, it was only in 1992 that clearer evidence emerged when Danish researcher Niels Skakkebaek and his colleagues published a review in the *British Medical Journal*[6] of 61 studies on sperm counts in a number of countries going back to 1938. They involved 15 000 men with no previous history of infertility. Average sperm count had fallen globally from 113 million per millilitre to 66 million over the 50 years to 1990. Furthermore the quality of semen produced in each ejaculation had fallen significantly and there was a threefold increase in the number of men whose sperm count had fallen below the 20 million level regarded as a threshold for fertility. Criticism of the way the data were compiled – it was impossible to standardise them for age of subject, etc. – prompted further research[7] which both bridged the gap and generally confirmed its findings.

No single factor has been identified to account for this decline. Studies by a group of scientists at Florida State University in 1987 however found that lower sperm counts were closely linked to the production of synthetic chemicals in that area, traffic density (as measured by vehicle registrations) and consumption of meat, fat and alcohol. In particular, other research suggests that widespread use of synthetic chemicals that mimic oestrogen, the female sex hormone could have severe and possibly irreversible effects on boys whose reproductive systems were not fully developed.

Over a period of some 30 years until it was banned in the early 1970s, some two to three million women in the USA received doses of diethylstilbestrol (DES), a synthetic oestrogen thought to prevent miscarriage. The actual cause of the ban was the finding that a small number of the daughters of these women developed a rare form of vaginal cancer at an unusually early age, but there also appeared to be serious side-effects amongst their sons – low sperm counts, undescended testicles and deformities of the penis.

Could the growing use of oestrogens in a variety of applications from skin creams to livestock raising, or the possible entry of ethynyl estradiol, the main ingredient of contraceptive pills, into drinking water via purification plants play a part in declining sperm counts? Male trout become feminised when exposed to concentrations of ethynyl estradiol too small to be detected. Phthalates, too, have been implicated as oestrogen mimics; these chemicals are used extensively to make plastics flexible – including those used for food containers.

At this stage many questions remain unanswered, and much evidence is circumstantial. We do not know, for example, whether declining sperm count has in fact been a contributor to declining birth rates for the past 50 years, which chemicals put us most at risk, and whether, if they were banned, it would be possible to undo their effects over time. *What is statistically clear, however, is that, given the wide variation of sperm counts around the mean, if counts continue to fall, an increasing proportion of the male population would approach the 20 million threshold of fertility, and birth rates could then take a real tumble.*

References

1 *Financial Times*, 18 February 1997.
2 Statistics Bureau; MHW, Sept. 1992, *Population Projections for Japan 1991–2090*.
3 *Financial Times*, 19 March 1998.
4 (March 1996.) 'Brazil's Fertility Decline 1965–95', *Population and Development Review*, Vol. 12, No. 1.
5 Guest, P. and Jones, G. W. 'Policy Options When Population Growth Slows: The Case of Thailand', *Population Research and Policy Review*, Vol. 15, No. 2.
6 Carlson, E., Giwercman, A., Keiding, N. and Skakkebæk, N. (12 Sept. 1992). 'Evidence of decreasing quality of semen during past 50 years', *BMJ*, Vol. 305.
7 For example: Irving S. *et al.* (24 Feb. 1997). 'Evidence of deteriorating semen quality in the United Kingdom: birth cohort study of 577 men in Scotland over 11 years', *BMJ*, Vol. 312.

ENCOURAGING
LARGER FAMILIES

Here I have to tread very carefully if I am to avoid the accusation of treating women like battery chickens with no power to regulate the size of their families. Demographic engineering in the past has usually been the province of megalomaniac dictators to the right and left, and has been done more with sticks than with carrots. Hitler began a programme of 'demographic rearmament' soon after coming to power in 1933. Mussolini had a target of 60 million Italians by 1950.

In 1974, Ceaucescu aimed at boosting the Romanian population from 21 million to 30 million by the year 2000 – a compound growth rate close to that of India. In this case, the combination of emigration and high infant mortality, in a country where health expenditure has been sacrificed for industrial production, has undermined this goal. The 1996 population is well below that of 1990 at 22.7 million.

What is so utterly distasteful in all these cases, and that of Russia when in a pronatalist mood, is not so much the financial incentives to have children – for example priority allocation of scarce housing to married couples was the main means of inducing early marriage in, say, East Germany – as the means adopted to ensure pregnancy. With few exceptions, such as East Germany, access to modern contraceptives or even reliable condoms was denied, and abortion and sterilisation made illegal. In Romania, the policy was carried to horrible extremes; in many enterprises, women were subjected to a monthly pregnancy check and could be prosecuted if, once pregnant, they failed to carry a baby to term. The demographic sigh that went up when this odious regime was swept away can be seen from the figures shown in Table 4.1.

Table 4.1 Fertility data, Romania, 1988–96

Year	Live births	Legal abortions	TFR
1988	380 043	185 416	2.31
1989	369 544	193 084	2.19
1990	314 746	913 973	1.83
1991	275 275	866 934	1.56
1992	260 393	691 863	1.51
1993	249 994	585 761	1.44
1994	246 736	530 191	1.41
1995	236 640	502 840	1.34
1996	231 348	456 221	1.30

Source: Council of Europe Recent Demographic Developments in Europe, 1997.

Such dehumanising treatment, like Indira Gandhi's sterilisation campaign, cannot be condoned, but these examples make it harder to advance arguments for encouraging larger families today, using incentives rather than penalties and loss of choice.

The recognition that no single theory fully explains the global decline in fertility does not mean that fertility cannot respond to economic incentives, at least in the short-term. While the UK government has maintained an Olympian disdain for such intervention, other countries have not. The examples of France after the Franco-Prussian War and Romania under Ceaucescu have already been mentioned, but in more recent times, some others, alarmed by the consequences of population decline are urging more far-reaching policies.

In effect, the ageing process is leading to an increasing transfer of national resources from the young to the elderly. Demographers such as Philippe Boucier de Carbon[1] argue that this will in turn lead to even lower levels of fertility – another twist in the spiral of demographic decline. His solution, to redistribute wealth back to families, may not even be politically feasible in a few years' time when the proportion of the elderly becomes large enough to swing elections. Retirees have more time on their hands and are more prepared to use their votes than younger age groups, and there is increasing evidence that how old you are determines how you vote on a range of matters. There may well develop a growing polarity between young voters seeking greater investment in education and job creation and retirees seeking investment in healthcare and State pensions.

Chesnais[2] highlights the difference in levels of family allowances to partly explain the widely differing fertility rates in Sweden (TFR 1991–5 = 1.96) and Italy (1.25). In 1992, *per capita* public expenditures devoted to children were respectively 1350 ECU and 150 ECU. Since 1974, both parents in Sweden can share parental allowances on the birth of a child equivalent to 85% of their former wage or salary for at least a year, and the real value of family allowance has been kept stable. By contrast, the share of child benefits within Italy's total security budget has fallen from 13.3% in 1970 to 3.9% by 1992, and there are no significant tax rebates for families with dependent children.

Even accepting this argument, the fact remains that despite the generosity of the Swedish system, birth rates are still well below replacement levels. The question must be asked – how much *more* generous must it become for this to be achieved? Moreover, the electoral climate in Europe is becoming more hostile to high-tax governments. Could electors be persuaded to support measures that would undoubtedly make the majority of them worse off for the sake of future generations?

Pronatalist policies?

Results of pronatalist policies in countries where means of birth control remain freely available have so far been only mildly encouraging, as the four examples highlighted below illustrate.

East Germany

Until the early 1970s, TFRs in East Germany closely tracked those of the Federal Republic, but then diverged under the impact of the 1972 policy initiatives introduced by Honeker. Abortion was liberalised and a wider range of contraceptives became available. At the same time, financial incentives for marriage and birth were offered and cost-free day care provided to the vast majority of parents for children older than one year. In 1976 this was further reinforced by the creation of a 'baby year' – a one-year leave for the mother giving birth and the guarantee of keeping her job. The combined effect of these measures was a strong rise in TFRs after 1974 which persisted at levels above those of West Germany until the shock of reunification.

Unfortunately, this recovery in birth rates, known as the 'Honeker berg' was not due to young women increasing their average number of children, but only to a change of timing.[3] The country has a chronic shortage of accommodation, and apartments were allocated according to a set of priorities. Priority status is acquired by (i) marriage, (ii) motherhood, and especially (iii) both. This factor explains why in 1989 the age of childbearing in East Germany was 24 *vs* 28 across the border.

Similarly, while college graduates in the Federal Republic postpone marriage and motherhood, there is little difference between graduates and the rest of the population in East Germany. By the time of graduation, three quarters of East German women were married, *vs* one-quarter in the West. Furthermore, one-third already had one or more children *vs* only 10% for women in West Germany. If housing becomes more readily available in East Germany, it could reasonably be assumed that the age of childbearing would rise towards West German levels.

France

During the period 1846–1946, the French population increased by barely 12%. Indeed the country encountered serious difficulties in finding manpower, not only to fight its perennial foe, Germany, united under Bismarck, whose own population was soaring, but also to man the factories of the Industrial Revolution. With a low birth rate, there was no pressure on land to drive peasants from the countryside into the towns. Governments did try to address the problem by encouraging families – typically, just after a war or just before one. Thus in 1920, the provision of information on contraception and the advertising or distribution of contraceptive devices was made subject to harsh penalties, while in 1939, the government enacted the *Code de la Famille,* which provides the basis for France's generous post-war family benefit system. Although TFR has been below replacement rate since 1975, it remains one of the highest in Europe.

In 1994, after TFR had dipped to a post-war low of 1.65, the government felt it necessary to reinforce the *Code* and enacted a number of measures designed to help families with young children or dependent adults. Despite a gloomy economic environment, TFR has recovered modestly from its recent low of 1.65 in 1993–4 to 1.72 in 1996, but is still almost 20% below replacement level.

Greece

Greece tried to arrest the decline with legislation in 1990 which provided monthly payments to mothers giving birth to a third child, and a life pension for mothers with five children or more. It is precisely these higher order births that have begun to respond, and even though the effect has been offset by a decline in first and second births, the net result has been to raise TFR from the 1993 low of 1.34 to 1.36 in 1994 and 1.40 in 1995. In 1996, however, TFR had fallen again to a new low of 1.31.

Singapore

At the time the People's Action Party (PAP) came to power in 1959, the population was rising rapidly (3.5% per annum), and if unchecked, would have put intolerable strain on a small island state. The new government therefore adopted a strongly antinatalist policy. Birth control was encouraged through provision of a network of clinics, and through wide-ranging penalties on families with more than two children. Birth rate has fallen sharply, although how much of this is due to the strong rise in *per capita* income is impossible to say. Despite similar economic growth rates, Malaysian birth rates have not shown such a steep decline. TFRs of Malaysian Chinese in 1994 stood at 2.53, a good 40% higher than for their Singapore counterparts.

By the mid-1980s, however, the trend had gone too far. Recalling the eugenists of the 1930s, Prime Minister Lee Kuan Yew was concerned not only that the population was not reproducing itself, but also that birth rates amongst university graduates were lower than those without higher degrees. A campaign was mounted to encourage female graduates to marry and also to permit such women to have a third child without financial penalty. A far more comprehensive programme of financial incentives was introduced in 1987, including substantial tax relief and priority given to children from three-children families in admission to schools, and to such families in public sector flats seeking to upgrade to larger units.

Such far-reaching social engineering has had some impact on births, with the number born to mothers with secondary and higher education rising, while the number born to those with primary or no qualifications has fallen.[4] This may however reflect in part the general rise in Singapore's educational standards, and a steady decline in the number of women with lesser qualifications in the younger, more fertile, age groups.

The number of third and higher order births has also risen perceptibly during the period. Even so, TFR, having surged from 1.62 in 1987 to 1.96 in 1988 has gradually slipped back and had remained below 1.8 since 1991. The age-specific fertility rates (ASFR) has also recorded a steady rise in the age of childbearing, perhaps reflecting the rising proportion of these higher order births. Finally, while 61% of women giving birth in 1992 had secondary or higher qualifications, they accounted for 52% of all third-order births and only 36% of fourth- or higher-order births.

Against this background it is clear that the government will not achieve its 1987 goal of reaching a stable population by 2030. Indeed, in its National Report for the International Conference on Population and Development (ICPD) at Cairo in September 1994, the Minister of Health and Development forecast a population peaking in 2025. By 2030, 24.6% of the 3.5 million population would be aged 60 or more with 43 elderly persons per 100 of working age (15–59), *vs* 14 per 100 in 1990.

It must be asked, therefore, if Singapore, with all the resources of the

State, combined with a tradition of Confucian ethics and respect for authority, is unable to increase family size to replacement level, even fleetingly, what hope is there for the *laissez-faire* countries of Europe?

America the exceptional?

If, as a very rough guide, birth rate tends to move inversely with *per capita* GDP, what are we to make of the position of the prosperous USA, where TFR is still managing to stay around replacement rate? Is it the exception that ruins our theory?

Probably not. For a start, the population receives a steady influx of young immigrants, particularly from traditionally high-fertility Hispanic countries, who are likely to marry within their own community. It may take some time before their fertility rates converge with those of the host country. For reference, average TFR in 1990–5 for Mexico, the source of the largest number of immigrants, was 3.12. It is worth contrasting the experience of Canada, a neighbour with similar living standards to the USA. Immigrants to Canada are more likely to come from Chinese communities in Hong Kong, Singapore or Malaysia, whose fertility rates are significantly below those of Mexicans (1.35, 1.8 and 2.5 respectively). Overall Canadian TFR is 1.85, around 10% below that of the USA, with the more urbanised Quebec and Ontario closer to 1.6.

Furthermore, as in other countries, rising educational standards are associated with later childbearing and lower fertility levels. For example, analysis of CPS data for the period 1985–9[5] yields a TFR of 1.5 for college graduates aged 15–41, around 25% below the national average. Over a 20-year time span, the same researchers estimate that the peak age of childbearing has risen by three years across the educational spectrum from high school to college graduate.

This may tie in with the high participation of women in the labour force, made easier by the availability of childcare. The proportion of fully employed mothers of pre-school children relying on organised childcare centres has risen from 5% in 1958 to 32% by 1988. Since childcare is costly, and since the incomes of younger women tend to rise with age, it is logical to assume that women postpone childbearing until their incomes can support this cost. This could explain why ASFRs up to age 25–29 have fallen between 1963–4 and 1975–9, but there has been little change since then. Furthermore fertility rates in ages 31 and above have not changed since 1970. Taken together, the increasing time spent in education and the convergence of immigrant fertility levels with US norms ought to depress TFRs, but perhaps not to the levels now experienced in much of Europe. Indeed the latest central population projections by the US Bureau of the Census are based on fertility rates of Hispanic Americans remaining stable at 2.98 (*cf* 1995 TFRs of white American women of 1.98).[6] On that scenario, overall TFRs actually *rise* gradually, and the proportion of the US population that is of Hispanic origin increases steadily from 9.0% in 1990 to 22.0% by 2050.

Revanche de berceau?

If, as German polls imply, hedonism is more important than children, and financial inducements don't work, what is left to prevent population decline? Some races, feeling themselves endangered species surrounded by suspicious or aggressive neighbours, have responded by spontaneously increasing birth rates, a phenomenon termed by some revenge from the cradle. This was true for French Canadians up to the 1970s, and is true for the Jews in Israel and the Tutsis in Rwanda today. In other countries there has instead been assimilation – for example the Chinese in Thailand and Indonesia, and, indeed, almost all the immigrants into the USA. In other cases, the Indians of East Africa and perhaps some Chinese in Malaysia, emigration has been the chosen option. If the EU takes hold as a *political* entity, will the erosion of the nation state lead to the erosion of national consciousness and any interest by its citizens might have in preserving and perpetuating their Britishness, Frenchness or Germanness through higher birth rates?

Summary

For over 20 years, the UK population has been reproducing at below replacement levels, and, against the expectations of many demographers, TFR, rather than showing signs of recovery, has declined further during the past five years. I have tried to show that the explanation is to be found in a range of factors which have combined to raise the age of motherhood – the single most important factor in determining family size. These include increasing financial burdens on couples buying their own homes, particularly first-time buyers, and the growing desire of women to be financially independent, which requires that they work rather than raise children. Finally, the massive expansion in higher education is providing the means whereby women can more easily gain higher salaries and greater financial freedom, while the rise in women's wages relative to men's increases the opportunity cost of giving up work to raise a family. These factors are unlikely to reverse, indeed, they are likely to become even more pronounced, and accordingly, TFRs in the UK seem more likely to continue to decline rather than recover over the next decade. Growing awareness of the impending bankruptcy of the State pension and healthcare systems throughout the EU may keep couples working to save for their future retirement, as well as for their mortgages, rather than starting families.

The fall in fertility is a worldwide phenomenon. Practically all of Western Europe is below replacement rate – TFRs in Germany, Italy and Spain being particularly low – while political uncertainties and the removal of social safety nets after the fall of communism have caused a collapse in fertility throughout Eastern Europe. Developing economies such as China, Brazil and Thailand may also have fallen below replacement levels. Attempts by a number of countries to raise their flagging birth rates have met with only a limited and temporary success, even in Singapore.

There is growing evidence that a number of man-made chemicals could be responsible for damaging sperm quality and reducing sperm counts. Although this may not have played an important role in depressing the ease of conception up to now, if the trend continues, it could become increasingly significant in years to come.

(For all these reasons, I would agree with commentators like Mathews[7] that future TFRs, and hence future population levels could be significantly below those projected by The World Bank. There seems no reason why all countries should converge towards a NRR of 1.0 by the year 2030, as the World Bank projects. There is nothing magical about either this number or that date. Many countries in Western Europe have remained below replacement rate for so long that it calls into question the expressed wish of women, in many years of opinion polls throughout the region, to have families averaging over two children. There has been little sign of recovery, and to make any assumption about a return to replacement rate is at least moot. Mathews' conclusion that the World Bank's lower variant is the most plausible is in line with the views expressed in this book.)

Remembering the arguments about the recovery in birth rates in the post-war period being linked to labour shortages arising from the low birth rates of the 1930s, it is reasonable to ask why history should not repeat itself. From around 2010 onwards the fall in the size of the population of working age in most countries of the EU will have eliminated the current high levels of unemployment, and, in theory, give younger workers significantly greater bargaining power than they currently enjoy. Logically, this should lead to greater job security, rising real wages and . . . perhaps higher birth rates?

Probably not. Over the next 30 years global competition will intensify, not only because of the massive devaluations amongst Asian currencies, but also because most of these countries have both abundant manpower and pension systems which do not inflict steadily rising costs on its employers. Workers in Europe will be unable to extract the advantage from their employers that they did in the 1950s because their jobs can simply be exported if wage demands are too high – and this applies to a growing range of services as well as manufacturing.

In the very near future, low European birth rates will translate into declining population. The consequences, which are the subject of Part II, are not pleasant.

References

1 Boucier de Carbon, P. (Nov. 1995) 'Population de la France: chronique d'une implosion annoncée', *Futuribles,* No. 203.

2 Chesnais, J-C. (Dec. 1996) 'Fertility, Family and Social Policy', *Population and Development Review*, Vol. 22, No. 4.

3 Conrad, C., Lechner, M. and Werner, W. (June 1996) 'German Fertility After Unification: Crisis or Adaptation', *Population and Development Review*, Vol. 22, No. 2.

4 Mui Teng Yap (Dec. 1995) 'Singapore's "Three or More" Policy: The First Five Years', *Asia-Pacific Population Journal,* Vol. 10, No. 4.

5 *Women: Setting New Priorities* (Jan. 1996) Whirlpool Foundation.

6 Day, J. C. (1996) 'Population Projections of the United States by Age, Sex, Race and Hispanic Origin 1995 to 2050', US Bureau of the Census, *Current Population Reports*, pp. 25–1130, US Government Printing Office, Washington DC.

7 Mathews, G. (Sept. 1994) 'L'avenir de la population mondial: quand les perspectives officielles se trompent lourdement', *Futuribles*, No. 190.

Part II

THE ECONOMIC
CONSEQUENCES
OF DECLINE

FALLING WORKFORCE, FALLING CONSUMPTION

Introduction

As a result of decades of birth rates remaining below replacement levels and a steady increase in life expectation, populations of countries throughout the world are ageing, and those in Europe will experience actual declines over the next 50 years. This chapter will cover the severely adverse consequences of this trend, which will increase progressively during the period.

Anyone caught in a traffic jam on the Périphérique around Paris or fighting for a parking space in Central London must occasionally cast an envious glance at the orderliness of Brussels. Smaller countries seem to order things better. Surely, if our population declined we would benefit from lower congestion, less pollution and a generally better quality of life? Maybe so, but in this life you don't get owt for nowt and the costs attached to this more spacious existence will be high.

In this section we will examine how some of the key components of all economies could be affected. If declining populations in Europe become incapable of running their own countries without substantial levels of immigrant labour, what will this do to the fabric of society? As European populations decline, those of Asia, particularly India and China, will carry on increasing, for at least the next 50 years. What will that mean for geopolitics? Finally, if this doesn't depress you, the following section shows how demographics will bankrupt the European social security system while the burden of rising taxation further depresses birth rates and encourages the younger skilled members of the workforce to consider emigration. (For those who believe that all doors are now closed to immigrants, I have a pleasant surprise in store – but you will have to read Chapter 14 to find out the country I have in mind.)

Austria: the shape of things to come?

We will start off by looking at Austria – small, prosperous, reproductively challenged and with a declining population. (I selected Austria partly because its economists and demographers had developed an integrated study of the consequences of an ageing population which has applications to other countries. Austria does not even represent the most extreme example of the crisis ahead.) The country's demographers have seen the future, and it doesn't work.[1] A recent projection to 2051 based on a NRR of 0.7 (consistent with recent TFRs), and a sharp decline in mortality, showed a 29.5% fall in total population but a 41.2% fall in the economically active population (participation) by the end of the period.

Things are fine up to 2011, then the rot sets in. Over the following 40 years, the proportion of the over-60s rises from 24.2% to 38.0% and the ratio of workers to pensioners falls from 1.9 to under 1.0. When coupled with medium-term macroeconomic models that link this demographic input with private consumption expenditure and gross capital formation, the results make gloomy reading. If the Austrian economy in the year 2000 had the same demographic conditions as forecast for 2051, then key economic indicators would show major declines compared to their performance under year 2000 demographics (*see* Table 5.1).

Table 5.1 Projected changes in Austrian economy in 2000 with 2051 demographics

Private consumption expenditure	−32%
Imports	−15%
GDP	−20%
Labour demand	2.714 million
Labour supply	1.967 million

Source: Joachim Lamel and Josef Richter, *Labour Market Implications of Aging – The Austrian Case.*

'So what?' you may say. *Per capita* consumption is not badly affected, and there is all the more *Lebensraum* for those who remain, so isn't a falling population a *good* rather than a bad thing? Emphatically not! Besides the severe crisis that it will provoke in the State pension system and the health service – the subject of Part III – falling consumption lowers the need for capital investment and the incentive to innovate. Such countries risk falling behind technologically, which means extinction in a global economy.

Furthermore, when the production and consumption variables are further used to calculate demand for labour in Austria, then *even in this declining scenario, there is insufficient domestic labour available on the basis of participation rates and retirement ages now prevailing.* Immigration at the rate prevailing in 1985–8 would be unable to fill the gap – it would only contribute an extra 500 000 persons of working age, *vs* a net demand of 750 000. Excluding immigration, the gap could only be closed by making the most heroic assumptions about increasing retirement ages and participation rates (which could itself trigger a further fall in birth rates).

If, however, Austria cut its production according to its available workforce of 2 million (assuming currently prevailing participation rates and retirement ages), it would have to cut exports by 37%, resulting in a 27% drop in imports and a 27% fall in consumer expenditure relative to the case where the gap is closed by supply-side measures.

Many of Europe's economies are in demographic trouble as deep as Austria's, but the gravity of the problem is still not fully recognised. There is a tendency in many quarters to believe that current low fertility rates in Western Europe are an aberration, and that we are at or close to the trough of a long cycle that will restore fertility to replacement levels. They point to Sweden as a country poised on a new fertility upswing that will in time carry the rest of Europe along with it. Unfortunately the most recent evidence does not support this view. TFR in Sweden showed the sharpest decline of all the countries in Western Europe in 1995; after a brief flirtation with replacement level, it fell back to 1.74 in 1995, and an even more disappointing 1.61 in 1996. Meanwhile in Austria, TFR has fallen to 1.39 in 1995, suggesting NRR is now below the levels used in the study.

Since this projection was made, Austria's population has received a boost from an unexpected source – the disintegration of Yugoslavia, which has brought in over 200 000 refugees – while a further 100 000 migrants have entered from Turkey, Asia and other countries of Eastern Europe. The latest Eurostat forecast based on low fertility (TFR 1.4) projects a population of 6.6 million by 2050 – down from 8.1 million in 2000 but significantly above the Lamel/Richter forecast of 5.3 million. Some 0.65 million of the difference is due to the higher base figure caused by immigration (which also feeds through into more births), and 0.25 million is due to lower mortality assumptions for those over the age of 60. Because of the lower average ages of immigrants, the old age dependency under the Eurostat scenario falls to 64.3% from the 75% forecast by Lamel/Richter for 2050. This might appear to alleviate the situation, but everything has a cost, in this case, rising unemployment which has fuelled a resurgent right-wing anti-immigrant nationalism.

With the benefit of this framework of research spelling out the broad consequences of population decline, we can now explore some of these aspects in more detail.

Society

Few countries in Western Europe have experienced actual population declines since the War, although many – Italy and Portugal, for example – have stagnated for a decade or more. It is possible, however to infer how decline could affect whole countries by examining the *internal* situation. The reason why so many French towns today are so attractively furnished with unspoiled centuries-old homes and public buildings is that most of the nation's population growth has gravitated to Paris, leaving the rest of the country with no perceptible increase. Between 1846 and 1946, the total population rose by a mere 4.9 million to 40.3 million, during which time the Paris region gained 4.6 million. By contrast, the total UK population rose by 27.9 million to 50.2 million between 1851 and 1951, necessitating a major expansion and rebuilding of the textile towns of Yorkshire and Lancashire, as well as the coal and steel towns of North-East England, Wales and Scotland, and the major ports of Bristol, Liverpool and Manchester.

Overall stagnation of the non-metropolitan French population conceals a mix of winners and losers, often reflecting improved communications or obsolete industries. For example, Alençon and Le Mans were of similar size by the mid-19th century, but with the coming of the main line from Paris to Brittany, the latter has now become three times as large.

The more isolated a community, the more likely it is to move to where job prospects and amenities are better and more varied. Between 1820 and 1943, 7% of the Swiss and 11% of the Italian population emigrated to the New World,[2] but within these countries, the poorer, more mountainous regions bore the brunt. Some 30% of the population of Sicily and Campania, and no less than 46% of that of Basilicata and the Abruzzis emigrated during this period. Although the era of mass emigration is over, the trend continues *within* countries today. The young, educated at the cost of their local area, are the first to go, giving an unpaid-for benefit to their new hosts, and leaving behind the less educated, the old and their dependants. A few examples may illustrate both the problem regions and the drift to the main cities such as Madrid (*see* Table 5.2).

Table 5.2 Regional demographic indicators, 1992

Country/region	Total increase (per 1000)	Population % below 15 years	Population % aged 65 years and above
Spain	1.5	18.7	12.8
Noroeste	−2.5	16.5	16.1
Noreste	−0.9	16.4	14.6
(Aragon)	−2.3	15.7	17.9
Madrid	3.1	18.9	12.3
Italy	3.6	15.8	15.4
Liguria	−2.3	10.5	21.7
Friuli-Venezia Giulia	−1.2	11.7	19.5
Portugal	0.4	19.4	13.8
Centro	−2.3	18.5	16.9
Alentejo	−5.7	17.0	19.7

Source: Eurostat, *Demographic Statistics 1995*.

France has few areas of population decline as marked as those above, but its urban inhabitants may well have parents who left the country for the town, and government takes seriously its responsibility for preserving the rural way of life, through a range of economic measures. Included in this is an excellent road network which enables rural workers to commute significant distances to work in the towns, reducing the need to move from their communities. With these advantages it might seem that the French countryside is holding together. At the micro-level, however, Breton farmers have had to give up their tiny plots and move to Aquitaine or the plains of south-east Paris, and their university-educated children may have to live in Brest or Paris to get jobs.

In the more rural *Département*s, stretching in a broad swathe from North-East to South-West, there is a continuing drift from country to town. Hamlets are being abandoned, shops and schools close down and scrub reclaims the fields. The French describe this with a vividly expressive word – *désertification*. It is no surprise that French governments of all complexions, recognising both the capacity of disgruntled farmers to stage demonstrations and disrupt communications and the public sympathy for their cause, oppose any toughening of the Common Agricultural Policy that could accelerate the trend. But with the entry of Eastern European countries into the EU, *désertification* seems set to accelerate.

As national populations begin to experience absolute declines, this trend is likely to accelerate, and will be aggravated by the push towards globalisation. Falling tariffs and deregulated transport mean that factories can serve far larger catchment areas than in the past. With more stable labour relations, companies are prepared to take the risk of concentrating production in fewer, larger factories located close to motorways and to population centres from which they can access workers. Car plants, operating on a just-in-time basis no longer want to risk disruption caused by a distant supplier, and 'encourage' them to relocate to factories adjacent to, or even in, their assembly plant. The net result is that industries specialising in related skills tend to cluster in relatively small areas – electronics in Silicon Glen, biotech startups around Cambridge, etc.

This is clearly not a new trend, it has been going on since the start of the Industrial Revolution, but selection of factory sites is now being pursued on a much more rigorous basis. The best locations are obvious to all, and attract the lion's share of new investment. The least favoured get little, and Brussels limits the amount of regional aid that can be offered to bribe companies to build in depressed areas. Major centres with concentrations of skilled labour and good motorway links get bigger, others may lose population to the extent that they can no longer supply large new employers with labour.

Labour force

The decline in birth rates is beginning to filter through to the size and composition of the workforce. As the population ages, an increasing part of the workforce moves into age-groups where participation rates are declining, due to ill health, early retirement or the departure from the workforce of people discouraged by long-term unemployment. In France and Germany, only 19.0% and 29.2% respectively of men aged 60 or over remained in the workforce in 1993, and the proportion has fallen further since then (*see* Table 5.3).

We can illustrate the problem with the particular example of Germany.

It is not hard to understand why the country has got itself into a high-tax, high-spend mode. The whole concept of a 'social state' was incorporated into the 1949 Federal Constitution, and has been interpreted since to mean that the State should provide indefinite support for a basic standard of living for those with no resources, or who are unemployed. Labour force participation in older groups is far lower than the

Table 5.3 Participation rates for selected OECD countries by age group, 1993

	UK	France	Germany	Ireland	Spain	Japan	USA
Males							
15–19	61.1	10.0	37.1	26.4	29.1	19.0	53.1
20–24	85.8	57.7	74.3	75.2	65.7	75.2	83.1
25–34	94.5	95.0	86.1	92.8	91.9	97.2	93.5
35–44	94.6	96.4	91.5	91.8	95.3	98.3	93.5
45–54	90.7	92.8	90.8	87.2	91.0	97.5	90.1
55–59	75.7	67.8	68.7	64.7	73.6	94.1	78.2
60–64	52.2	19.0	29.2	64.7	44.8	75.6	54.1
Females							
15–19	58.0	5.9	32.8	20.2	25.8	17.4	49.8
20–24	71.2	49.7	72.0	69.9	57.7	74.5	71.3
25–34	70.7	77.7	71.7	65.5	65.1	58.7	73.6
35–44	76.8	77.7	73.5	47.9	52.4	66.5	76.7
45–54	74.4	71.5	67.3	36.7	36.0	69.5	73.5
55–59	54.5	46.6	41.2	20.3	24.4	56.4	57.1
60–64	24.7	15.0	9.4	20.3	16.2	40.1	37.1

Source: © OECD Labour Force Statistics, 1973–93, Reproduced by permission of the OECD.

OECD average, because of generous provisions for early retirement. The standard age for retirement is 65, but around half the population retires earlier. Those with a long contribution record can retire at 63 while those who are handicapped or are unable to gain employment can retire at 60.

The West German pension system was legally extended to East Germany in 1992, and between 1992 and 1995 pensions in the new states increased by 127%. Until the end of 1992, East German workers aged 55 or over could, when dismissed, claim a special type of unemployment benefit until they qualified for an early pension at age 60 rather than 65.

A weak economy, combined with a savage rationalisation of obsolete smokestack industries in East Germany has caused a massive upsurge in early retirement in both parts of the country. In the worst year, 1993, the numbers grew by 66% in the West and over 200% in the East, and even in 1995, and on a larger base, the number seeking early retirement grew by 13% and by over 80% respectively. Altogether some 300 000 workers across Germany took early retirement on account of unemployment, and the number of new pension payments by all branches of the public pension system soared from 1 million in 1992 to 1.8 million in 1995.

As a result, labour force can decline even faster than the number of people in the 15–64 age group. Table 5.4 below extrapolates the size of the labour force in a number of OECD countries up to the year 2050 using World Bank population projections and assuming that participation rates for each cohort remain at the 1993 levels. It is derived by multiplying the number of people in each age group by their 1993 participation rates and summing for age groups 15–64. We will return to this subject in Chapters 7 and 8, when we will see how a declining workforce has to support a growing army of pensioners.

Table 5.4 Projection of size of workforces for major European countries (15–64), 1995–2050

Country	Workforce (000)			Change (%)	
	1995	2020	2050	2020/1995	2050/2020
UK	28 747	28 330	25 759	–1.5	–9.1
Germany	38 186	31 906	23 630	–16.4	–25.9
France	25 279	25 043	22 557	–0.9	–9.9
Italy	23 089	19 610	14 171	–15.1	–27.7
Spain	16 308	14 898	10 767	–8.6	–27.7
Ireland	1 391	1 639	1 603	+17.8	–2.2

Source: Data derived from World Bank, OECD statistics.

Some of the conclusions are astonishing – for example, *the workforce in Germany could contract by almost 40% by 2050, making it smaller than that of the UK at that date, while that of Ireland could increase by 15% over the same period. The top five countries in the list could see their workforces fall by 35 million in the absence of immigration.*

In an attempt to mitigate the problem, countries throughout the EU are raising retirement ages and reducing the number of years in university that are subsidised by the State. (France however has gone against the trend by granting lower retirement ages to striking transport workers – down from 60 to 55 for drivers with 25 years' service – at considerable cost to taxpayers.) These will have some impact, but could well be offset if birth rates continue to fall below World Bank forecasts.

More steps will be necessary to release manpower from other sectors; here are three unpalatable suggestions:

(i)   Abolish conscription and make all armed forces small professional units. France, the nation that invented conscription, announced this change in 1996.

(ii) Trim the size of the public sector – France has roughly 2 million more employees than the UK, but has been singularly timid in making them leaner and more efficient.

(iii) Ease the restrictions on retail chains setting up large new stores. In Italy, where it can take 10 years to get planning permission to develop a greenfield site, there are 900 000 small retailers, compared to 300 000 in the UK. (This would also reduce the size of the black economy – the highest in Europe at around 25% of GDP *vs* 13% for the UK, according to some estimates and boost government revenue.)

In addition, there must be more training and education for those whose jobs have been lost through the relentless march of technology and the closure of obsolete industries.

Falling birth rates are already having an impact on the number of people joining the workforce, and companies from McDonalds to Matsushita are changing their personnel policies to meet a growing scarcity. To attract and retain the graduates it needs, in Japan, Matsushita has developed a multi-tier pay scheme, under which new recruits can choose between three options:

(i) the same as the current schemes, in which basic pay accounts for around 70% of the total salary, the rest being bonuses (23%) and overtime (6%), with the usual fringe benefits and retirement pension;

(ii) surrendering retirement benefits in exchange for annual bonuses whose total present value would equate to that of the pension forgone;

(iii) experienced workers would be entitled to convert both retirement pensions and fringe benefits into income.

For an employee earning Y3 million per annum, option (ii) would be worth Y240 000 per annum, and option (iii) Y350 000 per annum.

In addition, Japanese companies are quietly abandoning the automatic link between salary level and seniority, and creating a merit-based gap between good and bad performers. In time, the steepness of the Japanese salary structure (in which incoming white-collar workers are paid a far lower percentage of, and workers in their fifties a far higher premium to, the average than their European counterparts) will flatten out. Wages of the former will rise while those of the latter will be held down. This will help mitigate the rise in both employee costs and defer the pressure on pension provisions as the workforce continues to age rapidly.

Private consumption

Private consumption is normally the largest part of a nation's GDP. Changes in the absolute level of consumption can affect the entire chain of manufacturers and their suppliers – their profits, investment plans and employment policies – and hence indirectly government budgets, as well as overseas trade.

Except over the short-term, when individuals can shore up their levels of consumption by borrowing, their ability to consume can only be financed out of income, which for the vast majority of the population means income from employment. People in retirement can finance consumption by running down savings, but in many European countries, retirees are overwhelmingly dependent upon State pensions, which are ultimately paid for by those in employment. As a first approximation, therefore, we can use the size and spending power of the labour force as a key input for national income available for consumption.

These workforce figures should also give a good lead to trends in spending power. Thus, even assuming a growth of real wages of 1% per annum, in line with pension calculations in Chapter 7, it is clear that *total real personal income from employment in Italy will show little growth for the next half-century.* As argued earlier, globalisation will prevent workers from using their growing scarcity to bargain for greater increases in real wages. When account is taken of the expected increases in payroll taxes and/or the cost of private pension schemes, the trend in disposable income shows little growth.

Most of the UK's productivity gains of the last decade were due to labour shedding in manufacturing and attention is turning to the more difficult service sector. There has been considerable progress in some areas. For example, while it is hard to see how plumbers, barbers and corner shops can be made more efficient, bank and building society branches are being cut by telephone banking, privatised rail companies are introducing flexible working that was impossible under British Rail and the crisis in the National Health Service is forcing hospitals to consider closures and mergers to eliminate duplication of resources.

In a less quantifiable way, falling communication costs and the rise of the Internet are speeding up the information flow and sharpening the competition among retailers. In the pharmaceutical industry, new techniques for screening drugs have advanced the productivity of research so greatly that mergers have taken place to cut research costs by closing whole laboratories, releasing scientists, trial and project managers who now form the nucleus of start-up biotechnology companies. In short, there is no *technological* reason to suppose that productivity growth in the future need be lower than in the last decade for much of the economy, although falling demand for goods and services resulting from a declining population and rising pressure on disposable income may blunt the incentive to invest, so that companies take longer to benefit from technological advances.

If total consumer expenditure is unlikely to grow much in real terms after 2010, at least we can get some guide to individual sectors that could buck the trend by turning to the CSO's *Family Spending* surveys. These show that, while households headed by 30–49 year olds spend most on a per household basis, on a *per capita* basis, spending is greatest for those headed by 50–64 year olds (*see* Table 5.5).

Table 5.5 UK household expenditure, by age of head of household, 1995–6 (£ per week)

	<30	30–49	50–64	65–74	≥75	Total
Persons/household	2.4	3.1	2.2	1.7	1.5	2.4
Av. age of head	26	39	57	69	80	51
Expenditure (£)	269.94	360.66	309.83	198.40	139.00	289.86
Per person (£)	111.31	114.86	143.20	117.76	95.83	118.78

Source: Family Spending, 1995–6, Office for National Statistics © Crown Copyright 1996.

We can see how changes in the absolute sizes of these age groups in years to come will lead to the rise of the grey consumer, whose purchasing patterns are quite different from those of younger age groups. As would be expected, the largest single outlay for households headed by the under-30s is housing (19.6% of the total *vs* 18.2% for the 30–49 group and 13.5% for the 50–64 year group). Because this group has yet to reach its peak earnings potential but has made considerable effort to getting on the housing ladder, there is little available for discretionary outlays such as motoring or leisure goods and services, or, to a lesser extent, household goods.

The key spending group is clearly the 50–64 age group, whose earnings may have begun to plateau or decline, but, with a mortgage substantially paid off and few dependent children to support, has a far higher level of discretionary income. Motoring, leisure, travel and entertainment all feature strongly. Surprisingly, on a *per capita* basis, 65–74 year-old households spend roughly as much as those headed by 30–49 year olds on household goods and services, motoring, leisure goods and services, and somewhat more on food.

Although the workforce may be declining, the number of households continues to expand, as the increasing incidence of divorce and single parent families, and the growing number of retired people, living either as couples or alone, reduces average household size. Indeed the extent of these trends has led to a consistent underestimation of household formation. The most recent projection is that the UK will require an additional 4.4 million new households by 2016, bringing the total to 23.6 million.

In theory, this would suggest on-going growth in demand for consumer goods, given that almost all households these days have telephones, TVs, refrigerators, etc; but divorce is a costly business, involving the financing of an extra home, whether rented or owned. It is unlikely that the 23% projected increase in UK households over the next 20 years will lead to a *pro rata* increase in consumption. As the annual number of deaths increases after 2020, more houses, cars and consumer durables will come to the beneficiaries, reducing demand for new ones. In countries such as Germany, Spain and Italy, the relative impact on consumption will come earlier and be more severe – especially because it will take place against a background of rising savings to finance private pensions.

It is also unwise to assume that in, say, 20 years' time, relative income and expenditure levels of the different age groups will not have changed, particularly as the value of State pensions is frozen in real terms, while real incomes continue to rise. Growing fears of destitution in old age and of the high costs of staying in a retirement or nursing home may well switch the balance from consumption to saving – indeed, this book is based on just this assumption.

Industry, retailing and property

As the previous section makes clear, a whole range of consumer-based industries and retailers is likely to be ground between the millstones of falling populations that are saving more, and a rising availability of bequeathed consumer goods. It should in part be seen as the reverse of the multiplier effect that results from a housing boom. Falling demand for homes indirectly impinges on not only construction and building materials but also everything from carpets to curtains, and furniture to fitted kitchens and bathrooms, as well as white goods. In addition, there will be a direct impact on demand for food, drinks and clothing, books and newspapers, and those who supply them will be severely affected.

Retailers, pubs and restaurants will be the most vulnerable, since they are both labour- and property-intensive and furthermore cannot reposition themselves to go for a new customer base, or attack export markets. The closure of major store chains will become widespread throughout Europe from 2010 onwards, and those investing in retail property, or lending money against the security of retail property should stay alert.

Even within the high technology growth sectors such as electronics and biotechnology, expansion may well be held back by a shortage of young skilled workers on which they depend for new ideas. The decline in the labour force in the 25–34 year cohort could cause problems in years to come. The figures below are derived by applying 1994 participation rates to World Bank population projections. Once again, Ireland stands out in resisting decline. It is, furthermore the only country besides the UK amongst those listed in Table 5.6 to be substantially increasing investment in higher education.

Table 5.6 Projection of labour force by country, 1995–2050

Country	Estimated labour force aged 25–34 (000)			Change (%)	
	1995	2020	2050	1995–2020	2020–50
Germany	11072	6997	5735	−36.8	−18.0
France	7560	6595	6179	−12.8	−6.3
UK	7741	6312	5805	−18.5	−8.0
Italy	7091	4194	3709	−40.9	−11.6
Spain	5201	3155	2868	−39.3	−9.1
Ireland	441	418	439	−5.2	+5.0

Sources: Data derived from World Bank, OECD statistics.

Overseas trade

The gradual dismantling of trade barriers within the EU has led to a strongly increased interdependence in trade. Most countries in the EU now undertake over half of their overseas trade with other members of the EU. With prospects of an accelerating decline in demand for a range of goods and services, from food and energy to white goods throughout the EU, this will increasingly become a handicap. Companies will be forced to refocus both their capital investment and export strategies. I offer a few suggestions as to how this may develop:

- the switch from high-cost low fertility countries (Germany, Italy and Spain) to the more competitive and less demographically challenged UK and Ireland will continue
- a steady rise in export ratios for all countries in the EU as domestic demand dries up
- a rise in the proportion of exports going to non-EU destinations
- a switch in the composition of both production and exports from consumer goods towards capital goods as countries in Asia and the EU experience growing labour shortages.

Imports too will be affected, and the EU's stature in world trade will decline relative to that of the USA whose population will continue to expand while that of the EU falls.

GDP growth and stockmarket risk

With one of the major inputs to economic growth, the size of the work-force, likely to fall over the next 50 years, and capital investment in more productive plant inhibited by falling demand for product, overall GDP growth will clearly suffer. OECD calculations[3] suggest that in the case of Japan, for example, the long-term annual GDP growth could fall from 2.9% (1987–97) to 1.5% (2000–2005) and 1.0% (2025–50). It is a truism that a rising tide lifts all boats – i.e., strong economic growth can bail out even badly run companies – but in a slowdown, only the best survive.

GDP growth of 1.0–1.5% per annum is not sufficient to bring down the PERs of most Japanese companies to acceptable levels, and the stockmarket remains vulnerable. The same argument applies increasingly to Italy, Spain and Germany from around 2005 onwards, a factor that will influence our long-term portfolios.

References

1 Lamel, J. and Richter, J. (1992) 'Labour Market Implications of Aging – The Austrian Case' in *Changing Population Age Structures, 1990–2015*, United Nations, Geneva.
2 Beaujeu-Garnier, J. (1978) *Geography of Population*, Second Edition, p. 227.
3 *OECD Economic Surveys: Japan 1997*, p. 115.

FALLING INFLUENCE OR RISING IMMIGRATION?

Population as power

This seems like a good time to examine the way the EU's falling population will affect its position in the world.

Not only religions enjoin people to go forth and multiply, national leaders do, too, although for different reasons. It seemed no coincidence to observers at the time that the Franco-Prussian War broke out when the German population was just overtaking that of France. The pronatalist policies adopted by subsequent French governments, bolstered by generous incentives, were intended to prevent a similar demographic conjunction recurring. As late as the mid-1950s, commentators such as Professor Kingsley Davis still saw population size as a key determinant of national power, not only for the economies of scale it brought to manufacturing and distribution, but also for its military implications. Closer to the present, when nuclear weapons have rendered large European armies obsolete, dictators such as Ceaucescu still persisted in the belief that it is necessary to have a good supply of cannon fodder.

Even in more stable and democratic societies there is a feeling that power and influence are related to population. Dr Mahathir, the Prime Minister of Malaysia, back in the 1980s, advocated a far higher population for the country. On the other side of the Causeway, Singapore's leadership is gloomily contemplating the future resorption of the country into Malaysia unless birth rates rise significantly. Their different demographic momenta – and hence their relative regional clout – is becoming painfully clear.

Table 6.1 Population projections, Singapore and Malaysia, 1980–2050 (million)

	1980	1990	2025	2050
Singapore	2.4	2.7	3.9	4.0
Malaysia	13.7	19.9	30.5	39.2
S%M	17.5	13.6	12.8	10.2

Source: World Population Projections 1994–5, IBRD/The World Bank, Washington, D.C., 1994.

The apologies made by Senior Minister Lee Kuan Yew for adverse remarks he had made about the state of Johore would have been unthinkable when Singapore still harboured an ambition to be the regional financial centre of ASEAN and was far ahead of its neighbours in the quality of its infrastructure, corporate management, bank supervision and corporate governance. Nationalism amongst its neighbours has prevented Singapore from achieving this goal, and the steadily deteriorating demographics has put the country increasingly on the defensive as regional countries become more vocal in their criticism. Singapore has therefore prudently altered course towards a policy of direct overseas investment, capitalising on the nation's strong management skills and huge savings ratio. A significant proportion of its capital investment is taking place *outside* ASEAN.

Compound interest is a wonderful thing. An economy growing at 5% per annum doubles its size in roughly 14 years; doubling the growth rate to 10% halves the time it takes. Singapore, a diminutive colonial backwater 40 years ago, now boasts *per capita* GDP of $21 800 – almost 22% above the UK's $18 494 – thanks to four decades of roughly double-digit growth rates.

Even small countries can drive hard bargains, providing they are growing rapidly enough to be important markets for Western goods. What is true of smaller countries is especially true of large ones. Big populations with rising spending power can mean big markets – particularly for exporters whose home markets are stagnating or declining for demographic reasons. The importing countries recognise that this gives them considerable bargaining power – not just in getting good prices and credit terms, but also in ensuring that manufacturers undertake to set up plants in their country to produce, say, cars or consumer goods in joint venture with local companies. Growing economic strength and regional interdependency combined with a relative decline in the importance of trade with the West have done wonders to the region's self-confidence. The ability to call the shots in trade agreements is increasingly leading to a more robust approach to international politics.

Not just Japan and China feel that they can say 'no' to the USA, and get away with it. Countries in South-East Asia have made it clear that they have no interest in Westminster-style democracy and no intention of letting Washington dictate their internal or regional policies. Even the threat of China aggressively projecting its power among the sea lanes of the region is unlikely to send neighbouring states screaming for Uncle Sam's apron strings. Instead, they are following a pragmatic two-pronged policy – continued investment in China to persuade it of the advantages of economic development, which could disappear in the event of hostilities, while at the same time quietly buying large quantities of warships, planes and missiles.

79

China, meanwhile is doing its best to show itself as a responsible and supportive member of the South-East Asian community. For a start it has contributed US$1 billion towards the rescue package for Thailand, the first time ever that the country has participated in such a regional deal. As to outstanding regional territorial disputes over the Spratley Islands, well, these should be resolved peacefully, if not by this generation, then by the next. China's premier, Li Peng, has also supported the 'visionary and courageous' proposal of Malaysian prime minister Dr Mahathir, to review the universal declaration of human rights at the United Nations.

Attempts to marginalise the influence of the West in South-East Asian affairs took a further significant step in December 1997 with a joint summit between the leaders of ASEAN and those of China, South Korea and Japan – the first at which the USA was not accorded even a token presence. Meanwhile the EU is so lamentably unable to speak with a single clear voice while its attention is focused on Maastricht that it is inaudible and unregarded in Asia.

On a Purchasing Power Parity basis, the Chinese economy could overtake that of the USA by 2020[1] (assuming annual growth rates of 7% and 3% respectively), probably sooner. Indeed, on OECD projections (admittedly made before the recent turmoil in Asia), the share of world GDP held by developing countries as a whole could rise from its 1995 level of 40% to 60% by the same date. What are the consequences of such continuing relative expansion?

All countries in the West have felt the impact of exports from the Far East on their own economies, but as their spending power is eclipsed by more populous developing countries, they become less relevant to the latter as markets. At the same time, they become increasingly dependent for their income on supplying developing countries. This combination of factors tilts the balance of advantage increasingly away from the West, which will become unable to dictate that the world adhere to its own brand of economic liberalism, while continuing to practise *de facto* protectionism against any imports deemed to harm its domestic manufacturers.

For decades, international agreements have limited textile exports from the Far East and the Indian subcontinent to the USA and EU. The West was able to lay down terms to countries such as Hong Kong, which were both heavily dependent on such exports, and moreover had neither the economic clout nor the political influence that goes with it. The boot will soon be on the other foot, even though the USA Administration in particular seems unable to recognise the fact. The sheer economic power of China, India and South-East Asia is already forcing Western companies to make fundamental changes if they are to secure orders.

Perry's black ships opened up the hermetic nation of Japan, and British gunboats forced similar concessions out of China. It would be a delicious irony if, early next century, the Chinese were to compel the USA to open up its markets to, say, Chinese-made supertrains by threatening to use US-designed protectionist measures against imports of agricultural or manufactured products. Indeed, as we shall see, China will become a major capital exporter, just at the time the USA needs foreign investors to finance its soaring budget deficit. The Chinese leadership will surely exact better terms than the Japanese did as their price for keeping the US government afloat.

Governments can very occasionally get too greedy. Exxon abandoned exploration in Malaysia in the 1970s when total taxes on every barrel of oil produced became way out of line with other countries, and IBM and Coca-Cola closed down in Brazil and India in the face of unreasonable demands. These days, however, the lure of China, India, Vietnam and the rest has made Western governments and capitalists more pragmatic. Far from backing away, Western multinationals have used the opportunity presented by current depressed asset prices to acquire strategic stakes in companies in the region.

At the same time, tariff barriers are falling within Asia, accelerating the already strong trends towards economic interdependency. Half the trade of the Asia-Pacific region now takes place within the region. Japan has been the catalyst, as the sharp appreciation of the yen forced its manufacturers to seek low-cost suppliers in the region. *Over the decade 1985–95 the proportion of Japanese exports going to the Asian Developing Economies rose from 19% to 40%, and that of imports from 26% to 37%. Because of this, Japanese trade with the region is almost as large as that with the USA and EU combined.* Clearly, in the short term, this interdependence will act as a brake to growth, but providing that the banking sector is restored to health, there is no reason why a strong recovery should not commence by 2000.

Japanese investment in the West has been a sobering experience. According to the Nomura Research Institute, between 1981 and 1994, Japanese overseas investment (particularly in US government securities) suffered foreign exchange losses of Y37 million – 28% of the accumulated investment. At the same time, Japanese companies have sharply reduced investment in the USA/EU, where operating margins are at best breakeven, and switched to developing economies, where margins are closer to 4–5%. Between 1988 and 1994 the proportion of total investment in North America had fallen from 70% to 35%, while that in the NIEs, ASEAN and increasingly China, had doubled to 36% over the period. More and more, this foreign direct investment was concentrated not on exports outside the region but on consumption within it, further reducing the ability of Western governments to dictate terms to these countries.

Europe's influence on the rest of the world as a major importer of consumer goods will continue to diminish as its population declines while that of Asia increases (*see* Table 6.2), and intra-Asian trade outstrips trade with the West.

Table 6.2 Population projections 1990–2050 (million)

Region	1990	2020	2050
East/South-East Asia	1788	2358	2644
China	1134	1434	1556
India	850	1304	1623
Africa	627	1304	1999
Latin America/Caribbean	435	654	804
Europe	723	744	721
France/Germany/Italy/Spain/UK	290	293	270
Russian Federation	148	153	153
North America	280	354	374

Source: World Population Projections 1994/5, IBRD/The World Bank, Washington D.C., 1994.

Providing that it uses its savings to build up profitable investments in growth economies, however, there is no reason why this should be a matter of regret. Switzerland manages quite nicely on financial services, investment income, tourism and a few key industries, arms, capital goods and pharmaceuticals, and has little international clout. On that set of yardsticks the EU could become Switzerland writ large. Indeed, by the middle of the next century, the pendulum may be swinging back to Europe, as Asia feels the full impact of labour shortages and accelerates its imports of capital goods, in order to reduce the labour content of its manufactured output.

Immigration: will the Moors recolonise Spain?
Discuss

Then I saw floating above the stem the Union Jack – the flag under which so many refugees, Russian, Italian, French, Hungarian and of all nations, have found asylum. I greeted that flag from the depth of my heart.

Prince Kropotkin

Not all emigrants are on the run from Tsarist police like Prince Kropotkin, but a depressingly large number are in a similar predicament. For hundreds of years, Europeans have been forced to leave their own countries for foreign lands under the pressure of political change or invading armies. The Second World War and its aftermath led to the displacement of millions. It is hard to recall that the building of a strong monolithic Germany has been achieved with a significant contribution from a large body of German-speaking refugees driven out by rising nationalism from Poland, Czechoslovakia and Hungary, and by the Russian armies who moved into East Germany.

Between 1946 and 1950 some 12 million *Vertriebene* (persons driven out) were expelled from East German provinces. Some 1.6–2 million were killed, starved to death or perished in the exodus. In 1950, 19.8% of West Germany's entire population were refugees, and on its eastern fringes, the proportions were much higher – 32.6% in Lower Saxony, 23.6% in Bavaria. The inward pressure continued afterwards – between 1950 and 1961, 2.6 million East Germans out of a total population of 17 million moved to West Germany. United by common ancestry, language and culture, and the pressing need to rebuild a shattered economy, they have become a homogeneous nation; Bavaria itself is a prosperous state with world-class auto and engineering industries.

Although the Berlin Wall closed off this flow for decades, the collapse of communism led to a new surge, culminating in 1989 with an inflow of 344 000, equivalent to 2% of the population and 3% of the workforce of East Germany. Between 1989 and 1993, 1.4 million East Germans and East Berliners settled in the West, although some 350 000 returned to the East during the period.

Assimilation inevitably takes longer for immigrants with different backgrounds to that of the host country. The huge loss of life amongst soldiers during the First World War left France with a labour shortage and a depressed birth rate. To fill the gaps in the workforce, some 1.9

million foreigners (of whom 33% were Italian, 32% Polish and the rest from Spain and Belgium), entered France between 1920 and 1931 to work in the mines, agriculture and construction.[2]

The Poles brought their families, their priests and teachers, maintained their own language and culture, and at the outbreak of war were still practically unassimilated, since the intention of the majority was to save sufficient money to return to a post-war Poland and become farmers. The war however prevented them from achieving their ambition; rather than return to a Poland under communism, they chose to remain in France, sent their children to French schools and have now effectively merged with the general population. In a similar manner, the Italians who came to the UK in the 1950s to work in the Bedfordshire brickfields are no longer an identifiable community.

Once a country does not need so many new workers to push forward the nation's frontiers or to bridge a labour shortage, assimilation becomes more difficult for newcomers, particularly when a dominant culture and language has emerged which is different from theirs. They will nevertheless continue to arrive, unless physically prevented, if prospects seem better than at home and there are fellow countrymen to whom they can turn for initial support.

Government may react to this by introducing restrictions on immigration, as the USA – a nation of immigrants – did in 1921. These tied permitted annual admissions to 3% of the population of each country resident in the USA at the time of the 1910 Census. When the inflow from Mediterranean and Slavic countries, who tended to have poor command of English and were more likely to intermarry than to marry native-born Americans, threatened to overwhelm the culture of the older waves of immigrants who had come mainly from the UK and Northern Europe, the quotas were tightened. In 1924, the Census date was changed to 1890, a time when the Anglo-Saxon proportion was more dominant.

Some countries such as Israel thrive on immigration, because the newcomers are united in their belief system, but in continental Europe, high structural unemployment, aggravated by the need to comply with the Maastricht criteria, is being blamed by its victims on competition from immigrants – particularly where the latter can be singled out by their colour, complexion or religion. Until recently, the French believed that there was no colour problem in France, but a significant change in the racial mix amongst immigrants is leading to increased tensions. In 1970, roughly 75% were Europeans; today, they represent only 40%, with Arabs and black Africans comprising almost 50%. The rise of Le Pen and his calls for repatriation of immigrants has struck a chord amongst the unemployed in Marseilles. Further East, Turks have been firebombed in Germany, while in Austria, anti-immigrant Haidar has done surprisingly well in the recent elections, as has Pia Kjaersgaard's Danish People's party in Denmark.

In the case of West Germany, post-war economic recovery was so successful that, even with the inflow from East Germany, labour shortages developed. They were met through the introduction of the *Gastarbeiter* – mostly from Mediterranean countries who were permitted to stay in West Germany for one to three years, then required to return home. Between 1960 and 1973 some 18–19 million *Gastarbeiter* worked in West Germany, of whom some 4–5 million overstayed. The severity of the 1974 recession caused the country to impose a virtual ban on recruitment outside the European Community, but 50–100 000 immigrants per annum still entered the country after 1974 on the basis of family reunion, under the protection of the Basic Law and the European Convention on Human Rights.

Furthermore, the generous provisions of the 1949 Asylum Law require that nobody arriving on West German soil and claiming asylum be turned away without receiving a fair and individual investigation. This loophole became the means whereby most immigrants entered the country, rather than applying for visas. In 1973, 57% of all applicants for refugee status were successful. Not only that, but those whose applications had been rejected could delay extradition for up to three years, during which time they received accommodation, food, schooling and a monthly allowance. Even those whose appeals were finally dismissed were seldom extradited – 60–70% of those rejected *de jure* were allowed to stay *de facto*.

Because of its history, Germany has been more receptive to immigrants than most. East Germans, refugees from the Yugoslav civil war and citizens from Kazakhstan of German descent have all been granted entry. Indeed, without this influx, Germany would have experienced a population decline since 1990. Official figures show the trends tabulated in Table 6.3.

Table 6.3 Rates of natural increase and immigration in European countries (per 1000 of population)

Country	Natural increase		Net migration		Total increase	
	1990–4	1995	1990–4	1995	1990–4	1995
USA	7.3	6.2	3.3	3.1	10.6	9.3
France	3.7	3.4	1.3	0.8	5.0	4.2
Germany	-1.0	-1.4	7.0	5.2	6.0	3.8
Ireland	5.5	4.8	-1.4	-1.5	4.1	3.2
UK	2.3	1.5	1.3	1.5	3.6	3.1
Spain	1.4	0.3	0.5	1.3	1.9	1.6
Italy	0.1	-0.6	1.9	1.6	2.0	1.1

Source: Eurostat Demographic Statistics, 1995.

In 1995 some 217 898 *Aussiedler* entered Germany, by far the majority from the former Soviet Union. They receive retraining, learn or improve their German and wait to be given an apartment of their own. They are generally older than native Germans – 22% were over 60 in 1995 *vs* 16.8% within Germany – and will therefore require higher levels of pensions and healthcare, although there is also a higher proportion in the prime working age band of 20–45 (37% *vs* 31%).

The cost of this amounted to some DM4 billion in 1995, and at a time when the taxpayer has to support over 4 million unemployed as well as bailing out the East German economy, resentment is growing. Oskar Lafontaine, leader of the opposition Social Democrats has proposed restricting the automatic right of *Aussiedler* to 'return home' as a first step towards a tighter immigration policy. Provisions were tightened in July 1993, and supported by Germany's EU partners who were worried that Germany could become a conduit for economic migrants and criminal elements. As a result, the number of asylum applicants has fallen sharply (*see* Table 6.4).

Table 6.4 Asylum applications in Germany, 1992–5

1992	438 000
1993	322 599
1994	127 210
1995	127 937

Source: Council of Europe, Recent Demographic Developments in Europe, 1995 and 1997.

Public opinion is still divided, however, as to whether or not Germany should be considered an Immigration country.

(It is ironic that research by the RWI in Essen concluded that, after allowing for the cost of unemployment benefits, family allowances, etc., amounting to DM18 billion per year, the 4.2 million new immigrants who entered Germany in the period 1988–92 contributed a net DM14 billion to government finances, and raised annual GDP growth rate by 1.5%. Such findings on the economic benefits of immigration are not unique to Germany. After 10 years in the USA, legal immigrants have higher than average incomes, are less likely to live in poverty, or if they do, are less likely than native-born Americans to go on welfare.)

In France, too, a recent parliamentary committee of enquiry recommended that the tough immigration laws brought in by Charles Pasqua when he was Interior Minister in 1993 should be made even tighter. It would introduce fingerprinting of all applicants for visas from countries with 'high migratory risk', punish employers of illegal immigrants and deny immigrants without valid papers access to public health care, family benefits and subsidised housing.

In both Europe and North America the earlier waves of newcomers contained a high proportion of professionals who found a ready demand for their skills. More recent arrivals include fewer professionals, and latecomers are finding it harder to succeed. Many immigrants are unskilled, but can occupy niches that the native-born population is unwilling to fill because of the low level of pay or poor working conditions. Smuggling is big business, and with the connivance of employers in the host countries, such illegal immigrants can be integrated into the workforce. Only when identification papers need to be presented is there a risk of discovery and deportation, and European governments have proved peculiarly reluctant to pursue a vigorous deportation policy.

In the short term, the recovery of the European economies will be insufficient to absorb the continuing redundancies from companies desperate to restructure, and unemployment will remain high. Attempts to create jobs by reducing the length of the workweek can only succeed if the greater flexibility and lower wage-cum-social security cost to the employer offset his lower plant utilisation. With workers unwilling to forgo income, it is hard to see a widespread adoption of this type of scheme. In other words, the conditions that underpin the likes of Le Pen and Haidar will persist for several years before a tightening labour situation begins, temporarily, to reduce the support for xenophobic nationalism.

The problem will not go away, however, and once the current high levels of unemployment decline, perhaps as soon as the end of the century for Germany, the stage will be set for a major confrontation between Europeans and immigrants. Putting it bluntly, if Europe is to maintain the present size of its workforce, an increasing proportion of which will be required to care for the sick and elderly, it will have to import huge numbers of foreigners. We have already seen that between 1995 and 2050 the workforce of the five largest countries in Western Europe could fall by 35 million. *Could the German public be seriously expected to welcome a workforce that was 40% foreign by 2050?*

When balancing the need for immigrant labour against the costs and possible risks incurred, we must consider not only gross numbers, but also the levels of skills required and perhaps even the age group of prospective incomers (Coleman, 1992).[3] The trend towards rising levels of skill has been in evidence for a decade or more in the West and is expected to continue. Indeed, even though an increasing proportion of the UK population is entering higher education, the demand for unskilled manual labour has been falling faster than the total number of those who have no qualifications; the lower the level of skill or qualification attained the higher the likely level of unemployment. *This in itself rules out relying too heavily on immigrants from countries where levels of skill and education are generally low – including the largest potential source of immigrants, North Africa.* Unemployment amongst immigrants in European countries is typically two to three times that of native residents.

It has been argued (*ibid.*) that there is such a reservoir of unemployed and underemployed people in the EU that additional immigrant labour is unnecessary; indeed *it is suggested that 30 million or more workers could be mobilised if governments could boost participation rates.* While this is *mathematically* plausible, governments have been lamentably unable to convert this into reality. Indeed it is their connivance with industry and unions to permit early retirement on spurious health grounds, rather than swell the roll of the unemployed, that has greatly contributed to the current situation. There is no sign that they have undergone any Damascene conversion, quite the contrary, if the antics of the Jospin government are any guide. With the exception of the UK, they seem constitutionally incapable of combining a carrot with even the smallest bit of stick to get people off benefit and into work.

The steady decline in the number of births throughout the EU has after a lag reduced the number of school leavers entering the job market, and in countries such as the UK, this number has been further cut back by the the rising proportion going on to tertiary education. Despite this, there has not, so far, been a disproportionate increase in starting salaries for the unskilled, partly because of the generally weak demand for such people, but also because companies such as B&Q are beginning to recruit older workers for jobs traditionally undertaken by teenagers. (By contrast, companies are starting to bid up salaries for the most promising university graduates, as has happened in the USA.)

If shortages amongst the younger cohorts of workers were to arise, then Western Europe might consider drawing on the population of Eastern Europe, which did not generally undergo either the 1960s baby boom nor the subsequent steady decline in birth rates until the early 1990s (*ibid.* p. 445). As a result of this, relative to its EU neighbours, the countries of Eastern Europe have a 'surplus' of those in the younger age groups (those now aged roughly ten to 25). These generally have some command of English (given a high priority after the fall of communism) and could perhaps smooth out, but not eliminate, shortages in countries such as the UK where unemployment has been in steep decline since 1992.

But, *where is one to find 35 million working immigrants* without damaging the economies of surrounding countries? If we are to assume that Europe will try to target immigrants from the White East rather than the Black South – how can it justify taking large numbers of the brightest and best from the poorer countries of Eastern Europe and the FSU, that are struggling to reach the economic level of the EU? Perhaps the only excuse is that, like Polish emigrants of 70 years before, these future migrants may wish to work abroad in order that, in time, they can afford to return home. Meanwhile, their remittances may make valuable contributions to their home countries, as has been the case with those from the Philippines, South Korea and the Indian sub-continent working in the Middle East.

However, in both Eastern Europe and the Russian Federation, the collapse in both State health services and pensions, and the decline in already low birth rates since 1990, point to a further fall in population and potentially a smaller influx of economic migrants to the West once their economies start to recover sufficiently to absorb current high unemployment.

The flashpoint over immigration is likely to be in the South, not the East where levels of education are high and no colour or religious differences to mark off an immigrant from a resident. The porous border between the countries of Southern Europe and North Africa however presents one of the most extreme gradients of wealth and demographic pressure anywhere in the world, and the gradients are getting steeper.

France, Germany and the Netherlands are so concerned by the apparent inability of the Italian authorities to prevent the influx of illegal immigrants from Tunisia and Albania, or to repatriate those they catch, that they refused to ratify Italy's full accession to the Schengen club of countries free of common border controls. (Recent anarchy in Albania, following the collapse of a pyramid selling scheme has greatly increased the number of economic migrants seeking a new life in Italy, and it remains to be seen how efficiently the Italian authorities deal with this problem.) They are similarly unimpressed with Spain, whose patrols seem equally unable to cope with Moroccans slipping across the border.

The 1995 TFRs in Spain and Italy confirm the seemingly relentless decline in fertility to levels well below World Bank expectations. In-built momentum will ensure a doubling of Morocco's population to 52 million by 2050, at a time when Italy and Spain will scarcely be able to muster 48 million and 35 million respectively (all World Bank estimates). Over this period, their combined workforces could have fallen by over 14 million, unless steps are taken to raise retirement age, cut early retirement and boost participation rates.

Is it likely that these countries will be prepared to rely increasingly on the labour of immigrants from such a different cultural background, and if so, will they permit them to acquire residency and citizenship rights? Are Europeans and their political leaders prepared to debate what type of society they want for the future? These are the questions that were never properly addressed in the 1950s and 1960s, and have come back to haunt us today.

As a postscript, it is worth pointing to the difficulties of getting workers to travel even *within* a country in Europe, where labour mobility is far lower than in the USA. Indeed, increasing demographic problems will greatly increase the risk of Italy splitting in two. The Northern region is prosperous and short of labour, the South depressed and suffering from high unemployment. But do Southerners move North? No. There is little incentive to do so while wage rates are largely fixed on a national basis. If, however, the two parts of the country split, and adopted separate currencies, it is clear that the Northern lire would be significantly stronger, greatly increasing the incentive for Southerners to move to the new North, and for Northern industrialists to invest in the new South, a win-win situation. Unhappily, with the single currency, this is not an option.

Not just a European problem

Any country that is perceived to offer a significantly higher standard than one's own is potentially a magnet for immigrants, but with labour shortages temporarily over for most developed countries, barriers to entry are being raised. On the other hand, some of the booming countries of South-East Asia have had to rely increasingly on migrant labour because economic growth has outstripped even the rapid increase in the domestic labour force. Here we examine the recent experience of Thailand, Malaysia and Singapore and draw a few pointers about their future.

The sharp decline in birth rates in developing countries will have an equally serious impact on the future sizes of the workforces in those countries. The difficulty in reconciling projected high levels of economic growth in Thailand with the tightness in labour supply, particularly since much of the possible transfer of workers from fields to factories has already happened, will lead to labour shortages from 2005. Indeed, the strong growth recorded up to 1997 has already attracted in around 1 million immigrant workers, mainly from Myanmar. With the current downturn, some 800 000 were told to leave in early 1998. *Once again, this raises a fundamental question about whether the Tiger economies can continue their torrid growth, or, whether like Japan, beset by an ageing population and soaring social costs, they will subside to far more pedestrian performances next century. When drawing up the guidelines for a personal portfolio, this choke point on future growth should be borne in mind.*

Malaysia has only been able to achieve its present rate of growth by harnessing the labour of perhaps 2 million immigrants of whom 1 million are thought to be illegal, and by mid-1997 had begun to experience the tensions that this creates. The government embarked on a high-profile campaign to deport illegal immigrants who are being blamed for the increasing incidence of crime and disease. The fact that they have undoubtedly helped to prevent the chronic labour shortage from getting worse, kept down wage inflation and probably made a significant net contribution to economic growth has been considered less important than their impact on harmony in a multiracial society.

By the end of 1997 Malaysia was reeling under the onslaught on its currency. It had been forced to raise interest rates sharply, imperilling a whole range of property and infrastructure projects, and causing wholesale layoffs of construction workers, a high proportion of whom are foreign, illegal, or both. Companies whose construction projects have come to an end have been ordered to notify government of any foreign workers in their employ, so that they can be repatriated. (Because of the high proportion of illegal workers on construction sites, this is unlikely to happen, but with employment opportunities vanishing in 1998, it is going to be increasingly hard for those made redundant to survive in the country.) Faced with an domestic electorate angered by loss of jobs and wealth, and now suffering from sharply higher inflation and borrowing costs, the government will at least try to ensure that the burden is borne by immigrants rather than by its own citizens, despite the tension it will cause to its neighbour, Indonesia.

Across the Causeway, Singapore, torn between chronic sub-replacement birth rates and the need for rapid economic growth, is even more dependent on immigrant workers than its neighbour. Between 1992 and 1997, their share of the workforce has doubled from 12% to 25%, a trend that shows no sign of being reversed. If the economy is to continue to grow at around its current rate of 7% per annum, it will generate additional demand for 100 000 jobs a year, only half of whom can be supplied by Singaporeans entering the workforce. Government must therefore choose between a future in which, according to Professor Hui Wang Tat of the National University,[4] foreigners could account for up to 44% of the workforce by 2010, and lower economic growth.

Because the economy is strong and unemployment low, the contribution of immigrant workers is accepted, since no Singaporean feels displaced by them in the jobs market. The government, too, is likely to act firmly against any violence towards immigrants. Indeed, if it so chooses, Singapore seems the country most capable of ensuring sustained economic growth, while remaining heavily dependent on immigrant labour.

Although the crisis will undoubtedly lead to massive loss of jobs in 1998, greatly enhanced competitiveness will ensure that economic growth resumes by the following year, and the problem of labour shortages will re-emerge, perhaps by the beginning of the new millennium.

The obverse to this problem throws up exciting investment opportunities in the West. If we assume that these countries wish to continue to grow at their historic rates, they will need accelerating productivity – in other words, heavy investment in labour-saving equipment, and this the West is well positioned to supply.

The problem of a declining population extends even further into the economic life of a nation. In most countries, State pension schemes are generally financed by a direct transfer of contributions from workers and their employees. So what happens when falling birth rates lead both to fewer workers *and* more pensioners?

References

1 'China Embraces the Market: Achievements, Constraints and Opportunities.' Department of Foreign Affairs and Trade, Canberra, Australia.
2 Beaujeu-Garnier, J. (1978) *Geography of Population*, Second Edition, p. 189.
3 Coleman, D. A. (1992) 'Does Europe Need Immigrants? Population and Workforce Projections', *International Migration Review*, Vol. xxvi, No. 2.
4 *Economist*, 17 January 1998, p. 67, 'Singapore: Foreigners still welcome'.

Part III

AUSTERITY OR STATE BANKRUPTCY?

PENSIONS

The babies born today will affect someone else's State pension 16–20 years from now. If you live anywhere in Europe, your pension is not safe. The demographics which made pay-as-you-go attractive in the early post-war period have gone into reverse. To bridge a yawning funding deficit, pension age will be increased, contribution rates will rise (prompting a switch to the black economy), and benefits will be allowed to fall in real terms. Governments make lousy investors anyway, so, if you can, start your own savings plan. P.S. Advances in biotechnology will have a major impact on life expectancy over the next decade; if you're reliant on a State pension, try not to live too long.

Introduction

Credit for the first national contributory old age insurance scheme goes to Bismarck, who established such a system for political rather than for social reasons. It must be said at the outset that ever since, politicians have used their control over the way State schemes are financed and over their benefits to bribe electorates, raid the funds and increasingly to renege on promises that could not possibly be kept from one generation to the next. By the start of the Second World War, some 17 countries had implemented national contributory schemes providing modest pensions at modest cost; pensions were typically 15–20% of the average wage and were means tested, while pensioners themselves were expected to live only a few years after retirement.

Following the publication of the Beveridge Report in 1942, Britain embarked on a more generous pension system financed by payroll tax collected on a pay-as-you-go (PAYG) basis. It was encouraged to do so by a combination of two favourable factors – a growing population and wages rising at historically high levels. Other countries followed suit, so that by 1980 the ratio of average pensions to average wages for 12 leading Western countries had reached 45% – roughly triple the payout offered in 1939.

The schemes are usually financed by payroll tax, sometimes topped up by contributions from general government revenues, e.g., income tax. Benefits are usually constructed on a two-tier basis: a flat-rate basic pension providing little more than subsistence and a second, earnings-related pension. However they are constituted, they have broadly failed in their principal aims of protecting the old against inflation and ensuring a degree of income distribution in favour of the poor, the USA being a major exception. The cause of failure is embodied in the formula linking benefits to contributions under a PAYG scheme. Assuming pensions are linked to wages and financed entirely by a payroll tax, the benefit rate B (as % of average wages) is given by:

$$B = \frac{C}{D}$$

where C = the contribution rate necessary to cover the pension, and D is the system dependency, i.e., the ratio of beneficiaries to contributors. Its implications are that the greater the ratio of contributors to pensioners the lower the contribution rate for a given level of benefit, or, more cynically, the higher the pension rate a government will promise for a given contribution rate. Once PAYG is in place, then providing the population continues to grow, so that the number of new contributors outpaces the number of retirees (when the age pyramid really *is* a pyramid), this, the ultimate pyramid scheme will deliver. Two factors have spoilt this – the falling birth rate has reduced the growth of the workforce, and pensioners are living longer. As a result system dependency rates are rising and pushing up contribution rates with them.

A British male born in 1931 would not, on average, have lived to see his retirement – his expectation of life was below 58 years. By 1961, near the peak of the baby boom, this figure had risen to 67.8 years, (i.e., 2.8 years in retirement), but by 1996, a newborn male would expect to live to 74.4 years, and hence enjoy a pension 3.36 times as long. Putting it another way, if hypothetically life expectancy had risen instantaneously from 67.8 to 74.4, then contribution rates would have had to rise by 236% to maintain the same benefit rate.

This rise in life expectancy is forecast to continue for at least the next 20 years, albeit at declining rates, reaching 78.2 years for males born in 2031. This is due in part to a fall in cigarette smoking and a move towards a healthier diet, particularly in Scotland. (Medical breakthroughs could lead to significant improvement in life expectancy for those suffering from diseases such as cancer, but this may be offset by increases in the incidence of such diseases of the rich as diabetes, where late complications considerably reduce life expectancy.)

We have already seen that a fall in European birth rates starting in the 1960s is rippling through the system, restraining the growth of the labour force while the number of pensioners continues to rise rapidly. The old-age dependency ratio (i.e., the number of pensioners divided by the number of people of working age, generally taken as 15–64) is rising steadily. By the beginning of 1995, those aged 65 and over comprised 18–24% of the population in the main countries of Western Europe. By 2030, however, this ratio will have risen above 30% for all these countries, even on the World Bank's optimistic birth rate scenario, and the impact on dependency ratios will be that much more severe.

That, unfortunately, is not the end of the matter, since, as mentioned earlier, not all those of working age actually seek employment, as they may be involved full-time in higher education or raising a family, or may suffer from handicap or chronic illness that prevents them from doing so. Furthermore this participation rate has been shrinking over a number of years in many countries as companies increasingly make use of early retirement to reduce their labour forces. The companies gain but the State pension system loses doubly, through reduced contributions and higher outlays. The net result is that the system is compelled to raise either payroll taxes or income tax to bridge the gap.

In the countries of Eastern Europe, this process has spun out of control. To prepare labour intensive companies for privatisation without swelling the headline unemployment figures, their governments have resorted extensively to early retirement, funded by rising payroll taxes. The ploy has backfired, since contribution rates have risen well beyond what would be expected for countries in their GDP range, with the result that other companies have been priced out of the market. They have reacted by shedding labour, or subcontracting to the black economy, the lower productivity of which puts a further strain on the nation's ability to compete.

The size of the black economy should not be ignored even in Western Europe. For example, in July 1997, the Italian statistical service, Istat, gloomily reported that almost 5 million people, or around one-quarter of the entire Italian workforce, were engaged in the black economy, and that the figure is rising – as is that of illegal foreign workers. Agriculture and services are the most affected overall. Not surprisingly, the problem is most acute in the south, where an estimated 40% of the construction workforce is in the black economy. The position is hardly better in law-abiding Germany, where IW, the research arm of the BDI, the Federation of Industry, estimated that over the period 1975–97, the size of the black economy had risen from DM103 billion to DM548 billion, i.e., from 6% to 15% of GDP. The cost to the State in 1997 was put at DM125 billion in lost tax revenue and DM110 billion in lost social security benefits.[1]

It is clear that those who cannot avoid paying taxes have had enough of carrying those who don't – even in famously *communautaire* Germany, where President Roman Herzog captured the mood in an interview with the weekly newspaper *Die Wocher* in which he was quoted as saying, 'I would like to see the German who still submits an honest tax declaration. Anyone abiding by the law must often feel an idiot.'[2] The official revolt has begun. Two of the richer states, Bavaria and Baden-Württemburg, have challenged the constitutional right of the federal government to transfer over 90% of the tax revenue originating in their territories to poorer Länder. On the very same day, industry leaders savagely criticised the recent decision to raise pension contributions from 20.3% to 21% – a record high – in 1998, and the continuing failure to deliver credible tax reforms.

Because of inadequate record keeping in some countries, or because, as a result of previous unwise promises, workers may be entitled to full pensions after working for as few as 10 years, there is every incentive to indulge in 'tactical' unemployment. In other words, after working just long enough to qualify for their pension they may opt out and join the black economy. The system dependency – the ratio of contributors to pensioners – takes a further dive, and the administrators are faced with three choices:

- a further increase in tax or payroll tax
- reneging on previous promises
- creating a new system.

By this stage, the first option is a non-starter because it would be counterproductive, but the second has been well exploited by a range of governments. A year (or more) can be skipped in indexing future pensions to wages (USA), or the basis of indexation can be changed from wages to prices (UK), so that pensioners preserve their spending power in today's terms but cannot participate in future productivity gains. The number of years necessary to qualify for a full pension can be raised as can actual retirement ages. If all else fails, a government can erode the real value of benefits through inflation.

Not all these ploys are successful. Legal challenges have established that, in Brazil and Italy at least, government must honour its obligations to pensioners whatever the cost. Italy's Constitutional Court found in June 1994 that the government should pay pension arrears to almost 1 million pensioners going back to 1983. While the backlog payable in

1996 will require the issue of L19 700 billion (£8.13 billion) the final total could reach L47 300 billion. There in no doubt that such sums can only be paid if the Italian government finds legal means to trim future entitlements. They must be looking nostalgically towards the USA where the Supreme Court ruled as far back as 1960 that social security recipients do not have a legally enforceable contract, and that the government can alter the benefits at any time.

Crunch time: 2030

The momentum of the demographic juggernaut will be unstoppable for at least the next 20, and possibly 50, years. Using the World Bank's figures, we can project the size of the population of working age, and that of retirement age, and hence derive the dependency ratio – the number of people of working age whose income can support a pensioner. In the case of OECD countries, we can go a stage further using participation rates to project the actual size of the workforce and hence the system dependency.

The figures point to a major meltdown of the existing welfare system resulting from much the same factors already apparent in Eastern Europe – rising contribution rates for existing workers and falling returns as they retire. For example, the ratio of pensioners to workers in Germany is projected to rise from 0.32 to 0.8 between 1995 and 2050. A World Bank simulation, based on actual data averaged across countries in three demographic stages from youth to maturity of the pension system confirms this (*see* Table 7.1).

Table 7.1 The life cycle of pay-as-you-go

Stage	Support ratio	Pension expenditure/ GDP	Payroll tax rate (%)	Coverage (%)	Surplus % of revenues	Simulated social security debt/GDP
1	17.5	0.6	8.0	15.7	47.1	5
2	11.8	3.3	13.7	45.4	34.9	40
3	5.3	8.5	24.6	89.4	−19.6	150

Source: p. 315, Table 6.1. *Averting the Old Age Crisis. Policies to Protect the Old and to Promote Growth* by World Bank. Copyright 1994 by The International Bank for Reconstruction and Development/The World Bank. Used by permission of Oxford University Press, Inc.

We already have a pointer to the future in Portugal, where the number of pensioners has risen from 100 000 in 1960 to 2.4 million by 1996, and there are now only 1.7 workers supporting each pensioner. Persistently low birth rates have played a part, but the situation has been made substantially worse by emigration. Between 1960 and 1990, some 1.7 million Portuguese emigrated – a huge number when set against a 1996 population of only 10 million. Many left because of the repression of the Salazar-Caetano regime and the chaos that accompanied its overthrow in 1974. Few have returned. As a result, social security contributions no longer cover the cost of the very meagre pensions, and the system only works because income taxes fill the gap. By 2030, with a further sharp fall in the support ratio, taxes will have to rise steeply, or the system will go bust.

As mentioned before, when a PAYG system is set up, the earliest cohorts of retirees do best. Actual studies show a spectacular difference in returns between this group and the latest ones. For example, US workers retiring in the 1950s received returns well in excess of what they would have obtained from investment in stocks or bonds while future retirees could well receive negative returns. This finding is being duplicated in other countries including Germany, the Netherlands and Sweden. Thus, whereas Swedes born between 1904 and 1914 received 3.75 times the present value of their contributions on retirement, those born between 1940 and 1944 will in real terms receive 40% *less* than their contributions.[3]

Greater realisation of this fact could lead to workers moving to the unofficial economy, putting further strains on the system, and forcing them to realise that they must find the means of preserving the value of their pensions from their own resources. Workers and employers will be in no mood to accept higher contribution rates. *It is likely that intergenerational tensions will increase, and elections may be fought over whether workers should continue to subsidise the old, when the value of their own future entitlements is diminishing rapidly. This is not a wild prediction – it is already happening in Italy.*

The management of public pension funds – could do better

Contributions received by the PAYG pension schemes may not go automatically to the pensioners. In some cases, a reserve is built up in the early years when the system is in surplus, to be run down as it becomes mature and ultimately falls into deficits. Under the law of most countries, these reserves are invested predominantly in debt issued by the government concerned, which can prove a mixed blessing. Governments gain access to funds at rates that might be unattainable if they had to compete for them in the open market – a fact that makes it a *de facto* tax on pensioners, whose real benefits may be further eroded by inflation. Such easy access to funds may also encourage governments to spend more than is prudent.

According to a range of studies summarised by the World Bank, most publicly managed pension funds lose money, largely because of two factors – low returns and high inflation. In countries of Eastern Europe and Latin America, funds have also been on-lent to finance residential mortgages at subsidised rates, benefiting the elite who can afford the loans and penalising the pensioners. Real rates of return have been as poor as –37.4% (for Peru, 1981–8) or –23.8% (for Turkey, 1984–8). Even the prudent and scrupulously honest Singapore has only offered pensioners a 3.0% real annual return over the period 1980–90, although in this case, much of the money is likely to have been invested overseas at far higher rates of return, helping to reduce the level of taxation, as well as spreading the risk. Singapore's foreign exchange reserves in November 1997 stood at US$74 billion, or roughly $25 000 per head of the population.

The contrast in performance between private pension funds and even the best of the publicly managed funds is damning (*see* Table 7.2).

Given the expectation that these trends are expected to continue, the case for examining the benefits of switching from public to private pension funds is a strong one. Indeed there is an economic case for such a switch provided that the real returns on pension fund assets exceed labour productivity plus the growth of the labour force – i.e., the growth of real GDP. A number of simulations have been done to check this, some being based on actual pension funds others on 'synthetic' pension funds composed equally of domestic equity and debt, and assumed to track domestic indices and interest rates. The latter (Miles, 1996)[4] show that the majority of Western countries have achieved this performance during the period 1962–94. The exceptions tend to be amongst those countries now facing the most severe demographic pressures – Japan, Italy, Spain and Portugal. The other approach (Davis, 1993)[5], covering the period 1970–90, highlights the fact that UK pension funds recorded the highest real rates of return – 6.1% *vs* an average of 3.8% for eight countries comprising the USA, Canada, the UK, Denmark, Germany, Netherlands, Switzerland

Table 7.2 Average annual investment returns for selected pension funds, 1980s

	Country	*Period*	*Returns*
Publicly	Peru	1981–8	–37.4
managed	Turkey	1984–8	–23.8
	Zambia	1980–8	–23.4
	Venezuela	1980–9	–15.3
	Egypt	1981–9	–11.7
	Ecuador	1980–6	–10.0
	Kenya	1980–90	–3.8
	India	1980–90	0.3
	Singapore	1980–90	3.0
	Malaysia	1980–90	4.6
	US OASI	1980–90	4.8
Privately	Netherlands*	1980–90	6.7
managed	US*	1980–90	8.0
	UK*	1980–90	8.8
	Chile (AFPs)	1981–90	9.2

* = Occupational schemes

Source: p. 95, Figure 37. *Averting the Old Age Crisis. Policies to Protect the Old and to Promote Growth* by World Bank. Copyright 1994 by The International Bank for Reconstruction and Development/The World Bank. Used by permission of Oxford University Press, Inc.

and Japan. This clearly illustrates the benefits of the high equity content, including foreign equities, compared to those on the Continent.

Private pension funds are good for you

The thesis I will advance here is that private pension schemes not only create a more reliable nest-egg for pensioners but may greatly help the overall economy. They cause a switch in expenditure from consumption to saving during the transition period, thereby improving the trade balance, while making available loans and equity funds to companies on terms that encourage them to invest. This steady growth in productive investment gradually brings about an acceleration in overall economic growth. The two examples chosen are drawn from opposite sides of the globe and from very different cultures and traditions – Chile, the trailblazer of Latin America, and Singapore, whose performance will be compared (favourably) to that of its fellow city state, Hong Kong. After that, we will see which other countries are following their example, before finding out how the switch affects government finances.

Chile and the domino effect

Chile in the late 1990s, the soundest country in Latin America, with a broadly based economy growing at a steady 5–6% compound, reasonable inflation and an aggressive internationally-minded corporate sector, is a far cry from the situation in 1980. At that time, the country was suffering from inflation of 30–35%, its economy was heavily dependent on copper, the inefficient industrial sector cowered behind tariff walls – and its PAYG State pension scheme was bankrupt. The demographics had deteriorated sharply since 1960, with the number of retirees having risen from 9 per 100 workers to 45 per 100 by 1980. The inevitable result was a strong rise in contributions to finance current benefits, and as these were paid by the State, led in turn to massive pressure on the Budget and tax increases that would have been impossible to collect.

Desperate times require desperate measures. Instead of retreating further into protectionism, government began to cut subsidies and demolish tariff walls, forcing companies to compete or go under, which many of them did. Lower tariffs cut inflation, leading to lower interest rates. State companies were sold off. Freed from subsidies and high borrowing costs, government finances began to improve. At the same time, it launched the private pension system, the essentials of which are as follows.

- New single-purpose companies, known as AFPs, were established to collect contributions from affiliates, manage their individual accounts, invest the pooled contributions and provide life and disability benefits. Workers could choose to stay in the State system, and in 1984, the last year in which this choice was available, some 19%, principally older workers close to retirement, elected to do so. By 1993, around 90% of the total labour force had become affiliates of one of the 21 AFPs in operation.

- Membership is compulsory for all employees but voluntary for the self-employed, the armed forces and foreign workers who are part of another social security system. Employers transfer 10% of a worker's pretax monthly salary to the AFP, subject to a prescribed maximum. The contributions which are free of tax buy shares in the fund which invests on their behalf. Affiliates who have made a contribution in the current month are known as '*cotizantes*'. Affiliates can make additional contributions, subject to the same ceiling, above which they are not tax deductible. Pension benefits are taxable at the time of withdrawal.

- Those workers who were formerly contributors to the State system also receive an interest bearing recognition bond which reflects the estimated value of their prior contributions. It is indexed to CPI and gives a 4% real annual interest rate. The bonds are lodged with the AFP in a separate account.

Over the period 1981–94, the growth of the private system has been staggering. According to the body that supervises the AFPs, at the end of 1994, the value of funds under management had reached US$22.3 billion,[6] representing 42.7% of GNP, even though only 57.4% of the 5 million affiliates were making contributions by that date. (Later affiliates are likely to be self-employed and are given considerable leeway in the timing of their contributions.)

From the contributor's standpoint, the switch to the private system has been an excellent move – over the period 1981–94 the real returns of the system as a whole have averaged 14.0%, well above the 4% guaranteed in the State scheme, and most State schemes worldwide.

Even more important is the impact on the economy. In the early years, the regulatory guidelines to the AFPs required that they invest the majority of their cashflow in government securities, mortgages or other fixed interest instruments, enabling government to fund its deficit without recourse to foreign borrowings. As more affiliates joined the system, however, cashflow began to grow faster than the government's borrowing needs, and those of the limited mortgage market. compelling the regulators to widen the range of permitted investments. The AFPs began to move into equities in 1986, and by 1994, 32.1% of total system value was in equities. The AFPs now account for over 20% of the capitalisation of all equities listed on the Santiago Stock Exchange.

The main stock exchange index, IGPA, based at 100 in 1980, reached 1167 by the end of 1990 and 5425 by the end of 1994. Even adjusting for inflation, this represents a real compounded rate of return of 12.6% (1980–94). This rapid rise, propelled first by the cash flow of the system, has been given greater impetus by the entry of foreign investment funds in 1989–90. Their combined effect has been to boost the ratings of domestic equities (PERs rose from 6.1 in 1989 to 19.6 in 1994), enabling them to raise money for expansion through the stockmarket on increasingly better terms, and helping the government to sell remaining stakes in former public utilities at high prices. Capital investment up, government debt down.

Cash flow has now begun to outgrow even the needs of the local stockmarket, and the AFPs have sought new outlets. They have forced the banks to compete for long term borrowers, by making available credit lines to industry at attractive rates, once again encouraging companies to invest. Indeed venture capital funds comprised 2.7% of their portfolios by August 1996. Since 1993, the funds have also been allowed to invest overseas. Although foreign assets now account for a modest 0.3% of total investments, they are forecast to reach 2.5% in 1998.

The companies themselves, having survived the transformation from overstaffed inefficient state organs to lean competitive and highly rated private companies, have now begun to employ their experience elsewhere in the region, particularly in Argentina, where Chilean utilities have made considerable inroads by buying into government companies undergoing privatisation. The pace of overseas investment is accelerating. By the end of 1994, Chilean companies had invested $5 billion overseas, but this total has now risen to around $10–12 billion, a staggering 14% of GDP, of which over 50% is in Argentina.

Encouraged by the return of economic and political stability, long-term foreign direct investment has also responded. By 1996, the annual inflow reached $4.5 billion, and a record $3.6 billion in the first half of 1997. Although 40% of all direct investment is in mining, Chile's growing integration into the region has led to strong growth in the industrial and service sectors. Looking into the next century, it is possible to depict Chile as a small but stable economy, still growing at 5–6% per annum but deriving an increasing part of this growth from overseas investments.

Imitation is the sincerest form of flattery – especially if it makes you money. What the Chileans started has been taken up after a lag by practically every other country in Latin America. Tariff barriers have fallen, governments have been selling off State companies, cutting subsidies, balancing their budgets and reforming their pension systems. The ripples from Chile have lapped in turn upon the shores of Mexico, Argentina, Peru, Uruguay and Paraguay. According to Salomon Brothers, some $1135.7 billion was under management by Latin American pension funds at the end of 1997,[7] and the figure is expected to grow to over $200 billion by 2000 and $600 billion by 2011. Table 7.3 gives the projected breakdown.

Comparing the projected investment in equities with the current capitalisations of the markets, it is clear that within a decade Latin American pension funds will become major players in years to come (see Table 7.4).

Table 7.3 Projected breakdown of Latin American pension fund
assets to 2015

Country	Stock market cap. ($ million)	Assets under management ($ million)			% assets under management in stocks	
	1997e	1997e	2000e	2015e	1997e	2000e
Argentina	51 200	8 818	20 963	156 653	23.5	30.0
Bolivia	900	790	1 564	3 997	94.6	90.0
Brazil	194 300	81 417	114 486	445 256	32.5	33.0
Chile	63 400	32 359	44 460	128 617	26.0	32.0
Colombia	8 800	1 607	4 014	51 776	8.0	25.0
Mexico	133 200	8 994	25 614	138 893	–	20.0
Peru	13 100	1 547	3 583	25 055	34.8	35.0
Uruguay	300	167	615	3 950	0.0	10.0

Source: Salomon Smith Barney, Private Pension Funds in Latin America, 1997.

Table 7.4 Pension fund investment in equities as % of 1997 stockmarket
capitalisation

Country	1997	2000	2015*
Argentina	4.1	12.3	91.9
Bolivia	83.0	156.4	399.7
Brazil	13.6	19.1	74.3
Chile	13.3	22.4	64.8
Colombia	1.5	11.4	147.0
Mexico	0.0	3.8	20.6
Peru	4.1	9.6	67.1
Uruguay	0.0	20.7	133.0

*Assuming the same proportion invested in equities as in 2000.
Source: ibid.

After starting well with deregulation and a successful privatisation
programme, Mexico which had tried to convince the world that it had
thoroughly learnt the lessons of the 'Lost Decade' precipitated by its
default in 1982, triggered another regional crisis in 1995.
Overdependence on short-term foreign borrowings to finance imports of
capital goods proved fatal when confidence was undermined by political
problems. The government failed to arrest the resulting collapse of the
currency, crippling the domestic banks and companies, which had
amassed heavy dollar obligations. A major US rescue package in 1995
stopped the collapse but confidence remains fragile because of continuing

political scandal, high real interest rates and delays in implementing a reformed pension system to restore savings ratios.

Argentina, with a more shallow economy and no NAFTA trade links to support it, could have suffered badly from the backwash of the Mexican crisis. In fact, it survived well because government kept its nerve and maintained its Convertibility Plan which linked the peso rigidly to the dollar, refusing to print money to offset a massive outflow of bank deposits and a huge rise in interest rates. Some weaker banks were forced to close and were taken over by better capitalised competitors, but the system survived. The interest rate sensitive construction sector collapsed and unemployment rose sharply, but there was no serious labour unrest. Fortunately the impact was mitigated by a buoyant trade position, thanks to rising oil output, strong grain and soya prices and healthy exports of cars to Brazil.

Having ridden out the crisis, Argentina set about pricing its companies back into world markets by reducing a number of workers' benefits. These measures reduced direct labour costs by 7–17% and were fully felt in 1996. At the same time the government has begun the reform of the State pension system. Authorised in late 1994, the private pension funds, known as AFPJs, already controlled $4.48 billion by September 1996. Benefiting from Chilean experience, Argentina has from the beginning permitted a high maximum of 35% of the funds to be invested in equities. The actual proportion invested in equities had risen from 5.9% in December 1995 to 14.8% by September 1996. Even then, this represented 5% of the free float of the equity market, and the monthly in-flow allocated for the purchase of equities reached 5% of September's traded volume in equities.

Projections by Deutsche Morgan Grenfell,[8] assuming a conservative 12% annual yield on the portfolio, in line with Chile, imply that funds under management could rise from $5.17 billion (end-1996) to $7.97 billion (end-1997) and $19.05 billion, by the end of 2000. By 2005, they could be neck and neck with Chile.

In all these cases, reform came from leaders realising that the economic crises they faced could not be solved by the discredited statism of the past and that they would only get the necessary support from international lending agencies if they completely abandoned the platforms on which they had been elected. Only countries like Brazil and Venezuela, shielded from financial sanctions by trade surpluses, have been able to indulge their penchant for voodoo economics longer than the rest.

110

(There's a lesson here, which I shall return to in Part IV, that is worth spelling out – politicians rarely do what is necessary unless forced to do so, so crises can be important in instilling a sense of realism. A sensible and co-ordinated response to a crisis by a government and its central bank has often been the factor that has launched an economy on a new trajectory and transformed the stockmarket from gloom to boom. For a period of around two years after their change in policy the markets of Mexico, Argentina and Peru were amongst the best performers in the world. *'Crisis' and 'opportunity' have the same Chinese character, and should be the same in any language spoken by investors, who should always be on the lookout for a good crisis from which to make money.* On the other hand, determination to avoid pain at all costs usually results in more pain for longer, as Russia has found out to its cost. Its GNP fell for seven consecutive years – 1989–95 – while Poland, which has taken its medicine has enjoyed six unbroken years of healthy growth.)

Finally, Mexico, the country most in need of boosting its savings rate, has been the most tardy in getting private pension schemes under way, partly because of the obstacles put in its path by IMSS, the inefficient State organisation that provides both pension and health services. The new private pension fund operators, known as *Afores*, began operations in early 1997, and by June 1997 some 3.4 million people – over one-third of those eligible – had signed up. By 2001, all private sector workers must have chosen an *Afore* to administer their pensions. As with other countries that switch from State to private schemes, a funding gap will open up which the government will have to fill by contributing directly to IMSS. This fiscal year (a half year), it will have to pay Ps21 billion, ($2.6 billion) to cover current pensions and make up for the subsidy on medical costs.

On Salomon Brothers' calculations, the sector should control $24 billion of investments by the end of the century. *Afores* will be able to invest in equities from the start, which should permit superior returns. Unfortunately, it is believed that a large part of the administration of the system will be entrusted to IMSS – a move that has been likened to 'getting the fox to guard the hens', in the words of Sebastian Edwards, former chief Latin American economist for the World Bank.

By reviewing the experience of other countries with private pension systems, we are now in a position to develop our first tool to screen countries for our long-term investment portfolio. *To be worth considering, a country must have a private pension system which permits investment in equities and has annual cashflow which is rising rapidly, is getting close to the public sector borrowing requirement and is significant relative to the free market capitalisation of the equity market.*

Singapore: Switzerland on the Equator

Many claims have been made for the success of the Chilean economy being tied to the development of the private pension system. Had Mexico begun its own system five years earlier it may have been able to avoid the 1993 meltdown. Unfortunately, it is hard to make a direct comparison with its Latin neighbours because of the decade of stagnation that they underwent and the different extent to which they were able to restore stability through renegotiating foreign debt and privatising State companies.

In the case of Singapore however it is possible to look over 30 years of almost unbroken growth, and compare it with that of its fellow city state, Hong Kong. To make the comparison fairer, I shall take the comparison only up to the mid-1980s, before the time that the Hong Kong economy began to benefit from the opening up of China, and reasonably far from the time the colony reverted to China in 1997.

Taking the period 1966–83, Singapore consistently showed stronger, less volatile growth and lower inflation than Hong Kong. Real GDP grew by 398% *vs* 270%, and the comparison was even greater on a *per capita* basis (285% *vs* 153%) owing to the sharply falling birth rate in Singapore. Excluding 1973–4, when both economies were distorted by the first energy crisis, inflation in Hong Kong averaged 5.3 points per annum over Singapore between 1970 and 1984.

Breaking down GDP by expenditure (*see* Table 7.5), there has been a massive shift from private consumption to capital investment in Singapore, which has not been matched in Hong Kong. Furthermore, despite the fact that substantially all Singapore's capital goods is imported, the trade position actually improved during the period, whereas that of Hong Kong deteriorated. A more detailed breakdown of capital investment reveals that a far larger proportion of Hong Kong's expenditure was in non-productive assets. Taking only plant, machinery and transport equipment (as a percentage of GDP at current prices) Singapore consistently invested at twice the rate of Hong Kong – 18.5% *vs* 9.6% between 1966 and 1982.

How did Singapore achieve such a performance? By boosting the savings ratio, which rose from 19.3% of GDP in 1970 to 40.1% by

Table 7.5 Breakdown of GDP by expenditure at current prices

	Singapore				Hong Kong		
	1968	1973	1978	1983	1973	1978	1983
Private consumption expenditure	73.7	63.7	60.0	47.3	70.0	70.5	67.5
Govt consumption expenditure	10.4	11.0	11.0	11.3	5.7	6.4	8.0
Gross domestic fixed capital formation	23.1	34.9	33.1	47.3	19.7	24.5	26.5
Stocks	1.8	4.3	1.8	–2.2	3.7	1.6	0.6
Net imports of goods/services	–6.6	–10.1	–8.2	–3.2	0.9	–3.0	–2.6
Discrepancy	–2.4	–3.8	0.1	–0.5	–	–	–
	100.0	100.0	100.0	100.0	100.0	100.0	100.0

Sources: Lyall & Evatt (Pte.).

1980, and a staggering 49.4% in 1994. The way this was achieved was through the State savings system, the Central Provident Fund, or CPF, originally set up in 1955 as a compulsory savings scheme to provide workers with monetary benefits when they reached the age of 55 or became permanently disabled. It is not a PAYG scheme. Both workers and employers are required to contribute a proportion of salary, with a limited number of exceptions for the self-employed and non-residents.

The deposits are largely invested within government securities, where they attract tax-free interest, and represent the main source of government funding. By the end of 1982 the CPF held 78.2% of all government registered stocks. There is no direct investment in equities, nor any international exposure.

As with so many other institutions in Singapore, the CPF fulfils a number of functions. For a start, it is an instrument of fiscal policy – if wages or consumption seem likely to get out of control, contribution rates are raised, but can also be reduced in times of economic slowdown, if this is felt to be due to a loss of competitiveness in export markets. Thus, while the rate was steady between 1955 and 1968 at 10%, it was raised progressively until by 1984 it stood at 46%, split equally between employer and employee. It is this which has been mainly responsible for the rise in savings ratio.

Secondly, it has been a means of transforming into a nation a disparate group of Chinese immigrants with more loyalty to their clan than to Singapore, by giving them a stake in it. From the time the People's Action Party (PAP) took control in 1959, the government has had as a priority the construction of housing for its population through the Housing Development Board (HDB). Initially these flats were rented at modest rates, but by the late 1960s the emphasis had shifted to direct sales. Since the land and building materials could be obtained at prices well below those of private developers, and the HDB did not require high profit margins, public flats could be priced attractively – at 30–40% of that of comparable private sector accommodation.

In addition, since 1968, CPF contributors have been able to use their contributions to make initial deposits and monthly payments on HDB flats. *Since homeowners could use both their own and their employers' contributions, employers were effectively subsidising the purchase.* The scheme was expanded in 1975 to cover other public sector flats. The success of the programme can be judged from the fact that between 1967 and 1981 the proportion of the population living in HDB flats had risen from 25.9% to 69.0%, and the proportion living in *owner-occupied* HDB flats from 1.7% to 43.7%.

Progress has continued since the 1980s, thanks to rising wages paid for from the sustained rise in productivity. With the majority of flats in Singapore now owner-occupied, the government has moved to make available other outlets for CPF savings. Members have been permitted to withdraw limited amounts for investing in a range of approved equities, or to finance education. As of 1 January 1997, unit trusts run by the CPF, into which members can divert some of their savings, may invest in stocks on regional exchanges up to 40% of the funds' values.

The government is also acutely aware of Singapore's limitations – small population, tiny land area and no minerals – and has acted to turn itself into a regional financial powerhouse, using the nation's savings to co-invest with local firms and multinationals into the region. The Economic Development Board (EDB) has targeted six countries for especial attention – China, India, Vietnam, Indonesia, Thailand and, despite the condemnation of the West, Burma. Direct investment totalled $6.95 billion in 1994 and the country is impressively high in the league tables as a foreign investor in all of them, ranging from eighth in India to fifth in China and second in Thailand.

The EDB has helped establish five regional industrial parks – in Suzhou, China, Batam and Bintan in Indonesia, Bangalore in India and in Vietnam. The government has reinforced this with considerable fiscal incentives for those co-investing with the EDB. Three years ago, Temasek, the main government holding company, formed a $800 million venture with American Insurance Group to finance infrastructure projects in Asia. In another development in January 1997, it set up a collaborative venture with Calpers, the California State pension fund which manages some $105 billion of investments. Its purpose is to attract Asian money into California as well as helping Calpers to diversify into Asia. In time, such capital investment will lead to a significant in-flow of dividends back to Singapore, and the nation, with its tourism, high-tech export industries and growing financial muscle, could justly stake its claim to be Switzerland on the equator, but a Switzerland with a greater sense of purpose, and a key member of the world's most rapidly growing trading bloc, ASEAN.

The success of the CPF scheme in mobilising savings has attracted the interest of a number of countries. Because of its common colonial history, Malaysia operates a similar scheme, but the real excitement comes from China and Hong Kong. The latter intends to establish a private sector scheme to be managed by independent fund management groups with freedom to invest in equities and other non-government instruments. China, however, wants a structure more along the lines of the CPF, and under tight government control. Whether China is prepared to give the assurances that it will not abuse its powers over the deposits will determine whether the scheme goes ahead.

Can Europe match this?

As all the unit trust disclaimers point out, the past should not necessarily be considered a guide to the future, but the performance figures recorded by European private pension funds have been considerably better than those of the average State pension funds for a decade or more. The gap should widen during the decades ahead – higher savings ratios could lead to falling inflation and a further rerating of equities, as happened in Chile, while returns on contributions to State schemes will decline, and could become negative, due to the sharp fall in the ratio of contributors to pensioners. Thus the implied yield on contributions to the unfunded compulsory French scheme, AGIRC, has fallen from 12.8% in 1980 to 9.2% by 1995 (against an average 15.6% compound over 15 years for private pension funds), and is projected to fall to only 7.2% by 2000.

115

Data on the private pension fund sectors of some 18 countries between 1983 and 1993, collated by UBS Asset Management, show returns in local currencies above the rate of inflation in all cases (*see* Table 7.6). Furthermore, the higher the proportion of the funds invested in real assets – shares and property – the higher the overall return. The research also highlights some countries with performances well away from the main trend – Singapore being the laggard at 2.3%, and France the star performer at 13.0%.

Table 7.6 Real returns of private pension funds by country, 1988–93

Country	Average real returns (% per annum)		Nominal exchange rates to US dollars*	
	In local currency	In US$	1983	1993
France	13.0	17.5	7.62	5.66
Australia	12.1	9.1	1.11	1.47
Ireland	11.2	13.3	0.81	0.68
UK	10.8	10.7	0.66	0.67
New Zealand	10.5	8.5	1.50	1.85
USA	9.6	9.6	1.00	1.00
Belgium	9.5	14.0	51.1	34.6
Spain	9.3	10.5	143.5	127.2
Denmark	8.8	12.4	9.14	6.48
Canada	8.8	8.4	1.23	1.29
Hong Kong	8.6	8.1	7.27	7.73
Norway	8.0	8.2	7.30	7.09
Netherlands	7.7	11.8	2.85	1.86
Sweden	7.6	7.5	7.67	7.78
Germany	7.0	10.8	2.55	1.65
Japan	6.7	14.3	237.5	111.2
Switzerland	4.1	5.8	2.10	1.48
Singapore	2.3	3.0	2.11	1.62

* Annual averages
Sources: UBS Asset Management, Global Pension Fund Indicators, Sept. 1994; OECD.

Looking at the league table, the bottom places are occupied by countries whose currencies have been the strongest over the period. Expressing these returns in US$, their apparent poor performance largely disappears (although this will be of little satisfaction to a German pensioner whose outgoings are in D-marks), illustrating the fact that globalisation is tending to even out returns between countries – something I will return to later.

There are two glaring exceptions – Switzerland and Singapore. Both have invested the bulk of their portfolios in domestic government bonds, even though domestic and international equities have shown far superior returns when expressed in local currency (*see* Table 7.7).

Table 7.7 **Investment returns 1983–93 (% per annum)**

Country	Domestic bonds	International bonds	Domestic equities	International equities	Av. pension fund
Singapore	3.9	11.0	11.0	13.4	3.9
Switzerland	6.3	10.7	13.8	13.1	7.3

Source: ibid.

In fact, *all* the poor performers are characterised by heavy reliance on domestic bonds. This may reflect the instinctive views of the regulators that the risks inherent in equities – especially in countries with illiquid or badly regulated markets – make them unsuitable for pension funds, despite their record of superior returns. Governments are also reluctant to give up access to sources of cheap funding. Institutions in countries with strong currencies also find it hard to invest in currencies weaker than their own – the higher returns may be wiped out by currency depreciation. By failing to switch funds overseas when speculative inflows push their currency to unrealistic levels, their policy becomes self-fulfilling, and performance suffers. Too much caution, it seems, is bad for returns. Who dares, wins.

How important are private pension funds in Europe?

If the returns from private pensions are so impressive, relative to State schemes, surely everyone is joining them. Well, not exactly. International comparisons show that with the exception of the UK, households in most Western countries keep a relatively small proportion of their financial assets in pension funds or collective investment schemes such as unit trusts. The value of household financial assets varies from a low of around 1.05 times GDP to around 3.0 times for the UK and USA.

Statistics would seem to support the conclusion that the most risk-averse nations – Germany, Italy, Spain and Japan – are the ones that keep the highest proportion of their household assets in cash, whether held

117

directly or through investments in pension funds, insurance companies or mutual funds. In the case of Italy and Spain, the large size of the black economy favours a high proportion of untraceable cash; as these economies are forced to become more efficient, and labour reforms and greater restrictions on early retirement cut into the black economy, a substantial proportion of this could be redirected into more 'orthodox' assets, to the benefit of their stockmarkets. Certainly, research by InterSec Research Corp. predicts that the most rapid growth in pension fund assets within the EU will come from these two countries.

Table 7.8 Global pension fund statistics, 1992–2002 ($ billion)

Country	Total			Change (%)		Non-domestic (%)		
	1992	1997	2002	1997/ 1992	2002/ 1997	1992	1997	2002
North America	3530	5756	7622	63.1	32.4	5	10	15
UK	643	1149	1645	78.7	43.2	28	27	28
Netherlands	242	321	445	32.6	38.6	12	24	28
Switzerland	144	211	280	46.5	32.7	8	11	15
Germany	116	118	165	1.7	39.8	4	5	7
Sweden	74	95	140	28.4	47.3	0	1	2
Italy	56	68	120	21.4	76.5	0	1	2
Spain	8	9	18	12.5	100.0	2	4	8
France	41	63	96	53.7	52.4	5	7	9
Ireland	14	34	48	142.9	41.2	37	34	35
Total Europe	*1413*	*2198*	*3199*	*55.6*	*45.5*	*17*	*20*	*22*
Japan	786	1112	1630	41.4	46.6	7	17	21
Australia	45	132	265	193.3	100.8	14	19	20
All Pacific Basin	*931*	*1432*	*2240*	*53.8*	*56.4*	*8*	*17*	*19*
Brazil	23	86	180	273.9	109.0	0	0	0
All Latin America	*41*	*142*	*290*	*246.3*	*104.2*	*0*	*0*	*0*
Africa/M. East/Asia	65	167	320	156.9	91.6	0	8	10
Total	*5980*	*9694*	*13 671*	*62.1*	*41.0*	*8*	*13*	*17*

Source: InterSec Research Corp.

Table 7.8 extrapolates continued strong demand for pension fund assets in Europe, even in the UK whose industry is far more developed than its Continental competitors, but the most spectacular growth will come from Australia, Brazil and other parts of Asia, such as India.

Although not shown in Table 7.8, the proportion of pension fund assets invested in equities is also rising steadily. For Europe as a whole, it was around 48% in 1996, but this overall figure conceals substantial variations across countries, with the UK close to 80% while Germany remains under 20%. Countries such as Finland have declared their intention of substantially raising the equity content of their pension funds over the next decade.

Within all major markets there is a marked trend towards international diversification, (the final three columns of Table 7.8), led by the UK, which has probably now reached a plateau. The smaller the economy, the greater the trend to foreign investments – e.g., Austria, Belgium and Ireland, with 32%, 36% and 34% invested overseas by 1997. The trend has been resisted by France and Germany, which have a fear of the exotic, and where union-appointed trustees regard foreign investment as treasonable. In countries such as Singapore, Malaysia and Latin America, overseas investment is greatly restricted, either for prudential reasons or to keep scarce capital within the country.

Even if the single currency increases international diversification, it will be decades before the pension funds of all EU countries converge toward similar geographic breakdowns, so asset allocators need not fear for their jobs just yet. The major groups in which they are investing are *themselves* diversifying regionally, so that by the end of our initial investment horizon (2005), investments will have congealed even more into distinct blocs – EU, US, Japan, India, Pacific Basin and Latin America – each with its own very different characteristics. It is precisely this factor that will enable to surf the demographically driven investment waves, and as they crest, to move across to the next wave as it builds up momentum.

As can be seen, France, Germany and Italy are well down the league table. Indeed, the UK accounted for over 52% of the EU pension fund assets in Table 7.8, with the Netherlands at 14.6%. When these assets are expressed as a percentage of GDP, the contrast becomes even more marked. The almost total dependence of the population of Western Europe on State pension schemes is probably the single greatest impediment to the introduction of any innovation that might appear to erode their safety or the level of benefits. The sensitivity of Europeans to politicians meddling with State pensions is as acute as that of the British to any tampering with the NHS. In Germany, Chancellor Kohl had to write a 'personal' letter to all pensioners to reassure them that their pensions were safe in his hands.

France recently capped its contribution rate, creating a long-term funding gap, and hence the need for top-up pensions, but government has become the victim of its own past policy of protecting their value. Workers may not be aware of the declining returns on their contributions, and regard PAYG schemes as government-guaranteed and safe, while private schemes are not guaranteed, and hence viewed with suspicion, despite a decade of superior returns. It is also true that the redistributional achievements of State pension schemes are lost in a switch to the private system – the better-paid can and do save more and can commit proportionally more of their income to plans where returns are linked to contributions. In time, this would widen the gap between rich and poor in retirement – a trend unions and socialist parties generally oppose. It is no surprise that it took six years of fighting before the government allowed Mr Jean-Pierre Thomas to present his proposals for an enhanced role for private pensions to the National Assembly.

Support for top-up schemes by the French government is at best grudging, however. Proposed tax concessions to contributors are mean. Furthermore, France's unions, who now co-manage the State pension schemes are pressing for active involvement in the new funds. If German experience is anything to go by, this risks the funds being largely confined to the domestic market, with inferior returns but possibly greater risk than if they were free to invest internationally.

The French government itself is vehemently opposed to any moves that could make it easier for pension funds to invest outside national borders. It recently complained to the advocate-general of the European Court of Justice about the European Commission publishing rules aimed at opening cross-border investment. The three least parochial investors in the EU, the UK, the Netherlands and Ireland, all supported the proposals. The sensible objections of the French would be substantially undermined by the success of a single currency, which would remove one major investment risk, but it is unlikely that any French government would give up its 'right' to avail itself of cheap captive funds, especially when the budget deficit has barely met the Maastricht guidelines.

(It is interesting that on the very day that Frank Field presented a Green Paper which contemplated compulsory saving for retirement in the UK through private and mutual providers, France's social affairs minister, Martine Aubry, announced her wish to slow down pension reforms in France, while Claude Evin, chairing the annual French conference on social protection claimed that there were already sufficient products for those seeking long-term savings for retirement.)[9]

The UK: still further to go

To understand how the UK has reached its present position, it is worth reviewing the way the State pension system has been modified over the past 20 years. All employed and self-employed persons earning more than a threshold income of roughly 18% of national average earnings are required to pay National Insurance contributions. These together with government contributions go to finance the State pension system, which in its present form is in two parts.

(i) Basic pension

A flat-rate basic pension aimed at providing 100% replacement of the lowest income level up to the lower earning threshold – i.e., around 18% of the average wage. It is payable in full from retirement age (65 for men, 60 for women) if contributions have been paid or credited for 90% of the working lifetime (16 to State retirement age) and *pro rata* for those with reduced contribution records. A married couple is entitled to a pension on the basis of the husband's contribution record, and the scheme also provides invalidity pensions, widows' benefits and unemployment benefits. Pensions are indexed to the Retail Price Index over the past 12 months and are not reduced if the pensioner has additional forms of income.

(ii) State earnings-related pension (SERPS)

Introduced in 1978 as one of the last acts of the Labour government, SERPS provides an additional pension linked to earnings. Over the first 20 years of the scheme, this would build up to a level of 25% of average earnings in the range between prescribed lower and upper earnings limits – roughly corresponding to 18% and 135% of national average earnings. The benefits are revalued to the level appropriate at the time of retirement.

Subsequent Conservative governments, concerned with the rising cost of meeting the future commitments to SERPS have used a combination of financial sticks and carrots to persuade individuals to contract out of SERPS and take on either an occupational pension or a personal pension, both of which would be fully funded, and therefore no burden on the State. The replacement rate for SERPS pensions for those retiring after 1998 was reduced from 25% to 20%, while those who contracted out of SERPS were allowed a rebate in their National Insurance contributions that could be applied to an occupational scheme. The size of the rebate is calculated for each five-year period on the basis of recommendations from the Government Actuary, who estimates the cost to the average occupational scheme of funding the accruing liability for guaranteed minimum pensions. Government may sometimes permit an additional rebate as a further incentive to contract out. As a result of these measures, while workers on average earnings retiring in 1998 can expect their basic State pension plus SERPS to equate to 37% of average earnings, those retiring in 2013 will receive a replacement rate of only 31%.

Who has a non-State pension?

Between 1953 and the peak year, 1967, total number of employees covered by occupational pension schemes rose from 6.2 million to 12.2 million, where they represented 53% of all employees. Since then, however, both their absolute number and penetration has shown a steady decline.

Table 7.9 Employees in pension schemes 1953–91, United Kingdom (million)

Year	Private sector		Public sector		Total members	Total employed	Percentage employed who are members		
	Men	Women	Men	Women			Men	Women	Total
1953	2.5	0.6	2.4	0.7	6.2	21.9	34	18	28
1956	3.5	0.8	2.9	0.8	8.0	22.7	43	21	35
1963	6.4	0.8	3.0	0.9	11.1	22.9	63	21	48
1967	6.8	1.3	3.1	1.0	12.2	23.2	66	28	53
1971	5.5	1.3	3.2	1.1	11.1	22.5	62	28	49
1975	4.9	1.1	3.7	1.7	11.4	23.1	63	30	49
1979	4.6	1.5	3.7	1.8	11.6	23.4	62	35	50
1983	4.4	1.4	3.4	1.9	11.1	21.1	64	37	52
1987	4.4	1.4	2.8	2.0	10.6	21.6	60	35	49
1991	4.5	2.0	2.3	1.9	10.7	22.5	57	37	48

Source: Occupational Pension Schemes 1991, Table 2.1, Government Actuary, Crown Copyright is reproduced with the permission of the Controller of Her Majesty's Stationery Office.

Table 7.9 shows a steady increase in membership by women offset by a sharp fall in membership by men. Breaking this down by industry group suggests that this is due in part to the rapid decline in workforce of certain State industries such as coal mining, steel, etc., where membership of occupational schemes was especially high. The transfer of State industries to the private sector, and the subsequent reduction in their workforces has cut the membership in the public sector without proportionally raising that in the private sector.

The membership of women remains low relative to that of men because of the disproportionate level of part-time work (*see* Table 7.10).

Table 7.10 Membership of current employer's pension scheme, 1975–95 (%)

	1975	1979	1983	1987	1989	1991	1992	1993	1994	1995
Full-time										
Men	63	68	66	63	64	61	62	60	60	58
Women	47	55	55	52	55	55	54	54	53	55
Total	59	65	61	59	61	59	58	58	58	57
Part-time										
Women	–	–	13	11	15	17	19	19	19	24

Source: Living in Britain 1994, 1995, Table 8.3, Office for National Statistics © Crown Copyright 1996.

It should be pointed out that since 1988 it has also been possible for employees to take out a personal pension plan, sometimes on terms more favourable than their employers' occupational schemes. As a result, by 1991 nearly 5 million people were contributing to such a plan. The following inducements were offered.

- The employee was allowed to transfer an amount equivalent to the rebate to be paid into the DSS from his National Insurance contributions into the pension plan.
- He was permitted to transfer the tax relief on his National Insurance contribution to the plan.
- A 2% bonus was added.
- The employee became the owner of his pension plan.

There has been a rapid increase in the number of policies issued since 1988, but it should be noted that of the 6 million members of the DSS schemes in 1994–5, about half pay nothing more than their rebates into the schemes. Furthermore Inland Revenue data suggests that for other schemes, the average contribution rate is only about 5% of average salary – hardly enough to provide a significant pension.

Table 7.11 Current pension scheme membership by age and sex, (GB, 1994–5)

Pension scheme members	18–24		25–34		35–44		45–54		55+		Total	
	1995	1994	1995	1994	1995	1994	1995	1994	1995	1994	1995	1994
Men full time												
Occupational	25	30	53	55	67	68	70	72	59	62	58	60
Personal	15	18	37	36	29	31	28	25	21	19	28	28
Any	40	49	91	90	97	99	98	97	81	81	86	88
Women full time												
Occupational	33	30	57	53	65	62	61	62	53	62	55	53
Personal	13	18	26	24	21	21	22	18	21	10	22	20
Any	46	48	83	77	85	83	83	80	74	72	77	73
Women part time												
Occupational	9	1	24	23	29	23	29	22	19	15	24	19
Personal	3	4	14	12	13	12	13	13	9	7	11	11
Any	12	5	38	35	42	36	42	35	28	23	35	30

Source: Living in Britain 1994, 1995, Table 8.1, Office for National Statistics © Crown Copyright 1995 and 1996.

Table 7.11 gives a breakdown of pension scheme membership in Great Britain by age and sex. Note the astonishing rise in the proportion of women covered by pensions over the period of a single year, while that of the youngest male age groups has fallen, confirming the longer-term trend shown in the Government Actuary's figures.

Even in the UK, coverage is by no means complete, although by the time employees reach 40 and turned from being dissavers into savers as wages rise and mortgage costs stabilise, they are generally covered by an occupational or personal pension plan. Taking a historical sweep, however, it is disappointing that the proportion of full-time employees covered by an occupational pension scheme has actually declined over the past 15 years, and that the proportion of firms not offering a pension scheme has risen since 1983 (*see* Table 7.12).

For recently retired pensioners, the contribution from occupational pensions is even more important at 26.3% of total income. Given that the figures show either that pensioners are working less after retirement, or are being paid relatively less well than in previous years, the need to rely on their occupational pension is likely to increase steadily. A total gross income of £14 269 per annum for a pensioner couple, who presumably have neither mortgages nor school fees still to pay, may appear adequate, but if 40% of it – the public component – is under threat, then the need to find ways of boosting the private side increases.

Table 7.12 Proportion of current employers not offering a pension scheme (1983–94)

	1983	1987	1988	1989	1991	1992	1993	1994
Men Full-time	22	22	19	19	21	21	22	24
Women Full-time	24	28	23	21	20	21	22	27
Women Part-time	40	44	42	40	39	39	38	45

Source: Living in Britain 1994, Table 8.4, Office for National Statistics © Crown Copyright 1995.

The value of occupational pensions can be seen from the way they contribute to average incomes (*see* Table 7.13).

Table 7.13 Average gross income of all pensioner units by source

	1979	1989	1993	1979	1989	1993
	£pw July 1993 prices			%	%	%
Benefit income	£69.20	£78.70	£90.50	61.0	51.5	53.2
Occupational pension	£18.20	£33.80	£42.30	16.0	22.1	24.8
Investment income	£12.30	£28.20	£27.40	10.8	18.5	16.1
Earnings	£13.10	£11.50	£ 9.50	11.6	7.5	5.6
Other	£ 0.70	£ 0.50	£ 0.50	0.6	0.4	0.3
	£113.40	£152.80	£170.20	100.0	100.0	100.0

Source: Social Security Statistics 1995. Table B2.01.

Those at risk

Even if we accept that participation of full-time employees of both sexes in private pensions is getting close to complete by the time they enter the 35–44 age group, there are large numbers who will not benefit. These include:

- female part-time workers;
- around 0.9 million self-employed;
- around 3.1 million who are paid wages below the lower threshold required for being included in the National Insurance scheme and SERPS;
- 0.5 million women paying the married women's contribution – at a rate far lower than the norm, but giving minimal pension rights.

To those should be added people who have dropped out of the workforce, perhaps through illness or after years of being unable to find work. Indeed, it is no surprise that *surveys suggest that between one-third and one-half of the population is likely to retire on incomes below those considered necessary to maintain their expected standard of living.*

If even British pensioners who have been accruing second pension rights for a decade or more are not fully protected, the potential for a meltdown in the rest of Europe, apart from Holland, is much worse, as the example of Germany shows.

Germany: caution can damage your wealth

Germans don't really believe in private pensions – yet. State, civil service and supplementary funds, all government-operated on a PAYG basis, together accounted for 83% of total pension benefits paid in 1993. Occupational pensions were an also-ran at a bit over 5% (*vs* over 30% in the UK), with personal life assurance accounting for 10%. These occupational schemes, worth DM461 billion in 1993, come in four flavours, reserve-backed schemes (56%), *Pensionskassen* (23%), direct insurance (12%), and support funds (9%), of which we will examine the two largest in more detail.

Occupational funds were set up following the passing of legislation in 1974 both to supplement the State system and, in practice, to encourage loyalty amongst employees, who generally receive no entitlement to benefits until they have been in employment with the company for at least 10 years, and are at least 35 years of age. They have been in decline for a number of years, both in terms of number and the number of employees promised a company pension. The reason for this depressing state of affairs is that the tax system discriminates against direct contributions into funded pension schemes (*Pensionskassen*) and life assurance schemes provided by the employer. Indeed the problem has worsened with an increase in the flat rate of tax from 15% to 20% of contributions from January 1996, or an effective 23%, taking in the solidarity surcharge and the church tax.

Reserve-backed schemes

Companies can and do, however, provide pensions through making book provisions on their balance sheets. These must correspond exactly to the present value of future obligations based on actuarial projections of mortality and risk of disablement. The rate at which these future obligations must be discounted to present values has been raised over time from 3.5%, to an unrealistic 6% thereby substantially depressing the size of the total provisions.

Even so, Deutsche Bank Research[10] has pointed out that the level of book reserves in 1993 was equivalent to almost 33% of the total capitalisation of the German equity market, and that the provisions made between 1982 and 1993 were equal to the market value of all equity issues by listed German companies during the period. Clearly, a reform of the system could help the entire structure of the corporate sector, by permitting companies easier access to equity finance as an alternative to bank loans.

From the companies' perspective, the book reserve system is highly attractive, because it is both tax- and cashflow-efficient, at least, while the workforce is young. Not only do they allow companies to make provisions without a corresponding cash out-flow, but the provision is allowable against profits tax. When the pensions become payable, the rundown in book reserves (counted as profit) can be offset by the actual cost of the pension (regarded as an operating expense). As a result, companies can defer payment of profit tax for a considerable period. Finally, the book reserves are counted as debt for balance sheet purposes, thereby reducing the value of company assets – and the cost of the asset tax levied on them.

There is, of course a downside. As the workforce ages, particularly so in the smokestack industries, there is a risk of an accelerating outflow of liquidity – unlike the case of funded schemes. Furthermore, there is no way for the beneficiary to test whether he is getting the best possible rate of return: in fact all his future is tied up in the health of a single company – hardly prudent, even if it is re-insured against the risk of bankruptcy.

Finally, accountants believe that companies are underproviding for future obligations by perhaps 20%, and in extreme cases, by up to 50%, because their book reserves do not allow for wage inflation. This is starting to become an issue as German companies adopt international accounting standards in order to seek funds overseas. In 1995, Schering, a major drug company, took a DM101 million charge to bring its provisions to international levels, while Bayer provided DM696 million for the same purpose. Takeovers can also be held up by disputes over pension provisions, as happened when Shell Agrar, a German pesticide company was taken over by Cyanamid of the USA, who contended that provisions of DM100m were 10–15% too low.

Pensionskassen

These differ from support funds in that contributions can be made by both employers and employees, and pensioners have a legal claim to the benefits. Employees are therefore liable to income tax on the employers' contributions (although these are normally paid by the employer), but their own contributions are paid out of after-tax income. Investment policy is regulated by the provisions of the Insurance Supervision Act (VAG). This limits such practices as loans to the sponsor, but also limits the returns by the restrictions it places on tied assets, i.e., those assets used to cover claims.

For example, risk capital (equities, equity funds and mixed funds) can comprise no more than 30% of tied assets. The VAG also insists that 80% of tied funds must be invested in the same currencies as those of the underlying obligations, a far more restrictive provision than in the UK. In theory, this would still permit a degree of diversification outside Germany. In practice, investment portfolios never get near these numbers because the funds are subject to co-determination. The representatives of the pensioners on the Executive Board tend to reflect the conservatism of German households, who keep only a modest part of their financial assets in the form of shares. Typically, therefore, domestic equities comprise only 6% of fund assets, with a mere 3% in foreign equities.

This state of affairs is unlikely to change without a thoroughgoing shakeup of the discriminatory tax system and a general change in perception of equity risks and rewards by pensioners and trustees alike. Two factors could help here: privatisation and Maastricht!

Although Deutsche Telekom has underperformed badly since flotation, a new generation has been introduced to the equity culture, and, importantly, has not lost money on their first investment. More privatisations are planned, including that other household name – Lufthansa – which should help to maintain the interest of private investors and by extension that of fund managers in equities. Secondly, despite the pain inflicted by the Maastricht criteria, implementation of a single currency will greatly extend the freedom of pension funds to invest across borders. The perceived risk of investing in other EU currencies will disappear, and the VAG will inevitably have to change its guidelines.

References

1 *Financial Times*, 3 November 1997.
2 *Financial Times*, 3 November 1997.

3 Stahlberg, A-C. (1989) in Gustaffson, B. A. and Klevmarken, N. (eds) *The Political Economy of Social Security.*

4 Miles, D. (June 1996) *Merrill Lynch Financial Research*, 'Savings and Wealth Accumulation in Europe.'

5 Davis, P. (1996) 'Pension Fund Investment,' in Steil, B. *et al.* (eds) *The European Equity Markets, the State of the Union and an Agenda for the Millennium.*

6 Superintendencia de AFP, 1996.

7 Salomon Smith Barney (Dec. 1997) 'Private Pension Funds in Latin America.'

8 Deutsche Morgan Grenfell, Argentine Research (7 Nov. 1996) *'Private Pension Funds and Equities.'*

9 *Financial Times*, 27 March 1998.

10 Deutsche Bank Research (9 Jan. 1996) 'From pension reserves to pension funds: an opportunity for the German financial market.'

THE DARK SIDE OF
THE PRIVATE SYSTEM

Government debt: can it be paid off?

PAYG means that cash is transferred between generations, but government has no permanent debt on its books, since future obligations to pay pensions will be financed by taxes and contributions as they arise. When, however, the system goes private, the contributions from workers to the State disappear, but the obligation to pay pensions does not. In other words, the government picks up the tab in the form of a massive long-term debt. This is one of the reasons why governments are often so reluctant to reform the State system by adding a private pillar.

The present value of this debt varies from 90% of GDP (for the USA) to over 200% (for France and Italy), figures that are in many cases two to three times the explicit national debt. To pay this off, *assuming no change in the current pension structures*, payroll taxes would have to rise by 15–20 percentage points for most countries, clearly an impossible proposal, and it confirms that other measures, probably including erosion of benefits and increase in retirement age will also become necessary. Can, indeed, this debt be paid off? Once again, demography helps find an answer.

Saving and wealth

A generally accepted starting point is the life cycle theory of Milton Friedman *et al.* which assumes that individuals tend to smooth their level of consumption over their lives whatever their income. They accumulate savings (or assets such as housing) in their earlier years which are gradually run down in retirement. Savings tend to rise steadily from the age of 30 onwards. *In the UK at least, the growth in the number of individuals in these age groups will outpace that of retirees until around 2010, implying that problems of funding retirement could be mitigated in the short term.*

Consultants to Merrill Lynch[1] have taken this further, extrapolating the level of savings and wealth accumulation for the four most populous countries in Europe – UK, Germany, France and Italy – using a model of earnings and savings based on this life cycle theory. Their first conclusion is that for the next 10–15 years, savings ratios in Europe will show a significant rise before declining steadily, then at increasing speed from around 2010. (As a corollary, if my view of birth rates remaining far lower than World Bank projections is correct, then the proportion of 0–15-year-olds, who, by definition must be dissavers, must also be lower, boosting savings ratios even more.)

Their second conclusion is that *because the stock of wealth owned by an individual peaks at retirement, an ageing population means that the Europe-wide stock of wealth will continue to rise, well after the savings ratio itself begins to fall. Indeed, the model predicts that over the next three decades, the private sector could generate between $5 trillion and $7 trillion of extra savings – sufficient to match the demand for funds to cover public sector pension liabilities over the period, based on current levels of benefit and contribution.*

Not all countries are alike in their behaviour. Japan and Italy show a rapid decline in savings rates from 1990 onwards, whereas those of France and Germany are projected to be broadly stable until 2015, and those of the UK and US rise strongly for the next ten to 15 years. There is often a mismatch between the level of savings generated and the level of public sector debt to be redeemed, and the gap will have to be bridged by changes in the current account.

To address criticisms inherent in the construction of the life cycle the researchers have built an econometric model to back-test actual savings behaviour of 14 European countries, together with Japan and the USA over a 30-year period. Not only does it confirm the strong correlation with population in various age groups, but it also shows that country-specific factors explain over 78% of the variance between countries. In other words, we cannot use the savings trends of different cohorts in one country to explain those in another.

A follow-up report in September 1996[2] refined these initial findings, and extended them to cover projected savings patterns in some countries, based not on a synthetic uniform pension regime, but tailored to the rules (retirement age, replacement rate, etc.), actually operating in the countries concerned. The trends of savings revealed by the two different approaches – the life-cycle and the econometric models – broadly agree, with the exception of Italy, where official data may well be distorted by the size of the black economy. Besides creating a league table of winners and losers, the report also relates the savings to the existing sizes of the private pension fund sectors in the countries concerned, assuming that all the extra savings were committed to insurance and pension fund assets. For example, the impact on Spanish funds is, relatively, far greater than on Italian funds, despite similar demographics, due to the far smaller capital values of the former. This will have a bearing on the investment strategy proposed later in this book.

Table 8.1 Impact of demographics on savings and investments

Country	Average extra saving per annum over 20 years due to demographics		Average annual extra growth in pension and insurance assets
	(% of income)	*($ billion)*	*(%)*
Austria	+1.9	3.9	+8.9
Belgium	+1.0	2.6	+4.9
Denmark	+1.1	1.7	+1.5
France	+1.1	15.6	+3.1
Germany	+1.2	23.7	+3.3
Ireland	+1.8	1.0	+2.2
Italy	+0.5	5.1	+2.4
Japan	−0.85	−40.6	−1.2
Norway	+1.7	2.0	+4.1
Spain	+1.8	9.5	+14.0
Sweden	+0.5	1.1	+0.6
Netherlands	+1.3	4.5	+1.0
UK	+1.8	18.8	+1.2
USA	+1.8	119.0	+1.9

Source: Merrill Lynch Economics, 11 September 1996, Dr D. Miles.

Some of the conclusions from the figures shown in Table 8.1 might seem surprising. For example, the impact of the demographics is more favourable for Germany than for the UK over this period, while the prospects for Austria, Belgium and Spain, all countries with unfavourable demographics seem very rosy indeed. In fact it is necessary to qualify Table 8.1 in three ways.

- The low level of impact on the UK reflects the fact that the UK pension fund industry is far more developed than most of its counterparts in Europe, apart from the Netherlands, also a low scorer in Table 8.1.
- The single currency should mean funds in smaller countries investing a proportionately greater part of their cashflow overseas, so that the impact on their own markets would be far less than Table 8.1 suggests.
- The real deterioration in the demographics begins after 2015, the end of the period covered by the study.

Even so, it is possible to derive a strategy that involves a relatively high portfolio weighting in certain European countries including France, Germany and Spain during the early part of this period, but switching later to the UK and Ireland for the long haul, when the demographics of the first group begin to deteriorate badly after 2010.

It is however evident that the Japanese will be accumulating assets over the period at substantially lower rates than in the past, while pension obligations will be rising strongly – hardly an auspicious background for Japanese equities. Even here, the conclusions must be nuanced to reflect the fact that foreign fund managers are having conspicuous success in getting mandates in Japan. They have been able to demonstrate superior performance through greater exposure to equities, including overseas equities. A recent survey of research skills by *Nikkei* newspaper, covering both Japanese and foreign fund managers, showed foreign brokers have taken seven of the top ten places.[3]

It is possible to envisage a scenario where the funds become net buyers of foreign equities while remaining net sellers of low-yielding Japanese bonds, a situation likely to keep the yen weak, to the irritation of the Americans. By January 1998, annual net purchases of overseas money market funds had doubled to Y1700 billion from the previous year, and the trend is likely to accelerate following the lifting of the remaining foreign exchange controls in April 1998, facilitating the marketing of overseas funds by brokers in Japan.[4] In March 1998, it was disclosed that in 1997 Nempuku, the largest public pension fund group in Japan, had allocated around half of its Y1000 billion of new money to foreign pension funds to manage.

Shooting at moving targets

The high present values of State pension debt/GDP ratios are daunting, but it should be recognised that these debt levels are not set in stone, and are highly sensitive to the underlying assumptions. Revision of rules governing replacement rates, changes in indexation of benefits from wages to prices, or in the official age of retirement can have a substantial impact on them. Unfortunately, in a Europe beset with rising unemployment, stagnant growth and dismal demography, the principal job of the politicians has been to keep contribution rates within acceptable bounds by tinkering with entitlement rates and eroding benefits. Periodic reforms which rein in projected increases in contribution rates have often been overtaken by events such as lower birth rates or participation rates, necessitating the introduction of further measures.

We can illustrate this with calculations made for the French State pension system[5] on equilibrium contribution rates (ECR) – the percentage of gross earned income that would exactly finance the pension expenditure for that year, irrespective of whether it is actually supplied as national insurance contributions, income tax or a combination of both. Bearing in mind the projection that under the contribution and benefit rules in force in 1991, over 40% of a French worker's gross income would have to be taken by government for State pensions by 2040, *vs* 18.9% in 1990, growing unrest in the workforce and the electorate seems inevitable.

The figures confirm that four factors are good for keeping ECR down:

- high fertility
- high participation rates in older age groups
- high real economic growth rates
- indexation to prices rather than wages.

The effect of changes in unemployment is less pronounced than the above factors.

Another lesson to be learnt is that, when unfavourable trends in these factors point to the need to reform the system, the changes should be carried out as early as possible because the system's inbuilt momentum means that it takes time to change direction. It is the early and gradual reform of the SERPS system that has enabled the UK government to keep pension expenditure down to a far smaller proportion of GDP than its European neighbours.

Going for growth?

If higher economic growth rates can alleviate the pressure on contributions, should we go for growth, and, if so, how do we achieve it? If countries in Asia have been able to rack up impressive growth rates over decades without inflation, then why can't we? Frankly, it won't be easy. Economic inertia means that growth rates tend to remain in a narrow range for decades. Asia benefited from the massive appreciation of the yen in the late 1980s, and it was also aided by a strong increase in the population of working age and a large agricultural workforce that could be transferred to factories. Europe, with the exception of Ireland, has neither advantage.

The only way out is to trade up, by investing heavily in education to develop the skills that may be lacking in Asian competitors. The success of Ireland, whose economy has become turbocharged since 1990, is due largely to its favourable demographics and its emphasis on higher education. The UK seems determined to learn from this and has made education a top priority, but it will take years to decide whether the strategy is a success. Meanwhile, Asia is not standing still, as the change in the composition of extra-EC imports makes clear (*see* Table 8.2).

Table 8.2 Regional structure of extra-EC imports of manufactured goods

		Total	*% of imports of total manufactured goods from each country or group of countries*			
		% of total extra-EC imports of manufactured goods	*Machinery*	*Chemicals*	*Clothing and textiles*	*High-tech*
USA	1980	22.9	26.4	9.1	4.3	24.3
	1995	21.6	30.8	8.9	2.2	33.5
Japan	1980	8.6	37.6	3.5	3.1	38.9
	1995	12.4	47.4	5.0	1.4	36.1
Developing	1980	27.4	4.7	6.2	23.7	7.4
countries	1995	36.4	13.7	4.7	23.7	17.3
DAE	1980	7.6	3.1	0.4	31.3	20.2
	1995	12.2	30.8	1.7	11.1	34.3
China	1980	0.9	0.8	13.5	44.1	1.9
	1995	5.7	9.6	5.8	23.9	21.3
Other Asia	1980	2.5	1.5	1.1	42.2	2.9
	1995	4.6	4.1	2.9	50.2	8.6
CCEEs	1980	5.2	9.8	12.7	16.9	3.6
	1995	11.6	14.0	7.3	17.5	9.0

DAE = Hong Kong, Korea, Malaysia, Singapore, Taiwan and Thailand
Other Asia include Indian subcontinent, Indo-China, Indonesia and Philippines
CCEEs include Eastern Europe and ex-USSR
Source: EU Commission European Economy 1997 Annual Report.

Not only are developing countries increasing their share of non-EC imports, but they are all increasing their technical content. The speed with which China is overhauling the other Asian Tigers means that a formidable new competitor is on the scene. While Table 8.2 covers manufactured goods, it should be pointed out that India is becoming an important source of software, an area previously the preserve of the West. For all these reasons, therefore, the countries of the West face a long hard slog in the years ahead.

What happens when private pension schemes mature?

Just suppose that by 2000 *all* countries in the EU switched to compulsory private pension schemes for those under the age of, say 40. Cashflow would initially be high, but probably rising at a decreasing rate over the following 20–25 years as the accelerating decline in the overall workforce progressively offsets the increasing proportion of the workforce entering higher earning wage groups. After 2020, when the first members of the scheme retire, outflows from the fund begin to rise while contributions fall at an increasing rate. At some stage, inevitably, unless birth rates recovered, there would be a net *out-flow* in the same way as from mature occupational schemes such as the British Coal Board today.

If the whole of Europe had by that time become net sellers of pension assets, would this damage the returns to pensioners? Probably not, for two reasons.

- Savings in other regions, particularly Asia, would be rising strongly by 2020, and could absorb some of the selling
- As the system moves towards maturity, it should be possible to move contributions progressively into less volatile investments – e.g., government securities. It would be prudent to reassess the prospective level of risk after 2020 and reduce the proportion of new money invested in equities.

References

1 Miles, D. (June 1996) *Merrill Lynch Financial Research*, 'Savings and Wealth Accumulation in Europe.'
2 Miles, D. (Sept. 1996), 'The Future of Savings and Wealth Accumulation: Differences Within the Developed Economies,' *Merrill Lynch Financial Research*.
3 *Financial Times*, 24 March 1998.
4 *Financial Times*, 26 February 1998.
5 Government of France (Livre blanc) (1991) National old-age insurance fund (CNAV), 1993 (after 1993 reforms).

HEALTHCARE: DON'T FALL ILL IN EUROPE

Not just the State pension system is under threat; the entire State health-care system is in danger of collapse, for reasons that will become clear as we review the growing crisis in the UK National Health Service.

Introduction

Before the discovery of penicillin, women frequently died of complications in and after childbirth, gardeners of tetanus from rose thorns, and tuberculosis, the old man's friend, enjoyed whole wards and sanatoria in which to spread. Mining and heavy industry were the dominant employers, coal the dominant fuel and smoke-filled rooms the norm. Not surprisingly people adopted a fatalistic attitude to their health. Every family knew someone with chronic health problems – bronchitis, pneumonia, back injuries, silicosis – and accepted that this was the norm.

Good health was not demanded as of right because people knew that no cures existed anyway. Apart from setting broken bones and isolating the infectious, the medical profession made little impact on the health of the nation. It was a clean water supply, universal sewerage and personal hygiene in the home and abattoir (nothing more advanced than carbolic acid) that kept disease at bay.

In the post-war period however, it became increasingly clear that medical advances really could now make a difference. Polio was beaten by the Salk vaccine, smallpox was finally eliminated in 1977, and TB began to be successfully treated with antibiotics rather than radical pneumothoracic surgery. In developing countries, DDT drove back malaria and the World Health Organisation (WHO) predicted that many other diseases would soon retreat before the advances of medical science. Indeed, so confident were health officials in the West that funding into diseases was sharply curtailed, laboratories closed and skilled teams dispersed.

In the matter of their health, British consumers were becoming aware of their rights. The provision of a universal health service free at the point of use, the medical advances mentioned above and the success of the Clean Air Act all combined to raise expectations. By the 1960s, GPs found that patients had come to regard antibiotics as an almost universal cure-all and were demanding that they be prescribed for the most trivial of infections. Within 20 years, the nation was being kept sedated and sane by popping billions of Librium and Prozac pills. In short, the public *expected* that a cure existed for their complaint and demanded that they receive it.

At the same time, the medical establishment was keen to try out new ideas – ultrasound for monitoring pregnancies or cracking kidney stones, lasers for treating skin blemishes, curing snoring and correcting eyesight, keyhole surgery to minimise post-operative recovery time. Conditions that had defeated the medical profession now became treatable and the number and type of treatment the NHS was called on to provide grew enormously. Many of these, such as organ transplants or NMR body scans, required expensive equipment. Furthermore, the drugs themselves became more expensive, partly because the increasingly exacting requirements of the regulators such as the FDA has greatly increased the number, size and cost of the trials necessary to get approval. It is also because Darwin was right about evolution.

Like every bull market, the advances in antibacterial drugs contained the seeds of their own destruction – the bugs, forced to evolve at an unprecedented rate or die, developed resistance. The speed with which they did so was undoubtedly accelerated by the overprescription mentioned above, and the failure of patients to complete the full course of treatment once they 'felt better' allowed residual bacteria to survive and multiply. The warning signs of resistance appeared very soon after penicillin was introduced but so many new antibiotics became available that it was not then realised that the battle against disease would settle down to trench warfare rather than the rapid advance of blitzkrieg. The hubris of the 1960s has now given way to a rueful reappraisal.

The cost of healthcare

The combination of rising demand for health services and the rising cost of providing them has resulted in health commanding an increasing part of the UK national Budget – up from 12.4% of expenditure in 1985 to 14.0% by 1995.

The NHS is the UK's biggest employer with a total workforce of over 1 million, and an estimated 1995–6 gross expenditure of £33.4 billion. It is divided as follows:

- NHS Hospital and Community Health Services (HCHS) which provide all hospital care and a range of community services;
- NHS Family Health Services (FHS) which provide general medical, dental, pharmaceutical and some ophthalmic services, and covers the cost of medicines prescribed by General Medical Practitioners;

- Central Health and Miscellaneous Services (CHMS) which provide services that can best be administered centrally, e.g., welfare foods, and support for the voluntary sector.

The relative importance of the various branches can be seen from the breakdown of the NHS Budget in Table 9.1.

Table 9.1 NHS gross expenditure 1995–6 (£ billion)

HCHS current	22.7
HCHS capital	2.1
FHS current, non-cash limited	7.8
CHMS	0.6
Administration	0.3
Total	33.4

Source: DoH The Government's Expenditure Plans 1996–7 to 1998–9. Crown Copyright is reproduced with the permission of the Controller of Her Majesty's Stationery Office.

Reflecting changing patterns of care over the life of the previous government, the proportion of HCHS expenditure accounted for by community health services has risen from 9% in 1983–4 to 15% by 1993–4. Table 9.2 shows how expenditure for the entire NHS has risen.

Table 9.2 UK national health and personal social service

Year	Gross expenditure 1978–9 to 1992–3 (£ billion)				
	£ billion	Hospital services %	CHS %	FHS %	Other %
1978–9	9.2	60.9	6.0	21.0	12.1
1992–3	41.0	55.8	8.8	22.7	12.7

Source: OHE Compendium of Health Statistics, 1992.

The extent of the volume growth in demand can be determined by deflating the total expenditure figures by an index of input costs. These show that for the decade 1983/4 to 1993/4, overall HCHS activity levels increased by 28% (2.5% per annum); but since HCHS input costs grew by only 13% over the period, 'efficiency', defined as the change in the real cost of treatment per patient, has risen by 15%. Some idea of how this was achieved can be gleaned from the DoH Expenditure Plans

1996–7 to 1998–9, which highlight the following acute, geriatric and maternity sector unit costs.

- Between 1983–4 and 1990–1, the average cost of treating an acute patient grew by 13%.
- The number of patients treated on a day case basis grew by 10% per annum, while the length of stay for patients occupying a bed overnight has been cut by over one-third to 4.3 days in 1993–4.
- The average cost of each geriatric case fell by 37% with the length of stay falling by around half.
- The average cost of a maternity case fell by 20%.

On the other hand, it is clear that some of the savings have been made by returning to the community certain patients deemed least in need of hospitalisation, retaining the most severe cases. Average daily costs for mental health and learning disability inpatients rose by 31% and 58% respectively between 1983–3 and 1990–1 and by 13% and 30% respectively between 1991–2 and 1993–4. Furthermore, the government's efficiency criteria say little about the quality of treatment. some patients may have been discharged prematurely, resulting in subsequent re-admission – swelling the throughput figures but damaging the quality of care.

It is hard to see how further improvements of this order can be made in the near future, especially after the economies that have already taken place. Purchasing experts from the private sector believe that savings of perhaps £300 million could be achieved by leaning harder on suppliers and by better stock control in hospitals, but even this is trivial against a total HCHS bill of around £23 billion, the bulk of which is labour. There is already a shortage of beds, particularly during the winter when accidents and the incidence of disease increase. By mid-1997, hospital waiting lists has risen by 13% – the largest rise since the foundation of the NHS – forcing the government to bring forward £1 billion of additional funding in time to meet the expected 1997/8 winter peak in admissions.

There is talk of amalgamating hospitals to optimise the use of specialised equipment, but it will take several years to find suitable sites, especially in London, and few such schemes are likely to reach fruition before the millennium. Few projects under the Private Finance Initiative (PFI) have yet commenced. A comparison with other OECD countries shows the UK at the bottom of the league in terms of physicians per thousand of the population and the gap has widened (*see* Table 9.3) since 1975, when the ratios were ~1.25 and 1.6 respectively for the UK and OECD ex-UK.

143

Table 9.3 Physicians per 1000 population for OECD countries, 1991

Australia	1.9	Denmark	2.8	Japan	1.6
Austria	2.1	Germany	3.1	USA	2.3
Belgium	3.4	Ireland	1.5	NZ	2.6
Canada	2.2	Italy	3.9	OECD ex-UK	1.5
France	2.7	Spain	3.8	UK	1.9

Source: © OECD. OECD Health Data (1991) (reproduced by permission of the OECD) and UK Department of Health.

It is fair to point out that there is a wide variation in these ratios between countries with similar levels of health expenditure *per capita* (Belgium, Denmark, Ireland, Japan, NZ and Spain), and little evidence that this affects life expectancy, but a 20% fall in the number of new medical students and newly qualified doctors is a disquieting sign of things to come. Nurses are increasingly having to take on some of the responsibilities of junior doctors, although it is too early to say whether they can bridge the gap – especially as the shortage of nurses is becoming more acute as the economy continues its rapid growth. The UK appears similarly lean in terms of annual expenditure on drugs compared to other Western countries, leaving little leeway for further economies, although rolling reviews of the efficacy of drugs prescribed and of treatments carried out should ensure uniform standards across the nation.

Within this annual growth in demand of 2.5%, there are two components – an intrinsic growth of around 1.5% representing new treatments or increasing demand from patients in particular age groups, and a significant demographic component.

While those aged 65 and over comprise only 16% of the population, they account for 42% of total HCHS expenditure (see Table 9.4). Over 40% of expenditure on acute care and significant proportions of expenditure on services for the mentally ill and on other community services are for those aged 65 and above. Clearly, the older we get, the more our bodies show signs of wear and tear, and the more time and money is involved in putting them right, if possible, or easing the discomfort if it is not. 'The extra years of life gained by the elderly are extra years with a disability, not extra years of healthy life' is the conclusion of a 1995 OPCS study. Once over the age of 65 and health costs start to soar. If we relate HCHS costs by age group to the size of population in that age group, we can get a better idea of the problem (*see* Table 9.5).

Table 9.4 HCHS gross current expenditure by age, 1993–4

	£m	%
All births	1147	5.3
0–4	1365	6.4
5–15	1210	5.7
16–44	4757	22.3
45–64	3942	18.5
65–74	3277	15.3
75–84	3600	16.9
85+	2063	9.6

Source: DoH Crown Copyright is reproduced with the permission of the Controller of Her Majesty's Stationery Office.

Table 9.5 HCHS gross expenditure per head of population in age group, 1994–5

	£
Births	1857
0–4	435
5–15	195
16–44	251
45–64	377
65–74	817
75–84	1502
85+	2205

Source: ibid.

Pressure on health costs

As the population ages, therefore, so does the pressure on health costs. In the mid-1980s, this resulted in an annual increase in costs of up to 1.1% per annum, simply because of the increasing proportion of the elderly, even though the overall population was almost static. Since then, there has been a steady decline in pressure from this source, which will reach its low point by the end of the century, but will regain momentum from then to 2030 – i.e., *just at the time when there will be the greatest pressure on the State pension system. It is also worth noting that if these costs had to be borne directly by recipients rather than the National Insurance contributions of the next generation, they would account for 11.5% of the State pension of a couple aged 65–74 and 31% of that of a couple aged 85 or over.*

It is not possible to obtain detailed cost breakdowns by age for all the other main countries in Europe, but we can get some idea of how health-care costs can increase over the next 30 or 50 years by applying HCHS costings, assuming that the same proportion of each age group requires the same medical treatment as in our base year. In Table 9.6, I have departed from my normal practice by using Eurostat rather than World Bank projections, since the 'low birth rate' scenario of the former seems more consistent with recent experience than the 'central' projection of the latter, which assumes a steady recovery in fertility back to replacement rate.

Table 9.6 Change in costs due to demography (%)*

	EUR15	Germany	Spain	France	Ireland	Italy	UK
2020/2000	7.2	5.8	5.9	10.9	7.9	5.3	4.8
2050/2020	−2.9	−4.3	−4.9	4.9	−3.2	−6.3	1.6
2050/2000	4.1	1.2	0.7	16.3	4.4	−1.4	6.5

* Calculations based on Eurostat Low Fertility scenario and HCHS Costings

At first glance the results might seem encouraging, with demographic pressure on EUR15 not exceeding 0.35% per annum up to 2020 – far below the rates obtaining in the 1980s – and actual declines during the following 30 years. Unfortunately, it is time to remind readers of the other component of demand – the increasing *per capita* demand for medical services from individuals in a number of age groups. At its simplest, this may be typified by the growing incidence of asthma amongst children due to pollution. It is normally alleviated by drugs bought on prescription and paid for partly by the user. To get some idea of the *real* scale of the problem, however, we need to look elsewhere – the rising importance of one of the diseases of affluence, diabetes, and growing incidence of Alzheimer's disease. The first of these is a chronic condition, expensive to treat and subject to complications ranging from blindness to heart disease and which may result in the need for limb amputation. The second brings increased need for carers and health visitors.

These examples should illustrate the growing pressures on resources at a time when workforce will be in decline. *In other words, while the demographic pressures on UK demand over the next 50 years will be less intense than in the past decade, the ability of the workforce to finance them will become increasingly strained.*

LONG-TERM CARE

Introduction

In the UK, long-term care (LTC) consists of the provision of nursing and care services to those incapable, to some degree, of looking after themselves. It specifically excludes care provided to short-term convalescents. Historically, the bulk of such care has taken place within institutions, but with the implementation of the 1990 National Health Service and Community Care Act, it has moved back into the community. The budget for supplying these services is set by central government but administered by the local authorities, and specifically excludes non-care costs such as that of residential accommodation. The financial reason for the new Act can be seen from the fact that Income Support payments for nursing and residential homes rose from £10 million in 1979 to £2.5 billion by 1992 – the last year before local authorities had full responsibility for providing such care.

The conditions requiring LTC are many and varied: the result of sudden illness or of degenerative disease; they may be episodic, with periods of remission when patients can return home or care provision reduced, or chronic. Attempts have been made to create standardised scales by which the appropriate degree of care can be measured. The one devised by the OPCS was used in a survey on long-term disability conducted in the mid-1980s which revealed the statistics shown in Table 10.1.

Table 10.1 Estimate of disability by degree of severity and age group

OPCS category	Likely care need	Estimated number of disabled lives in GB in 1985 (000)		Estimated prevalence rate (%)	
		16–59	60+	16–59	60+
1–2	Low – occasional	667	1371	2.1	12.0
3–5	Moderate, probably less than daily	716	1446	2.2	12.6
6–8	Regular, probably daily	422	1005	1.3	8.8
9–10	Continuous	121	454	0.4	4.0

Source: Financing Long-Term Care in Great Britain, S. R. Nuttall *et al.*, Journal of the Institute of Actuaries, 121, 1, 1994.

Anything requiring both long-term demographic perspectives and assessments of long-term costs and liabilities is usually of interest to actuaries, and various teams have tackled long-term projections of healthcare costs. The model developed by Nuttall *et al.* (based on 1991 population projections) shows projections to 2031 (*see* Table 10.2).

Table 10.2 **Number of disabled adults over 60 (000)**

Care need	1991	2001	2011	2021	2031
Low	1451	1403	1549	1737	1943
Moderate	1532	1491	1653	1856	2107
Regular	1074	1097	1260	1450	1691
Continuous	482	575	720	872	1080
Total	4539	4566	5182	5915	6821

Source: ibid.

The principal conclusions are that, while there will be a brief respite up to 2001, there will then be 30 years of steady increase, due *entirely* to growth in demand from the over-60s. Furthermore the rate of increase in the number of disabled over time rises progressively with the degree of disability. *By 2031, over 90% of those needing continuous care will be over 60.* When the number of disabled is expressed as a ratio to the population of working age (taken as 20–60) it is clear that the burdens will increase significantly. On the central forecast the ratio of total disabled/population of working age will rise by 50%, and for those needing continuous care by 100% by 2031. (Taking the 1994 projections by the Government Actuary, which are based on far lower fertility rates, the ratios are even less favourable.)

When the team turns to the financing of LTC, the prognosis is one of impending crisis. Taking a 1991 cost of £7 per hour for all carers, whether institutional, professional or informal, and assuming the number of hours per individual rose from 5 hours per week for those with low needs to 45 hours per week for those with continuous needs, total cost amounted to £44 billion, broken down as shown in Table 10.3.

Extrapolating to 2031 on the basis of the central assumptions on mortality and incidence, there is a roughly 50% increase in real costs to 2031, and a somewhat higher increase per person of working age (*see* Table 10.4).

Table 10.3 Financing of long-term care

	£ billion
Institutional care	7.0
Professional homecare	3.1
Informal	33.9
	44.0

Source: ibid.

Table 10.4 Total cost of LTC in constant 1991 £

	£ billion	% of GNP	Cost/person 20–60 (£)
1991	42	7.3	1345
2001	44	7.7	1365
2011	49	8.5	1485
2021	55	9.6	1689
2031	62	10.8	2014

Source: ibid.

If costs grow by 1% per annum less than GDP, they would remain stable in real terms. Given, however, that the bulk of costs represents labour, and that there is little scope for economies of scale, especially if overall demand for labour throughout the economy tightens as the workforce contracts, such cost reduction is unlikely if services are to be maintained at current levels.

The growth in demand from those needing regular or continuous care – i.e. 30 and 45 hours per week respectively – will cause severe problems for the State sector. There is a risk that the informal sector may be unable to meet the increased demand because of the difficulty of combining such care with a normal job. According to the 1990 General Household Survey, some 15% of people aged 16 and above were already carers, of whom nearly one-half were looking after a parent or parent-in-law. Over one in five carers spent 20 hours per week or more looking after someone, and the proportion was higher for those looking after someone in the same household. *If, pessimistically, supply from the informal sector were to be static up to 2031, then care costed at some £15 billion would have to be bridged by the State or the private sector.*

Indeed, it could be argued for the reasons above that the gap will be even larger.

Can the inheritance effect pay for the care of the fragile elderly?

Always looking for the bright side of the demographic problem, Tory politicians have for decades painted a future in which, as home ownership increases, house prices rise and the population ages, growing quantities of inherited wealth will come cascading down through the generations. Given also that family sizes have fallen steadily, we would intuitively expect this growing transfer of assets into a progressively smaller group of beneficiaries. Detailed studies (Holmens and Frosztega, 1994[1]) give grounds for cautious optimism, for the patient.

On the one hand, there has been no increase in the annual number of deaths since 1970, thanks to a temporary slowdown in the growth of the number of people aged 65 or over – up from 5.5 million in 1951 to 8.5 million by 1981, but with only a modest increase to 9 million by 1995 – and increasing life expectancy. Home ownership among the elderly has risen, however, and by 1994 55% of this accommodation was owned outright. The combination of rising ownership levels and rising house prices has caused a dramatic rise in total housing equity held by the over-65s, which reached an estimated £173 billion in 1988, when it represented a remarkable 29% of the nation's owner-occupied housing stock, and £220 billion at the 1991 peak.

The actual number of estates passing at death has been static or declining since 1968/9, the first year for which separate data for housing in estates was published. Surprisingly, the number of estates containing property has also been static since that date at around 140 000 per annum, despite the rising levels of home ownership, and the increase in their value is due almost entirely to price inflation. This showed its most dramatic increase in the decade to 1980–1, when the value of housing in estates passing at death rose from £530 million to £3057 million (19.1% per annum), and to £8579 million by 1990–1 (10.9%); after the 1989–90 peak of £9460 million, there has been a small decline to £8016 million in 1992–3.[2] Not all this value is actually transferred to beneficiaries on death: roughly one-third is owned by married couples and passes to the survivor, implying that around 90–95 000 units per annum currently pass to beneficiaries. Estates with house property passing in 1991–2 averaged some £76 250.

Holmens and Frosztega estimate the total value of all assets inherited by individuals in 1989–90 at £11.3 billion. This might seem an impressive rise from the £4.6 billion estimated for the early 1980s, but it represents under 1% of total estimated marketable wealth of individuals, put at £1290 billion in 1988, excluding the value of life policies and consumer durables. Up to now, therefore, it has not made a significant impact on the overall distribution of wealth.

This does not mean however that it has no real impact on legatees at particular points in their careers. If we were to assume simplistically that today's elderly commenced their families by the age of 25, have bequeathed everything to their children, and that the surviving parent died in their mid-seventies, then the most likely age group of the beneficiaries would be 45–54, a time of life when the cost of servicing mortgages and raising children is starting to take a rapidly declining share of disposable income. Perhaps because of this, recent surveys show that over half the inheritance received is saved and that homeowning legatees devote much of the remainder to improving their existing home. In the future, such windfalls could well be used to top up pensions or buy health insurance.

Looking ahead, the projected increase in total deaths will be comparatively modest up to 2021, before rising by around 30% over the following 30 years. Unfortunately, the proportion of non-married men and women living in institutions or in homes in which they are not the heads (and are therefore assumed to have sold their housing to pay for their accommodation), is expected to rise sharply. Despite this, prospects for the legatees look bright, as current high levels of home ownership in younger age groups flow through in time to the over-65s. Calculations by Holmens and Frosztega point to a 47% increase in non-married male and 22% increase in non-married female owner-occupiers by 2011 to a total of around 149 000.

We can also get some idea of the trend in the net value of owner-occupied house property in estates left by non-married men and women. In constant 1989–90 prices, the researchers project a 58% rise in value between 1996 and 2011. Although their forecasts stop at that date, it is clear that the 30% rise in total deaths forecast from 2011 to 2051, accompanied by a further rise in the proportion of owner-occupiers from perhaps 65% to 75% over the period will allow another significant increase in the real value of bequests flowing to the next generation. Furthermore, thanks to the declining birth rate, families are becoming smaller, and hence, assuming no change in the proportion of estates bequeathed to direct descendants, the rising real value of bequests will be spread amongst a decreasing number of beneficiaries. Without attempting the same sophisticated analysis that Holmens and Frosztega have, it is possible to get some idea of the magnitude of change likely by comparing projected average total UK deaths in a 10-year period with the average number of people in the 45–54 age group. After a 20% decline in this ratio between 1991–2001 and 2011–21, *there is a 70% rebound from then up to 2051–61, and presumably a similar rise in the ratio of bequests per beneficiary. When overlaid with the rising proportion of homeowners in the over 65 age group, this points to an important rise in income for the beneficiaries.*

When the same exercise of working out the ratio of projected deaths to the number of potential beneficiaries in the 45–54 cohort is applied to other countries in the EU, it is found that the ratio rises earlier and the percentage increase between 1995 and 2050 is generally far higher than in the UK. Given that household savings ratios are also much higher in most of the EU, this could suggest that the impact of the inheritance effect could be even more pronounced.

This may not be the case however, since a lot depends upon the nature of the estate – the breakdown between property and financial assets, price levels and the rate of inflation in property prices since acquisition, etc. For example, house prices tend to be lower in France than in the UK, despite higher *per capita* GDP. The value of private pensions is also significantly higher in the UK. The French see gold much more as a store of value than do the British, while both share- and home-ownership levels are far lower in Germany than in the UK. Even allowing for these differences, it is reasonable to suppose that, other things being equal, inheritances will play a more important part in cushioning spending power in the EU than in the UK. As we shall see, however, the state of government finances by 2030 may be such that these windfalls become targeted for increased inheritance or wealth taxes.

A more immediate threat is the rising proportion of the elderly forced to sell their homes to pay for long-term care. This has been taken into account by Holmens and Frosztega in their calculations up to 2011. It is worth studying this in more detail and projecting further into the future. We can get an idea of the potential scale of the problem by looking at the proportion of the elderly in residential homes, length of stay and total cost relative to the value of their estates. In 1994, there were some 273 000 residents in homes for the elderly in Great Britain; the figure has risen by 11% since 1986 but still represents only 3% of the population aged 65 or over. By far the majority of these are in private residential homes – 153 000 in 1994. The proportion of residents in English homes for the elderly aged 85 or over has risen from 47% in 1989 to 54% by 1994, and they now represent 14.7% of the 1 million people in this age group. Their average length of stay is estimated at 2½ years by consultants Laing and Buisson,[3] implying around 110 000 new residents per annum.

Following the implementation of the Community Care Act of 1993, the cost of financing residential accommodation and nursing care for the elderly now falls largely on the recipients. In theory, the outgoing Conservative government allowed individuals with limited incomes to preserve assets of £8000 from being applied to the cost of their residential care. A High Court ruling that local authorities have no obligation to waive their entitlement to these assets and that in practice, no such protection exists has been overturned by the Court of Appeal. In 1991, residential home fees averaged £250 per week and nursing home fees £300 per week in England (Laing and Buisson), implying a total outlay of £32 500–39 000 during the average stay. While this amounts to over half the value of the average estate with a dwelling, it should be remembered that, even accepting that the ageing of the elderly population will result in a higher proportion of them entering a retirement home, only perhaps 10% of the over-75s will be affected by 2030.

As a guide to the growth of this population, we can perhaps use Nuttall's projections for those over-60s needing regular or continuous care (30 hours and 45 hours per week respectively) mentioned on page 149. In 1991, these totalled 1.556 million, or say 1.6 million by 1994, of whom 273 000, or 17% were in residential homes. By 2031, this figure is projected to rise by 73% to 2.771 million, suggesting that the number in residential homes would reach 473 000. Putting this in context, there are projected to be 18.3 million aged 60 or over, and 6.4 million aged 75 or over at that date. By then the rising level of home ownership will result in a sizeable increase in the value of the average estate available to the next generation. On that basis nursing home costs might absorb only 5% of the total value of inheritances containing a dwelling, and while it could represent a far larger bite out of small estates, many will be sheltered to the extent of £8000. In other words, this is one fear that has become exaggerated, *unless the level of unpaid voluntary care fails to keep pace with the growth in the number of the fragile elderly, forcing an increasing proportion of the latter into residetial homes.*

We have shown how, even in the case of the UK, the costs of maintaining State pension benefits, health services and the care of the fragile elderly at current levels will soar in years to come. Chapter 11 puts the problem into context across the OECD group of countries. It examines the hard choices their governments will face, between maintaining these services (and letting their debts balloon to dangerous levels), squeezing the taxpayer, and/or cutting pensions and State health services. It concludes that demographic circumstances are so different across the OECD that, while some countries such as the UK and Ireland will escape almost unscathed, others such as Italy face decades of austerity that will put intolerable strains on their governments, and make economic growth grind to a halt. It may ultimately even threaten the stability of the EU.

References

1 Holmens, A. E. and Frosztega, M. (1994) 'House Property and Inheritance in the UK', Department of the Environment, HMSO.
2 Inland Revenue *Annual Reports*.
3 See Ref. 1. Laing and Buisson are consultants cited in Holmens and Frosztega's paper.

THE SOUND OF
SQUEAKING PIPS

Annual income twenty pounds, annual expenditure twenty pounds ought and six, result misery.

(Mr Micawber)

Introduction

In the last chapter, we saw that Merrill Lynch had concluded that the increased personal savings generated in the UK, Germany, France and Italy over the next three decades would match the demand for funds to cover public sector pension liabilities over the period, based on current levels of benefit and contribution. While this may seem to suggest that fears of impending doom are groundless, I have already warned that the World Bank fertility projections on which they are based are optimistic. The growth in the workforce, and hence in the number of taxpayers, will therefore be lower than forecast, and either tax rates or government debt will have to rise to match the liabilities. There are, moreover, other reasons for caution.

The Merrill Lynch research confines itself to examining solely the relationship between demography, private savings and pension obligations, although it fully recognises that there will be other calls on household savings. There are reasons to suppose that other services now provided by the State will be increasingly sloughed off onto the private sector – in particular, healthcare. Building this into the model could seriously modify the conclusion that a wall of savings, to the tune of $15–20 trillion over 30 years, will be available to pension funds. *The size of the future healthcare obligations has been calculated by the OECD, and for many countries it is significant relative to State pension obligations. On average, it adds 25% to the incremental State pension burden by 2010, 33% by 2020 and 43% by 2030.* The figures in Table 11.1 are calculated as projected spending, based on policies prevailing in 1996 and projected demographic changes, minus spending based on no change in the respective expenditure to GDP ratios after the year 2000.

Table 11.1 shows that, in general, the countries where population is ageing most rapidly (Italy, Spain) are among those that will suffer the most from this double impact on government expenditure. Others, such as Germany and Japan seem to escape surprisingly lightly, while Finland and the Netherlands look like spiralling out of control. By contrast, the UK is barely affected, and the position of Ireland can only be described

Table 11.1 Estimated impact of ageing population on government expenditure on pensions and healthcare (% of GDP)

	2010			2020			2030		
	Pensions	Health	Total	Pensions	Health	Total	Pensions	Health	Total
USA	0.3	0.1	0.3	1.0	0.7	1.7	2.4	1.8	4.3
Japan	3.1	0.5	3.5	6.0	1.1	7.0	6.3	1.2	7.5
Germany	0.2	0.0	0.2	0.7	0.1	0.9	5.0	0.8	5.8
France	0.0	0.2	0.2	1.9	1.0	2.9	3.8	1.8	5.6
Italy	0.6	0.1	0.7	2.6	0.5	3.1	7.7	1.7	9.4
UK	0.7	0.2	0.8	0.6	0.3	0.9	1.0	1.1	2.1
Canada	0.2	0.3	0.5	1.8	1.4	3.2	3.9	3.1	7.1
Australia	0.0	0.1	0.1	0.6	0.7	1.3	1.5	1.8	3.3
Belgium	−1.0	0.0	−1.0	1.0	0.8	1.8	4.2	2.2	6.4
Denmark	1.2	0.4	1.6	2.9	1.0	3.9	4.5	1.6	6.1
Finland	1.3	0.3	1.6	5.8	1.5	7.2	8.4	2.7	11.1
Iceland	0.0	0.0	0.1	0.7	0.7	1.5	1.9	1.9	3.8
Ireland	−0.3	0.0	−0.3	−0.1	0.4	0.3	−0.1	0.7	0.6
Netherlands	1.0	0.5	1.5	3.7	1.7	5.3	6.9	3.3	10.2
Norway	1.1	0.0	1.1	3.7	0.9	4.6	6.0	1.9	7.9
Portugal	1.2	0.0	1.2	2.7	0.3	3.0	6.1	1.0	7.1
Spain	0.2	0.1	0.3	1.5	0.6	2.1	4.2	1.8	6.1
Sweden	1.3	0.2	1.5	2.8	0.9	3.7	3.9	1.6	5.5
Total OECD	0.8	0.2	0.9	2.1	0.7	2.9	3.9	1.7	5.6

Source: © OECD. OECD Economic Outlook, June 1996, p. 25, Table 12. Reproduced by permission of the OECD.

as remarkably healthy. Such major differences in what are effectively transfers from taxpayers into non-productive activities will have a sizeable impact on the relative attractiveness of these countries to both direct and portfolio investors.

When these figures are translated through to government budgets,[1] they show a frightening and exponential rise in levels of debt compared to GDP for most of the 20 OECD countries in the study – Australia, Canada and oil-rich Norway being the main exceptions. In the case of Japan, for example, net financial liabilities rise from 11% of GDP in 1995 to 317% by 2030, Germany from 44% to 216%, and France from 35% to 165%. By contrast, Canada actually becomes a net lender over the period, and the projection for Ireland – stable debt/GDP for 35 years – has been overtaken by events; thanks to unprecedented economic growth, the ratio for Ireland is now closer to 54% than the 74% projected for 2000.

It is clear that the urgency of the European Commission to achieve Monetary Union by 1999 must be based in part on the need to meet the 60% debt/GDP ratio as early as possible, before demographic pressures begin to bite early next century.

Researchers separate out the effect of this demographic component on net financial liabilities as shown in Table 11.2.

Table 11.2 Pure ageing effects on net financial liabilities, 2000–2030 as a percentage of GDP

	%		%
United States	41	Australia	34
Japan	180	Austria	162
Germany	42	Finland	199
France	60	Ireland	2
Italy	103	Netherlands	132
United Kingdom	26	Norway	127
Canada	38	Spain	61

Source: OECD Economics Department Working Paper No. 168.

The contrast between, say, Ireland and Finland is enormous, and gives a good idea of the tasks facing the different governments in their attempts to prevent deficits from getting out of control. If instead of other policies, the governments elected to keep the ratio of debt/GDP constant after the year 2000 (assuming they had achieved the fiscal consolidation projected by the OECD at that date) by changing taxation, there would have to be some swingeing tax increases for many countries – particularly for Japan, France, Germany, Italy, Austria, Finland, the Netherlands and Spain – towards the end of the period when the demographic pressure is most intense.

Avoiding the problem

How can countries avoid such problems? Conclusions without recommendations are only half the story, and the researchers have put forward the following proposals under three separate headings:

- policies to increase the effective size of the workforce:
  - (a) raising retirement ages
  - (b) discouraging early retirement
  - (c) increasing immigration

160

- policies to improve the overall budget position
- policies to restrain the growth of expenditure on health and pensions.

Under the first group, it is clear that the rush towards early retirement has become a stampede; in the UK, head teachers and chief superintendents of police are queueing to leave their professions before the rules change. In France, striking lorry drivers actually forced the government to concede early retirement at the age of 55. It is hard to see countries in Europe forcing through legislation to counter this trend while unemployment levels are so high, and the same is even more true for any moves to liberalise immigration, in the face of a right-wing upsurge in France. Only in raising the statutory retirement age have they been successful, but it should be pointed out that no country so far has accepted the OECD researchers' proposed target of retirement at 70.

The OECD makes the point that, in budgetary matters, where you start has a critical bearing on where you get to. In other words, to get the most favourable balance in 2030, countries should try to ensure that by the year 2000, they have achieved the best possible primary balance – the higher the surplus, the better, since this permits the repayment of existing debt, reducing future interest burdens. In general terms, if the primary surplus is assumed to be 1 percentage point higher than the base case in the year 2000, the primary surplus by 2030 could be 25–50 percentage points of GDP lower. The stagnation in Europe over 1994–6 has been the principal reason why the OECD has revised sharply downwards the primary balances expected by 2000, and hence its projections to 2030.

Up to now, the UK has been taking the lead in reining in State pension and health expenditure, switching contributors out of SERPS and into private pension schemes, and also in tightening costs in the National Health Service. Short of medical breakthroughs, it is hard to see significant progress in cutting health costs further, but a number of steps can be taken to trim pension liabilities, and the OECD has examined four scenarios:

- cost containment (pensions frozen as percentage of GDP from 2015);
- later retirement (increasing retirement age by 0.5 years each year from 2005 until the age of 70;
- targeting (reducing the proportion of retirees eligible for pensions to 30% over the period 2015–30, while freezing the replacement rate at its 2010 level);
- indexing pensions to wages.

The first three make a significant impact on expenditure, although the third, designed only to provide a pension to the most needy 30% of retirees, is unlikely to survive any democratic election, and encourages both financial irresponsibility and deceit among potential recipients. For both these reasons, it should be discounted as a viable policy. Later retirement must also come up against the fact that after the age of 55, participation rates in the workforce are very low, and that after the age of 65 the proportion of people suffering disabling illness rises sharply, making employers reluctant to offer jobs to those in this age group. Governments may well find that a large part of their expected tax and National Insurance in-flow from the 65–69-year-olds actually becomes an unemployment benefit out-flow. The final scenario has little effect on expenditure, except in the UK, since most countries link pensions to wages not prices anyway.

It could get worse

The researchers rightly point out the 'heroic' nature of the assumptions that they are forced to adopt in order to create a manageable model, which is also extremely sensitive to apparently small changes in assumptions. Like butterflies' wings, they can cause distant financial hurricanes. Unfortunately, the base assumptions themselves are acknowledged to be optimistic and in need of modification.

For a start, all projections begin at the year 2000, when it is assumed that the countries have all achieved the trajectories laid out in the Secretariat's Medium-Term Reference Scenario (MTRS). These are based on a favourable interpretation of governments' fiscal plans and their ability to achieve them. Clearly, in the case of the European countries seeking economic convergence under Maastricht, growth has been sluggish, and unemployment levels, and hence budget deficits, have been far higher than projected by their governments. In other words, the fiscal positions at the year 2000 are likely to be worse than the Working Paper suggests.

Secondly, they still rely on the World Bank demographics that assume that fertility rates in Western Europe will return to replacement rate over time. The impact on projections of taking a more pessimistic fertility rate can be seen in a different context from separate studies on the Japanese State pension system. There, the ageing of the population shows no sign of being arrested, and dependency rates are rising sharply.

Even on the Central TFR assumption used by the Ministry of Health and Welfare, contribution rates will have to rise from a 1995 level of 17% to 29.8% by 2030 – and that is after 1994 reforms had cut the 2030 rate from 34.8%. Assuming the pessimistic TFR scenario mentioned on page 42, the rate would reach 32% by 2025. Applying a low-fertility scenario to these OECD studies would lead to a growing decline in the solvency of the State pension systems of the countries concerned from 2015 onwards.

Wanted: One dozen Iron Chancellors

There are two components of any government budget – revenue and expenditure. If the latter exceeds the former, then the result, if not 'misery', is at least a higher debt burden for repayment in later years. The consequent higher borrowing costs hang like an albatross about the necks of future Chancellors, cutting their scope for independent action, since debt represents an on-going obligation to service interest and capital until redemption.

How does this relate to Europe? For all the public satisfaction expressed by European leaders over the pace of convergence of their Budget deficits towards the Maastricht criteria, it is becoming increasingly clear that their optimism will be short-lived and within 30 years the deficit will become a nightmare if no action is taken. If State pensions, health and long-term care are going to swallow up an increasing share of national income, what does the future hold in store? Will workers be condemned to decades in which no improvement in personal living standards is possible because all their incremental income is appropriated by government to feed the voracious demand of this trio? Will other areas be run down to make way for their relentless growth? Will government think the unthinkable and cut back this growth below the rate dictated by demographics, causing uproar amongst the electorate as hospital waiting lists soar and the elderly are evicted from nursing homes as their money runs out? Can workers afford privatised pension and health insurance, since many will have to pay twice – once for themselves and once to support those already in retirement?

To get some feel of the options available, we will look at both sides of the UK Budget, starting with expenditure, which is dominated by three sectors – education, health and social security, whose combined share has risen from 44.5% of the total in 1985 to 50.3% by 1995.

The squeeze on government expenditure is well advanced. Over the period, the share taken by defence has fallen by 4.6 percentage points to make way for expansion in the police, health and education. Housing has been slashed and the commitment to mining and agriculture probably reached its low point by 1995, given the cost of compensating farmers over BSE. The sale of State assets which cut debt servicing from 10.9% to 8.7% of expenditure during the past decade has practically come to an end.

How much more can be trimmed?

Here are a few suggestions.

Defence

In July 1997 the UK defence secretary announced a shake-up of the annual £9 billion procurement programme with the intention of cutting costs by 10%, or £900 million, borrowing best practices from countries such as the USA. These might involve adopting the budgetary practices used by the private sector, making use of civilian equipment that could be adopted to the military market, and increasing partnership with the private sector.

Even though UK ministers are adamant that they will never surrender defence policy to Brussels, economic circumstances will compel all EU governments to pool their hardware requirements in a way that will lead to a rationalisation of suppliers, elimination of duplicated R&D and production capacity, and hopefully lower costs. The chauvinistic nonsense of 'national champions' will have to give way to economic realities, and open tendering must bring about genuine competition.

In Spain, the Ministry of Defence is disposing of its surplus land holdings, while in France the 1998 Defence Budget is scheduled to fall, even in current francs, in order to raise funds to reduce youth unemployment.

Education

If one believes the World Bank projections, the size of the school population will show no decline over the next 30–50 years, so there are few prospects of trimming the UK school education budget in line with falling enrolment. Furthermore the government is determined that the expansion in further and higher education will continue. On the other hand, university students will be expected to pay for an increasing proportion of their tuition fees. Current proposals are that students pay £1000 per annum, irrespective of the course pursued, to be financed by loans, repayable once the student is in employment, with an annual salary above a certain threshold. In Australia, charging students roughly one-quarter of the average cost of all university courses enabled the government to increase the number of places by 4% without deterring applications from poorer students. No downturn has been detected in UK applications after the new fee structure was introduced.

In the UK, the conversion of polytechnics into universities has led to problems. Not only has the expansion led to wasteful duplication, but not all can offer quality education across the board. Weak departments should be closed: indeed in areas of London where former polytechnics cluster cheek by jowl, there may well be scope for horse trading. According to Geraint Jones of Lancaster University, such moves to specialisation could cut the cost base by 40%, or £2.5 billion.[2]

Things are also stirring on the Continent. The Italians are overhauling their school system for the first time in 70 years, and in Germany, where around 10% of German 29-year-olds are still in education, the standard length of many courses is to be cut by a year, but will still take four to four-and-a-half years.

Health

Rationing of services will become commonplace. Already, health authorities in Birmingham are considering removing fertility treatment from the services available free on the NHS because of the low success rate and high cost (£5000 per baby born), saving some £0.4 million *per annum*. Others may well follow suit. In both health and education, the need to rationalise premises to optimise scarce resources will lead to a review of the guidelines for the private finance initiative, and this could be extended into other areas. Finally, the UK Health Secretary has asked his team to 'think the unthinkable' in a far-reaching review of NHS spending, not excluding charging patients for services, in flat contradiction to the principles on which the service was established. Given that managers in the NHS consider that the cost of repairing hospital buildings is close to £2 billion – four times the government estimate – it is clear that unpleasant measures will have to be taken.

Social Security

Table 11.3 Social security expenditure, 1980–1 to 1994–5 (£ billion)

	1980–81 £ billion	1990–91 £ billion	1994–95 £ billion
Total benefit expenditure	22.7	56.4	85.2
Contributory	14.9	30.5	40.1
Non-Contributory	7.8	25.9	45.1
Total benefit paid to			
Elderly	12.1	28.6	37.9
Sick and disabled			
Total	3.2	11.2	20.4
Short-term sick	0.7	1.4	0.8
Long-term sick and disabled	2.5	9.8	19.6
Family	4.1	9.7	15.9
Of which lone parents	0.9	4.7	9.1
Unemployed	2.4	5.3	9.1
Widows and others	0.9	1.5	1.8

Source: Social Security Statistics, 1995, p. 3.

Table 11.3 shows an astonishing increase in payments to the long-term sick – up from 11% of the total in 1980–1 to 23% by 1994–5 – despite the fact that a number of the more hazardous industries, such as mining, steel, shipbuilding, etc., have given way to service industries. This could well include the impact of early retirement on grounds of health or stress, an area where the government is keen to tighten the qualifying criteria. The other area on which ministerial guns will be focused will be lone parents, whose benefits have soared ten-fold in 14 years. Here the emphasis of the new government will be to find ways of bringing them back into the workforce by reducing the high marginal tax rates faced by those on benefits when they enter work, perhaps improving the availability and cost of nursery places. The previous government did little to change the way the tax and benefit systems interact to produce high effective marginal tax rates when those on benefit return to work and the benefits are withdrawn.

The problem of reform has been aggravated by the two systems being based on different criteria – taxes on *personal* income, benefits on *household* income. It is admitted, however that there will have to be significant expenditure *before* any savings are achieved.

Finally, the scope for reducing unemployment benefits is limited, given

Table 11.4 Total number of people (000)
with marginal tax rates above:

%	1985	1995/6
100	70	5
90	130	105
80	290	360
70	290	645
60	450	655
50	680	660

Source: DSS. Crown Copyright is reproduced with the permission of the Controller of Her Majesty's Stationery Office.

the marked fall in unemployment in the past two years. They now represent around 10% of total expenditure.

Other savings?

There are a number of public sector activities whose cost is insensitive to the size of population or workforce, and are thus especially vulnerable in a demographic downturn. Think, for example, of the running of libraries, art galleries, museums and swimming pools, where the level of fixed costs (heating, lighting, insurance, repairs, etc.) far outweigh the cost of manpower. Already libraries are cutting back expenditure on new books. Soon, however, they will have to choose permanent closure, unless they can persuade the public to pay substantially more for the services they provide. Similarly in the utility sector, whether public or private, the cost of maintaining a power station or a network of underground water mains or sewers, gas or electricity supplies is also largely fixed. Whatever the regulators say, these utilities will be unable to keep down tariffs when their customer base begins to contract next century. Joe Public's discretionary spending power is going to get increasingly dented.

<u>Who pays?</u>

There's no such thing as a free lunch – or a free operation, free unemployment benefit, free State pension or free homecare. Since governments have few income-generating assets of their own (usually they have accumulated debts), the costs must largely be borne by the workforce through direct taxation on income (26.9% of UK government receipts in 1995),

National Insurance (15.6%), indirect taxation on consumption or excise duties on tobacco, alcohol and petrol. Comparatively little income derives from such areas as corporate profits (9.0%).

Governments have responded to the fact that the most rapidly growing part of the economy is the service sector by going after air travellers, insurance and the National Lottery. Given the popularity of the Internet, which is leading to a sharp rise in telephone traffic, and satellite and cable TV, they may seek extra revenues from these sources, although proving where an Internet transaction originates – and hence where tax can be levied – is likely to remain a major headache for taxmen worldwide. *The fact remains, however, that well over 60% of government revenue is collected from individuals, and if the workforce declines, so will government revenue.* (As we shall see, Ireland, with a rising workforce, is generating rapidly rising government revenue, and budget surpluses.)

The previous sections give a warning that, even in a country as demographically fortunate as the UK, and even before the problems really begin next century, government will be fighting to hold back the budget deficit by cutting services, raising taxes and forcing the general public to shoulder an increasing share of the cost of the services provided. How are *less* fortunate countries coping? Here are two examples.

Take Italy – the EU's Achilles' heel

Italy today typifies the problems that much of the EU will face from around 2010 onwards. Unfortunately for the Italians, their period of austerity will begin almost immediately, The ability of successive governments to maintain the present course may determine whether the single currency survives.

By dint of heroic measures, the government of Romano Prodi has cut the budget deficit from around 7% in 1996 to below the Maastricht threshold of 3% in 1997 and (hopefully) 1998. Cumulative public sector debt stands unfortunately at over twice the level permitted by the Club rules (122% *vs* 60%), and the other EU governments are seeking reassurance that future Italian governments will continue to bring it down.

It *can* be done, claims the treasury minister, Carlo Azeglio Ciampi; just give me time. In fact, he means 12 years to 2009, and even that depends on maintaining a primary budget surplus of 5.5% *per annum* over the period, leaving little over to help families or restore crumbling infrastructure. Twelve years of austerity, with perhaps further measures to trim the pension entitlements that continue to swallow an increasing proportion of GDP, is good neither for birth rates nor for one's chance of being re-elected. Sensibly, the government is looking to raise money in other ways, particularly through privatisation, but continuing resistance to labour reforms from the trade unions and the former communist party make it difficult to cut losses in State-controlled companies by trimming labour.

At any time during the next few years, as austerity begins to bite, the calls to abandon monetary union in order to save the Italian people will grow louder, and the money markets will react accordingly. Interest rates will soar, making it hard for the treasury to keep to its targets, perhaps precipitating the same collapse as has happened in Asia. As for the claims that it will be impossible for a country to exit from monetary union once it has joined, well, they *would* say that, wouldn't they? It is nonsense. If banks and individuals become so alarmed about the political situation that they remove money from Italian banks, or refuse to lend money to, or buy securities from, the government, then it cannot refinance any maturing debt. Remember the Asian crisis. Watch this space.

Meanwhile in Tokyo . . .

The problems of countries running primary deficits have been spelled out earlier – by adding to government debt, they cause future borrowing costs to spiral. In the case of Japan, the situation is extreme because:

- the population is ageing rapidly and the demographic pressure on future budgets is intense;
- governments have spent massively over the past few years to try to rekindle economic growth, without much success.

After a period of steady improvement in primary balances through the 1980s – from a deficit of 3.4% of GDP in 1980 to a surplus of 3.6% in 1990 – the budget has plunged into increasing deficits again, reaching 3.6% in 1996. As a result, general government gross financial liabilities rose from 62.3% of GDP in 1991 to 87.4% in 1996, and are projected by the OECD to be approaching 100% by 1998, even before the real cost of ageing hits early next century.

Drastic action had to be taken. In May 1997, sales tax was increased from 3% to 5%. A month later, the government forced through a package of healthcare measures that will double the cost of medical treatment for those belonging to the national health insurance scheme from September 1997. This will raise an estimated Y2 trillion, equivalent to 0.4% of GDP, or a quarter of government health expenditure in the year to March 1997. The same month, it adopted a programme of severe spending cuts designed to lop Y200 billion, or 0.5% off general expenditure in the fiscal year beginning April 1998.

Unfortunately, private consumers reacted disproportionately to a sales tax increase that should have had only a marginal impact on behaviour. Department store sales fell, as did sales of cars and consumer electronics. The unfolding Asian crisis removed a major export market and increased competition for Japanese groups both in third markets and within Japan itself. At the same time, it undermined the already precarious position of Japanese banks. As a result, the government, increasingly a hostage to events, was forced to change tack again and pump money back into both the banking system and the economy in order to coax it into life again. By June 1998, an increasingly frustrated group of Asian countries, together with the EU and USA, were pressing Japan to take further steps to restore its economy now sunk into recession.

What if it doesn't work? Japan will simply have added to its rapidly escalating debt burden, just at a time when the size of the workforce, and hence the tax base, is about to decline appreciably – by 13% between 1995 and 2020, almost as much as Italy's 15.1%. Japan's seniority system means that those who are now entering retirement are those earning the highest salaries, and hence their retirement will mean a far more significant drop in income tax than in the UK, where salaries generally peak at around age 45–50.

The burden on the State pension system will be further aggravated by the high participation rates of older workers, in part because this seniority system ensures a relatively high pension, since it will be hard to increase them from current levels. It also means that the ratio of pensioners to workers will deteriorate more rapidly in Japan than in Italy, which has a far lower fertility rate. Taking World Bank population projections and assuming current participation rates, we find that the ratio of Japanese pensioners to workers doubles between 1995 and 2020 (from 0.30 to 0.62), while for Italy the rise is only 61% (from 0.41 to 0.66), and National Insurance contributions will follow suit. The pressure on net pay will intensify in both countries.

The perils of high taxation

It is clear that if pension entitlements are to be maintained at current levels, taxes in the EU and Japan will have to rise sharply. For example, most conventional estimates suggest that for France they will result in an increase equivalent to about 6% of GDP by 2020 and 15% by 2050. A recent Working Paper of the International Monetary Fund[3] concludes that this could be a serious underestimate because it fails to take into account the impact of rising tax rates on investment and economic growth. Factoring this in, the researchers find that, *in the case of France, the share of public expenditure in GDP could rise by not 15 but 35 percentage points by 2050, and that economic growth could eventually grind to a halt.* While their findings are heavily qualified because of their sensitivity to the underlying assumptions, they make the reasons for the overhaul of the State pension system even more pressing. Are you listening, M. Jospin?

Social security costs – rescued by 'deflation'?

Like beauty or GNP, inflation is in the eye of the beholder. For centuries, it really meant the price of corn, reflecting the fact that the staple diet of the labourer was bread and beer. As society has become more complex, the basket of goods used by the statisticians to calculate price indices has been getting progressively larger and more difficult to value. The relative importance of food and clothing has declined and their places have been taken by a range of services for which changes in both quality and price complicate the calculations. For example, if BT cuts phone charges, do you make more phone calls? Even in the case of food, if there is a glut of plums, do you switch your purchase from apples to plums? And what if apples are in the consumer price index but plums are not?

More seriously, how do you allow for improvements in quality? A 1997 car with computerised engine control, anti-lock brakes, a heated windscreen and corrosion warranty is a far cry from one from 1960. Many of the improvements may be imperceptible to the buyer – more precise machining of components, better quality steel for the bodywork, lower drag co-efficient – but nevertheless contribute to making a better vehicle.

The reasons for raising these points are not trivial ones. Even though wages are no longer index-linked rigidly to inflation, other important items such as State benefits and pensions are. The USA is a case in point. The 1995 base case projection by the Congress Budget Office shows a massive increase in deficit and debt due to the rapid escalation in Medicare and Medicaid payments, and the interest on the compounding debt itself. Without reform, the Medicare trust fund was projected to be bankrupt by 2001 and reach a cumulative deficit of $408 billion by 2005. Things have improved since then, but the problem continues to grow in the longer-term.

It is here that the structure of inflation shows us a way out of looming bankruptcy. For years, economists have puzzled over why the USA, the country that has done the most to develop computerisation, IT and the Internet, should apparently have shown the least impressive growth in productivity of all the major countries since 1990. At the same time other economists were worrying that the Consumer Price Index (CPI) didn't seem to be picking up the trends in quality mentioned above. If, however, it is agreed that inflation is actually lower than represented by the CPI, real output and hence productivity are correspondingly higher. The circle is squared, and with one bound the US government is free from huge future social security obligations.

Is this too good to be true, a financial version of the Indian rope trick? The idea is being taken increasingly seriously, and not only by government and economists. Already the Grey Panthers are snarling at the economists, and are threatening congressmen who might support reforms that would erode their inflation-indexed benefits. Alan Greenspan, Chairman of the Federal Reserve, has thrown his hat into the ring by supporting the view that the current CPI overstates inflation, and has asked Congress to appoint an independent commission to determine the annual cost-of-living increases for government benefits. By late 1997, however, even he had to admit that the complexities of the problem could keep them busy for a very long time.

Despite the fact that Europe is further behind the USA in its consumption of high-tech services, similar overstatement of CPI on grounds of quality improvement probably occurs; unfortunately, even if CPI were adjusted for this, it would not help government liabilities significantly since, with the exception of the UK, benefits are indexed not to prices but to wages.

A new equilibrium?

What would happen if, faced with the impending bankruptcy of the bulk of the European State pension, all these nations were to give the private sector free rein? At the start, private consumption is likely to decline relative to investment, something that could pose a serious threat to world trade, because of the imbalances between the types of goods produced and traded among different countries. For example, countries in the Far East export consumer goods to the USA and EU in return for import of capital goods. But if the latter cut down their consumption (as has happened in the EU because of Maastricht), the former suffer badly. The lags between export of consumer goods and import of capital goods mean that the countries in the Far East fall into deficits while their Western trading partners move into surplus. Furthermore, companies in the Far East are accustomed to a healthy growth in demand and plan capacity accordingly, but when demand fails to grow as fast as installed capacity, operating ratios fall and profit margins are hit. Indeed this was also reflected in the lacklustre performance of Far East stockmarkets in 1995/6, and was an important contributor to the currency crisis of mid-1997.

At the same time, the opportunity to invest all the available savings at a particular rate of return should diminish, because of the reduced need for plant to produce consumer goods. Accordingly investors would have to accept lower rates of return – or conversely, existing assets offering rates of return above that available for new investment would be bid up in price. *In other words, both bonds and equities should be further rerated globally.* This will be covered in more detail in Part IV.

References

1 OECD Economics Department Working Paper No. 168.
2 Jones, G. (May 1997) *Economic Journal*.
3 Habermeier, K. F. and Lenseigne, F. (1998) 'French Public Finances: Modeling Long Term Prospects and Reform Options', IMF European Department WP/98/12.

Part IV

A FINANCIAL SURVIVAL COURSE

THE DYNAMICS OF THE STOCKMARKET

Chapter 12 will look at the global influences currently driving down inflation and boosting share ratings – the single currency, globalisation, the Internet. Chapter 13 provides a framework for both a medium- and a long-term global investment strategy. For the former, countries are screened for risk and factors affecting international competitiveness and profitability. For the latter, we will look at the demographics and the privatisation of State pension funds, both of which influence the cash available to go into the market.

The market merry-go-round

Let us be clear what moves markets – it's cash, lots of it. Whether this comes from wealth generated by people or companies, or from the sale of other assets is not immediately relevant. Providing that the cash directed at a marketable security exceeds the supply available at a given price, its price will rise. Equilibrium will be reached when investors believe that the risk-adjusted return at some higher price is no better than for other investments, and so stop buying. This is why totally new money is better than that generated from the sale of other assets judged to have less potential. As the latter fall in price, the expected return at the lower price will rise. Eventually the returns will reach a level where selling dries up and the share price stabilises.

The more buoyant the economy, the higher the government's tax receipts and hence, hopefully, the lower its borrowing requirements. The fewer the securities it has to issue to cover the deficit, the higher the price, or the lower the interest rate, it can offer to investors. As yields fall on government securities, the more investors will switch into other assets, such as equities and property, whose profitability is also rising with the growing economy.

No tree grows to the sky. Even the most buoyant market tops out: indeed, they tend to do so just when things look most bright. It's an axiom of the stockmarket. Here's another. Each bull market carries the seeds of its own destruction. The rising level of corporate profitability and a tightening of capacity, whether of plant, property or people triggers a wave of new investment. But because of the inevitable time lag between ordering new equipment and it being installed, companies face an interim period where they cannot easily increase sales volume. If demand remains high they may be able to put up prices, fuelling national inflation, while trying to squeeze out more production by increasing overtime working, thereby boosting incomes and threatening a consumer boom. Alternatively, shortage of capacity could lead to an upsurge of imports, damaging the trade position and weakening the currency. In economist parlance, Britain's 'high marginal propensity to import' has been its downfall in many previous cycles.

It is at this point that the government or the Central Bank steps in, taking excess steam out of the economy through higher taxes and interest rates. Those leads and lags become the enemy of the market – the new capacity finally comes on stream just when demand is topping out because of government action, so the higher fixed costs (depreciation and interest on the new plant) bite into profitability. Indeed the more capital intensive the company, the more volatile the profits – i.e., the greater the risk for investors, who accordingly compensate by putting a lower rating on the shares. Thus the shares of cement companies are rated more modestly than those of supermarkets.

Finance directors also seek to raise money by issuing new shares at the highest possible price – i.e., when investors are most optimistic about the prospects. Existing companies have rights issues and new ones seek listing. When however companies have entered a contract to buy new plant or make a takeover, they come under pressure to secure finance. As they see other companies coming to the market to raise funds, they become increasingly anxious that they themselves may miss the boat and rush through their rights issue before the market dries up.

This fear in fact becomes self-fulfilling since it leads to an upsurge in capital raising just at a time when investors are starting to become nervous about future earnings prospects, anticipating rising wage costs, higher interest rates on borrowings and a fall in operating capacity. The market begins to fall and demand for new issues evaporates. Latecomers may be unable to raise new funds, even on the most generous terms, and may have to postpone expansion plans. Eventually, the supply of new capacity peaks out, demand begins to rise, price-cutting comes to an end and profit margins begin to rise. Share prices bottom out and the merry-go-round is about to start again. All aboard!

The forces of deflation:
Brussels, the single currency and the Internet

Inflation and share ratings (PERs) sit at opposite ends of the see-saw. High inflation leads to low PERs, and *vice versa*. So, any investment strategy must take a view of the future course of inflation, where surprising things may be taking place.

For most of the past 300 years, inflation did not exist in the UK, apart from brief episodes resulting from war or harvest failure. For example, Winchester College paid the same price for cloth, 120s a piece, between 1612 and 1791.[1] Prices actually drifted down over the period 1660–1760, rose continually over the period covering the American War of Independence and the French Revolution until they peaked during the Napoleonic Wars, before resuming their steady decline. Insofar as it is possible to compare two consumer baskets 250 years apart, price levels in 1913 were similar to those in 1660. The huge rise in population that coincided with the Industrial Revolution, which might have been expected to put pressure on resources, and hence on their prices, did not do so.

During the 20th century, however, union power was able to raise wages significantly, particularly in post-war periods when labour was scarce, in exactly the same way as, after the Black Death, serfs were able to improve their contracts with their lords. In many countries, they were able to secure the automatic indexation of wages to prices, as in Italy or Brazil, a move that may have helped industrial peace in the short term, but, by institutionalising inflation, made it harder to tackle. The inflationary spiral was given a further twist by the growing shortages of industrial commodities. The Malthusian equations built into *The Limits to Growth* seemed to be vindicated by the quadrupling of the oil price in the early 1970s, when governments monetised their soaring trade deficits by printing money, adding petrol to the inflationary fires.

By the 1980s, governments had learned that this policy was a mistake and reacted to the second oil crisis by reining in demand, starting a process which has gradually brought inflation back under control. For a start, companies make more efficient use of raw materials through better design and more recycling, while the nature of the products themselves has changed. They are based less on heavy metal electromechanical controls and more on electronics, and demand itself is moving towards ideas-based products. More significantly, in the UK, Thatcherism has brought about the streamlining of the union-dominated heavy industries through privatisation or closure by forcing them to compete in the global marketplace without the crutch of subsidies. Their place in the economy has been taken by non-union service industries.

GATT, the Uruguay Round, the EU, the single currency and the

Internet – what do they have in common? That they make it more difficult for countries to pursue an independent course of action, that they extend and intensify competition and drive down prices. Finally, that their influence on inflation has been gathering momentum over the past decade.

Even in the 1960s and 1970s, being out of step with the rest of the world could bring on a financial crisis. The none-so-subtle engineering of pre-election booms by countless Tory Chancellors, or French reflation when surrounding economies were slowing down, have led to humiliating climb-downs as foreign investors withdrew funds, interest rates soared and devaluation often became the only way out. These days, as countries become increasingly bound up in a web of international treaties, the scope for individual independent action is becoming an even more remote prospect – at least in the EU. The increasing independence of Central Banks, modelled on the Bundesbank, is keeping the politicians honest.

In the good old days, countries conducted their affairs to suit themselves. If the UK found gas in the North Sea and taxed it in a way that enabled ICI to produce petrochemicals cheaply, then that might be tough on Bayer or Hoechst, but there was nothing that they could do about it. If a government wanted to stimulate the shipping sector by granting accelerated depreciation on ships so that their owners would be tax-free for decades, that was their affair. And if it wanted to attract foreign investment to a depressed area by outbribing other countries it could do so. Companies could stay snug and uncompetitive behind high tariff walls, while consumers were ripped off with shoddy goods at high prices.

Times have changed, not only because of a general reduction in tariff barriers under GATT, but also because within Europe the bureaucrats are busy rolling out bumps in the playing field. Bribes for attracting foreign investors now have to be approved in Brussels, and the more egregious ones have been rejected. Customs formalities have been streamlined, non-tariff barriers reduced and national monopolies opened to competition.

Brussels has achieved steady progress, despite entrenched opposition, especially from Germany, the country currently most wedded to subsidies and protection, because of soaring unemployment in East Germany. After failing to bring Volkswagen to heel for accepting DM241 million of aid from the state of Saxony in 1996, Brussels got its revenge in 1998 with a record fine of Ecu102 million for preventing its Italian distributors from selling cars to foreign buyers. In another landmark ruling in

October 1997, the French government agreed not to renew an aid pro-gramme worth FFr1.8 billion per annum which reduced employers' social security contributions for lower-paid workers in the textile, cloth-ing and shoe industries. These declining sectors, which still employ some 300 000, are suffering severe competition from the Far East. This will intensify following recent devaluations, making the loss of subsidy espe-cially hard to bear, and job losses could accelerate, offsetting the government's job creation schemes.

Despite some setbacks, markets are opening up, and investment is gravitating to the most competitive countries. The massive in-flows of Continental investment into the UK and US investment into Ireland underlines the attractiveness of countries where low labour costs and sen-sible labour laws have combined to produce profit margins well in excess of those available in much of Western and Central Europe. It is unfortu-nate that the response of politicians and unions in France and Germany is to seek to impose on the UK their own discredited system and blunt its new-found competitiveness, rather than implement much-needed reforms at home. Meanwhile their major companies are voting with their feet, and leaving.

What will the single currency do for business and the consumer? If it survives, it will make life easier for all concerned. Besides the savings on currency transactions, put at $5 billion per annum, it will enable larger companies to dispense with perhaps half their employees involved in monitoring them. The downside is that it will make it far harder for com-panies to sustain different pricing structures in different countries in Europe. Germans may find both German-made cars and aspirins cheaper in Italy than back home for the moment, but in future, such price differ-ences will narrow. Certain drug companies are introducing a single Europe-wide price for some new products. Virgin Records is reviewing its European pricing policy to stem losses from parallel imports. Indeed, efforts of companies to prevent parallel imports may well be outlawed. The net result will be pressure on manufacturers' margins, but benefits for the more imaginative retailers – particularly ones that know how to use electronic marketing.

The Internet – the great leveller

At a time when the hype about intelligent agents, virtual malls and elec-tronic money has been shown to be very wide of the mark, or at least premature, and only a fraction of consumer transactions take place on the Net, it may sound odd to view the Internet as the crowning touch to globalisation, the golden spike at the end of the railroad track. But there are already signs that it *could* be, and, in the process it will transform the way we live and work.

Leading the charge are not the nerds, nor even consumers, but big business, looking for ways of buying in supplies faster and more cheaply than by traditional methods. In the vanguard is General Electric, whose Information Services division now does $1 billion of business a year with some 1400 suppliers on the Net – more than the entire consumer sector. The software on their web site, Trading Process Network (TPN) enables suppliers to receive specifications, including technical drawings, automatically managing the bids when they return, notifying the bidders of the result and providing an on-line form of contract for the winner. Besides cutting the bidding process at GE's lighting division from 21 to 10 days, it has created spare capacity at the GE end, enabling it to widen the range of its suppliers. Foreign suppliers now account for 15% of orders. The net result is that the increased competition has lowered the cost of supplies by between 5% and 20%.

GE has begun to offer its TPN system to other groups, and the expectation must be that its suppliers will in time negotiate with *their* suppliers, with the benefits ultimately flowing through to GE in even lower component costs. With such benefits, and such low costs of getting on the Net, it is not surprising that the value of such transactions is expected to soar, with Price Waterhouse forecasting $400 billion per annum by 2002.[2]

The Internet will throw into sharp relief those firms that can compete by keeping prices low – the world becomes their oyster. They can reach more customers faster and more effectively than anyone would have dreamed about only a decade ago. Airlines, for example, are finding they can cut out travel agents and deal direct with customers over the Net, offering lower prices by cutting out agents' commissions. In the USA, and increasingly in the UK, agents are selling houses over the Net, and car distributors are beginning to worry that the single currency and the Internet will bring a regime of lower and more uniform prices for both new and second hand cars. German companies now complain that the Internet is cutting into their markets since customers can check the prices from a range of suppliers for the cost of a local phone call. To cut costs, the Japanese flag carrier, JAL, is now tendering for supplies internationally over the Internet.

As to the adage that 'On the Net, nobody knows you're a dog', the response is that they will very soon find out if all you can do is bark. What the Net does is expose your shortcomings. Those who can't cope will only be kept alive by orders from those not themselves trading on the Net, until they themselves succumb. The gulf between winners and losers will open more rapidly and become more extreme, and the stockmarket will judge them accordingly. Evolution is fast on the Net, and these electronic niches get filled rapidly. Amazon's web site for the sale of books electronically already dominates the market, with latecomers like Barnes & Noble picking up the crumbs.

Privatisation: reform through the back door

Even the Germans are now touting the single currency not as an unalloyed blessing in its own right, but as the catalyst for further reforms. One such reform, which will have far-reaching effects beyond the mere balancing of government books in the run up to Maastricht, is *privatisation*. Adam Smith didn't see much of a role for government in creating wealth. All that it need provide is 'peace, easy taxes and a tolerable administration of justice'. The invisible hand would do the rest. Unfortunately few politicians have been keen to leave it at that, and their fixation on State control has certainly done away with 'easy taxes', at least as far as the Continent is concerned.

Public ownership has a deadening effect on business; State monopolies generally give no choice to the consumer and all idea of service, accountability and efficiency go out of the window. In many countries, the public sector industries are used to soak up the unemployed, and by so doing, government creates a growing constituency of voters that it dare not offend at election time with any talk of productivity, return on capital or redundancy. In effect, it has a tiger by the tail, and daren't let go. Compare the politics of France, where one in four workers is employed by the government, to those of the UK where the ratio is closer to one in seven. At the same time, nationalised industries provide jobs for retiring politicians once they 'descend from heaven', so they too have a vested interest in perpetuating the existing system. Not surprisingly, such a system rumbles on until losses become unsustainable due to foreign competition, budget deficits reach crisis levels that need shock tactics to restore international confidence, or a Thatcher appears.

Privatisation does more than just reverse the pernicious effects of monopolistic public ownership. For a start, it gives government ready cash for what is often, in public hands, an unprofitable asset. This in itself could be used to reduce debt, and hence borrowing costs. Ultimately, by making it easier for government to control future deficits, it can bring down interest rates, to the benefit of the public and private sectors alike. More importantly, it allows the entity to develop commercially.

Introducing the element of competition into a monopoly industry forces companies to reassess their relationship with customers and suppliers, to develop new services and keep down costs. On privatisation, Telmex, the Mexican telephone giant, refused for months to sign any agreement with its suppliers until they had conceded massive reductions in the price of their equipment. British Steel and British Airways became the most profitable entities in Europe in their sectors after privatisation by slashing costs, improving quality and listening to their customers. Having learnt to compete successfully at home, many of these companies have put their hard-won skills to work elsewhere, particularly in bidding for overseas companies in the course of privatisation. For example, Chilean private power utilities became major shareholders in Argentina's newly privatised power sector, and Britain's National Power, British Gas and several water companies are now well-established overseas.

With all these benefits to recommend it, it is disappointing how slow countries in Europe have been to pursue privatisation more aggressively. Opposition by unions and the vested interests of politicians have slowed the process. Unfortunately, the risk of missing Maastricht is not considered a sufficient reason to privatise state companies, especially in France – quite the reverse. Better to avoid the risk of industrial action which could dent economic growth than grasp the nettle and stare down the unions. If all else fails, then the government can resort to creative accounting instead. Only the fact that the French deficit was getting wildly off-course prompted the Jospin government to abandon its rhetoric about the sale of France Télécom. Even here, the privatisation is grudging, and government is only selling a minority stake and making sure that the main buyers are *not* from the private sector.

By contrast, the privatisations that took place in Mexico and Argentina were far more transparent. In Brazil, the government forced through the sale of CVRD, the nation's crown jewel, in the teeth of opposition and blizzards of lawsuits. Italy, too, is selling off all its remaining 44.7% stake in Telecom Italia, raising some $14 billion. Furthermore it has appointed professionals to run other State companies, rather than elite bureaucrats answerable to the State rather than to shareholders. It is a pity that Jospin is not more courageous.

Is zero inflation really a good thing?

All the above factors, together with the Asian crisis, are working to cut inflation. In both the USA and the UK, the rate of unemployment below which inflation starts to rise (known in the UK as NAIRU, the non-accelerating inflation rate of unemployment) has been falling from peaks of 11% and 8% respectively to perhaps 5–7% and 6%. Is there a chance that the twentieth century is an aberration as far as inflation is concerned, and that the Millennium will usher in a new non-inflationary age? And if so, should we celebrate? It is easy to instance why high inflation can be a BAD THING. The hyperinflation of the 1920s that Germany engineered to pay war reparations in debased coin wiped out the savings of the middle classes and the living standards of those on fixed incomes, paving the way for Hitler and untold miseries to come. But does that mean that high inflation is automatically bad and zero inflation therefore an unalloyed good?

As regards the former, the answer is 'Yes', but not unequivocally so. Inflation is the instrument with which unscrupulous governments can destroy future obligations, particularly State pensions, by not indexing them fully to inflation. Its effect is most devastating in economies which suddenly experience a bout of high inflation for which they are unprepared, often due to a sharp jump in the budget deficit, as in Argentina or Russia, and where large numbers are on fixed incomes. On the other hand, if all prices, wages and pensions are fairly indexed to inflation, then everybody seems to be riding up escalators at the same speed. After all, Brazil has managed impressive real growth rates despite high inflation and a shambolic political system.

Apart from the obvious comment that it is a huge waste of everybody's time to have to work with different prices every day, the real criticism of high inflation is that it prevents long-term planning. A bank is most reluctant to lend money over a long period if it fears that a burst of inflation while the loan is outstanding will make it worthless by the time it is repaid. For example, it is rare to have a financial sector that offers attractive mortgages in a country with high inflation – interest rates are high and repayment terms short – so people tend to buy for cash. Companies also find it difficult to plan and finance capital investment and may be forced into inappropriate strategies by short-term considerations.

It was noteworthy that when inflation was high in the late 1980s, peaking at almost 130% in 1987, the most important executives in Mexican companies were not the sales directors or production directors, but the finance directors, whose job it was to juggle loans and working capital to 'manufacture' profits. Companies temporarily lost sight of the fact that their real reason for existing was to produce and sell. It was only after inflation subsided to more normal levels in 1989 that they could return to their proper function.

On the other hand, zero inflation can also be double-edged. If you have money to lend, then zero inflation means that its value is better preserved, but it also increases the risk of not being repaid. Think of UK building societies in the mid-1970s happy to lend a high proportion of the cost of a house, confident in the knowledge that rising wage inflation would make it easier for the borrower to repay, while rising property prices would improve the value of the collateral in the event of a default.

In the late 1980s, however, the growth in wages slowed down, and real interest rates began to rise. For latecomers, buying homes at the top of the market with only a small deposit, borrowing costs became a major part of household income. In many cases home-owners defaulted on mortgages and their homes repossessed and sold. Because house price inflation had turned from positive to negative the sales proceeds were often below the size of the loan they had contracted, leaving them with no home and debts to repay. Tell *them* that negative inflation is a good thing!

In other words different rates of inflation simply mean different sets of winners and losers. During the German hyperinflation of the 1920s, Hugo Stinnes used heavy bank borrowings to build an empire of interests stretching from banks and hotels to paper mills and newspapers, as well as joint ventures in heavy industry and electrical engineering. When inflation collapsed in 1924, the real cost of these borrowings soared, and the empire was dismantled as quickly as it had been assembled. This should warn us that however good the story all bull markets come to an end.

'This time it's different'

Typically, the entire stockmarket cycle takes around four years from start to finish, but there have been occasions when either the cycle has been extended or prices have been carried to extremes, and this is when things become dangerous. Hubris, the overweening pride that attracts punishment from the gods, follows the stockmarket cycle. In the pit of the bear market, when it is impossible to sell a one-pound coin for 50p, the financial columns muse the death of capitalism – profits will never recover, the workers will dictate terms to companies, bankruptcy looms, etc., etc. At the top of the bull market frenzy, economists proclaim that the secret of combining growth with low inflation has finally been cracked. Booms and busts are gone forever, and with the dawning of an era of greater certainty, shares will be steadily rerated, allowing all investors to ascend to the sunny uplands of personal prosperity.

Oh, yes?

At best we can say that the present bull market, still enjoyed by most countries apart from Japan and South-East Asia, has been given a period of grace, because of a heady combination of globalisation, the 'lightening' of output, an unquantified feeling about rising productivity and falling inflation . . . and fear of the future, which has driven US individuals to pour billions into retirement plans, and hence into the stockmarket. The first factor, whether in the form of the single market or competition from the Asian Tigers, has switched the balance of negotiating power from workers to management, and from companies to the consumer. On the one hand, fewer companies can be held to ransom if they can relocate their production or supply the market from plants in other countries. On the other, globalisation and privatisation bring competition. The one restrains wages, the other prices, and in theory, low inflation which leads to market rerating.

The second point, the 'lightening of output', deserves explanation. Industry is switching production away from products with inherently long lead times, e.g., cement plants or steel works, towards, say consumer goods and services. At the same time, it is both speeding up production cycles through CAD/CAM (computer-aided design and manufacturing technology) and just-in-time deliveries of parts, and spreading the risk by widening the export content. Because of this, any supply/demand imbalances can be ironed out more rapidly than in the past. Furthermore, as a nation's output switches from goods to services, the cycle becomes faster and more flexible still. If nobody wants to buy cement, the plant cannot be used for anything else. But if *Windows '99* flops, the programmers can switch to other projects with the minimum of disruption.

These factors, combined with the rising productivity from computerisation are keeping the lid on inflation and lessening the risk that the government or Central Bank might take action to cool the economy and puncture the bull market.

Murphy's Law of stockmarkets

'How can cocoa go down?' said the Great Winfield.
– The Money Game, Adam Smith[3]

Those who enjoyed *The Money Game* know the answer. What applies to cocoa applies equally to equities. There are a number of reasons why equity investment can never enter a virtuous circle, even in an era of low or zero inflation. The greatest risk comes from the 'animal spirits' of its participants. Declining inflationary fears and increasing hopes of stable growth leads to rising optimism amongst investors who drive up market ratings to higher levels, as has happened in Brazil in 1996/7, when inflation plummetted. Companies then succumb to temptation and raise increasing sums of new money for expansion or acquisition, or for sheer opportunism – i.e., because the money's there for the taking at low cost. Eventually, oversupply of stock or overcapacity reappears, and the market tops out, although perhaps at higher levels than in economies experiencing higher levels of inflation.

Other factors can strike markets out of the blue, particularly crises affecting the financial sector, since this provides lubrication for the whole economy. If banks stop lending because their balance sheets are awash with bad debts from, say, property loans, then everybody suffers. The UK secondary banking crisis in the 1970s, the collapse of Japan's 1990 property bubble and the 1997 problems in Thailand, Malaysia and the Philippines are testimony to this. Capital investments are postponed for lack of funds, economic growth slows and profit margins tumble. The global financial system was, in theory, strengthened by the Basle Agreement which set minimum levels for certain balance sheet ratios of banks and finance companies, but this did not prevent the latest crisis in South-East Asia.

Claims that the sophisticated hedging techniques developed by the rocket scientists of the major broking houses can now contain such risks are probably wide of the mark. Murphy's Law dictates that the more links there are in the chain of transactions, the more likely that it is the link that was overlooked that will break first. The melt-down of the Hong Kong market in the 1987 Crash was the result of so-called 'riskless' arbitrage going wrong, because one group of counterparties – private individuals – did not have the financial resources to pay their mounting obligations and defaulted, leaving institutions sitting on large paper profits they couldn't realise and the brokers in turmoil.

The Pan-Electric crisis that brought down Singapore's leading brokers in 1985 was due to the dishonouring of forward contracts to buy back shares, originally sold by a client to a broker, at an agreed higher price at some time in the future. When the market fell, clients refused to repurchase the shares as agreed, and the brokers suffered massive losses. The aftermath revealed that the most respectable of local companies had been involved in these dubious transactions to make a turn from their surplus cash.

Metallgesellschaft lost heavily on speculative currency transactions. Sumitomo's chief trader in copper concealed mounting losses from his superiors over many years until they reached massive proportions. Deutsche Bank had to bail out its UK subsidiary and compensate its investment clients to the tune of £230 million for unauthorised dealings by a fund manager. The UK insurance sector has had to make huge provisions to compensate individuals who had been mis-sold personal pensions. Crédit Lyonnais and GAN have been brought to their knees by bad debts. The list is endless.

Fortunately, in these more recent cases, the groups concerned, or the French government, were large and rich enough to swallow their losses. In future we may not be so lucky. *All we can be sure about is that for each market cycle, the losses recorded by the less fortunate will be far larger than for its predecessor.*

Murphy's Law warns one to expect the unexpected. In the current bull market, the mantra that is propelling ratings ever higher is 'falling inflation'. Earlier we examined the factors that are contributing to its decline and found them persuasive, but that does not mean that further declines are bound to be smooth and linear. There are both short- and medium-term risks to the trend. A short-term risk relates to Japan, where money supply is being pumped in to stimulate flagging consumption as the country heads for recession. At some stage, demand will re-ignite, and domestic interest rates will begin to recover, reducing the flow of money into US deposits, and given the soaring US current account deficit, US rates may also begin to firm, undermining the basis on which the stockmarket is rated. At the present time, admittedly, this risk seems fairly small.

A medium-term risk is the prospect of a third oil shock. Oil industry consultants Colin J. Campbell and Jean H. Laherrère have made detailed appraisals of global oil reserves and, more crucially, their production profiles.[4] They conclude not only that official reserve figures are significantly overstated, but that global oil production from conventional sources will peak by 2010 – even allowing for the introduction of new technologies (4-D seismics, horizontal drilling, etc.). Between 1984 and 1996, Middle Eastern producers increased their share of world output from 20% to 30%. Given both rising demand and a downturn in production from North Sea fields starting around 2000, their share could well rise to 50% by that date – a level well above that prevailing at the time of the first oil crisis in 1974.

Even though Western economies are far less oil-dependent than they were 25 years ago, a sharp rise in the oil price would have a number of consequences. Spending power would be transferred from consumers to producers, cutting demand for goods boosting inflation and denting corporate profits. While there are immense reserves of gas, tar sands and oil shale that could in time be developed as new energy sources, their exploitation is highly capital-intensive and the long lead times for new projects to reach production mean that could take several years for the supply/demand balance to be restored, and economic growth to resume its former trajectory.

Those who get downhearted at this point should remember the story of the motto inscribed on King Solomon's ring, to make him happy when he felt sad, and sad when he felt happy:

This, too, will pass.

Remember – you're investing for the long term.

The currency kicker

Analysts thrive on anomalies, and are at their happiest when they can find an undervalued currency, because, by buying bonds or equities in the country concerned, they can get a double kicker – currency *and* capital appreciation. Such speculators are often roundly condemned by governments and their central banks, since the net effect may be to push currencies to levels that damage the underlying economies, sucking in imports, depressing exports and putting massive pressure on industry to adjust over a short period. Or the reverse can happen. (During the recent crisis in South-East Asia, the Prime Minister of Malaysia claimed that foreign speculators were conducting economic sabotage against his country in order to re-establish a form of neocolonialism.)

If, on the other hand, the central bank wishes to maintain its currency within a prescribed range, it must neutralise the inflows without boosting money supply and kindling inflation. In short, it seems a lose-lose situation for the countries concerned. The same is true on the downside, as the recent crisis in South-East Asian markets has shown – investors sold both the equities and the currencies, forcing central banks to run down their reserves, often to perilously low levels, to support their exchange rates.

The most severe pressures are felt by countries that are dependent on a particular commodity whose price makes a strong and sustained move, for example the UK during the second oil crisis. At that time the country was a net exporter of oil and hence benefited while most other Western countries suffered. Money flowed into the UK, boosting sterling, making industry uncompetitive, just as soaring oil prices destroyed consumer spending power, through most of the world. Corporate profits collapsed and a large number of the more marginal manufacturers went to the wall. Mercifully, the government chose not to throw good money after bad in a vain attempt to bail them out, as happens in much of Western Europe.

The markets might therefore be accused of gross irresponsibility in their effects on economies, but although currency traders never seem to have attention spans of more than 30 minutes, combined with a political outlook to the right of Genghis Khan, they actually force governments to behave responsibly in running their economies. For example, a government that lets its economy overheat will in time be forced to tighten money supply, thereby raising interest rates, causing the currency to strengthen. The market may anticipate this and act accordingly, driving up the exchange rate and signalling to the government that they expect it to address the problem sooner rather than later. The longer the delay, the greater the loss of confidence, the more the markets will punish the currency and the longer the economy will take to recover from the downturn induced by an overvalued exchange rate.

How will a single currency affect asset allocation?

The single currency is going ahead. At some date in the future, exchange rates will be set between national currencies and the Euro. These rates will determine the value of assets throughout the EU in a common currency, and will be set at levels that, in theory reflect their relative competitiveness. Once this takes place, the way is open for some major restrictions on overseas investments to be lifted.

What has inhibited truly international investment by European insurance companies and pension funds is the prudential requirement of matching assets and liabilities *in each currency*. If you write your policy in sterling, then it may be a bad idea to have your assets in lire if the policy suddenly requires to be paid out. The exchange rate may not be favourable at the time, and costs are incurred on the foreign exchange transaction.

Eliminating currency risk within the EU through a single currency will encourage such funds to invest beyond their borders and will put increasing pressure on national governments to change the rules that compel them to keep their money at home. However much political parties and trade unions try to brand international investment as a form of betrayal, as the UK miners once did the Coal Board pension fund, their ability to prevent it will be swept away by companies taking their complaints to Brussels and winning.

The impact of the single currency will vary from country to country. For example, the Dutch stockmarket is dominated by two major groups, Royal Dutch Shell and Philips, which distort investment and increase portfolio risk. Once Dutch pension funds are free to invest abroad, it is clear that they will sell down their holdings in both and switch to non-oil shares elsewhere in the EU. Conversely, Germany has no major oil companies of its own, and its pension funds may therefore sell domestic non-oil shares to invest in Royal Dutch! There is obviously scope for a lot of horse trading between institutions to rebalance their portfolios.

Boring EU markets?

With the elimination of exchange rates within the EU and the convergence of inflation and bond yields, a substantial element of volatility is being removed from markets. Furthermore, many of the major groups are spreading their activities across the whole of Europe, and therefore becoming more like each other. Does this mean that markets are going to become more boring in the future? Not a bit of it – at least for some time.

There are a number of reasons for this. For a start, nobody would call the US market dull and uniform, despite it operating under a single currency. There are major variations within the USA – for example, the Texan economy still depends heavily on energy and is highly sensitive to the price of oil, while that of California is driven by technology. Even within one industry, conditions differ markedly between states.

Secondly, with the start of the euro, world trade coalesces under only three currencies – US dollar, euro and yen – and the degree of volatility could become greater once speculators have only three targets to aim at. Finally, whatever the plans of European governments to create jobs, their companies are still vigorously restructuring, shedding workers and moving overseas. In the short-term, the associated costs have dented profits badly, but the scope for recovery is substantial. For example, Scandinavian banks that incurred massive losses in the 1980s have risen phoenix-like from the ashes. On that basis, there is even hope for Crédit Lyonnais. This has been a major factor driving the European markets in 1997 and 1998, and should continue to exert a favourable influence in the years ahead.

References

1 Deane, P. and Coale, W. A. (1969) *British Economic Growth 1688–1959*, 2nd Edition, Cambridge University Press, p. 13.
2 *Financial Times*, 18 April 1998.
3 Smith, A. *The Money Game*, Random House Inc., New York, 1967.
4 Campbell, C. J. and Laherrère, J. H. (March 1998) 'The End of Cheap Oil,' *Scientific American*, Vol. 278, No. 3.

AN INVESTMENT STRATEGY FOR THE DEMOGRAPHICALLY DEPRESSED

In the long run, said Keynes, we are all dead, but we might prefer to die in relative comfort than in poverty. With the erosion of the State pension system, the time for living for the moment like the grasshopper of fable is over. So, consider the ant, thou sluggard, and invest!

Getting started

I am assuming in this section that those of you who have followed my arguments so far now want to find some means of securing your financial future in retirement besides your occupational pension, if you have one, and your (soon to be worthless) State pension. I am also assuming that you recognise that this is a long-term investment, and that you are not prepared for the hassle of daily monitoring, nor the upfront cost of insurance agents' fees that can wipe out a few years' contributions.

Before getting into the details, it is worth saying a bit about the two main advantages of planning a regular monthly commitment. The first is obvious – if you get used to budgeting this amount each month, you will soon adjust your expenditure pattern. The second relates to the benefits of pound-cost (or DM-cost, etc.) averaging. For a fixed monthly outlay one buys proportionately more shares when prices are low than when they are high, which brings down the average cost per share.

We must also consider how to minimise risk not only by spreading the investment over time but also over a range of different assets. First of all, it is important to decide what degree of risk you feel you can handle, and for this we can make some comparisons between the way US and UK investors run their affairs.

Across the pond, fear is the key

The US mutual fund industry, with end-1997 assets of over $4700 billion is 'seriously large', and continues to hoover in money at an incredible rate. In 1996, mutual funds, the US equivalent of unit trusts, attracted a net $223.3 billion, almost $100 billion more than the previous best in 1993, a mere $129.6 billion. Low inflation, stable economic growth and good corporate profits certainly helped, but it was fear of the future rather than greed that was the driving force. The social security system is heading for bankruptcy and private individuals are therefore making their own retirement plans by ploughing all their surplus cash into 401(k) investment accounts. Between 1986 and 1995, the total value of 401(k) assets has risen from around $162 billion to $1300 billion, and they are growing at 15–18% per annum with no sign of slowing down. By 1996, some 96% of companies employing over 5000 workers offered such plans.

Employees in the USA have much more say in the way their accounts are managed, and since they are predominantly defined *contribution* plans – i.e., the actual benefits are neither defined nor guaranteed – they place the risk squarely on the beneficiary. This leads to less volatile investments, which are likely to produce lower returns, as the contrast in Table 13.1 with a typical UK defined *benefit* scheme shows.

Table 13.1 Investment preferences in UK and US schemes

UK defined benefit scheme		US defined contribution scheme	
Asset class	%	Asset class	%
UK equities	57	Equity funds	40
Overseas equities	24	Short-term fixed income	34
UK bonds	6	Balanced funds	14
Overseas bonds	4	Intermediate/LT bonds	8
Index linked	4	Employee stock	4
Cash/other	5		100
	100		

The choice is yours. The higher the equity content, the higher the risks as well as the expected rewards. As people age, they tend to become more cautious, so as the *workforces* age throughout the West, we should expect a general switch toward lower risk assets over time. *It must be pointed out however that because of the demonstrably higher performance of equities over fixed interest securities over the long term, this section focuses entirely on equity investment. Indeed as Wall Street continues its almost unbroken seven-year run, US investors have become more courageous; in 1990, only 25% of the assets of US mutual funds were in equities, but by 1998, the proportion had risen to over 50%. As we will see, the case for equities is becoming even stronger.*

Paradoxically, a revolution is taking place in US government thinking about the way payroll taxes for social security should be invested. At present, they are invested entirely in government bonds. The social security system has been designed to generate an annual surplus, currently around

$60 billion, that forms a reserve which can be gradually run down over time. This surplus however will end by 2012 as the post-war baby boomers retire, and by 2029, the system will be bankrupt, with payroll taxes covering only 76% of promised benefits.

As with other countries, the way is open for government to change the level of benefits or raise retirement age, but its instincts are more to tackle the looming crisis by improving returns on investment. Specifically, it is examining whether this can be achieved by switching some of the cashflow into equities. Members of a 13–member advisory council on social security failed to reach agreement on a unified plan in January 1997 but significantly the three competing plans all included the recommendation to invest in equities.

Believe it or not, they may be beaten to it by the Egyptians, who announced in September 1997 that the surplus in the State pension system, currently running at E£77 billion (£14.2 billion) is to be invested in domestic equities, as well as venture capital, real estate (pyramid buying?) and international equities. The Egyptian stockmarket at the time of the announcement was capitalised at a mere E£67 billion. The government regards the fund as playing a key role in providing investment capital to accelerate the country's development. Which leads us on to . . .

. . . Funds for blue-eyed Arabs

During the various oil crises of the 1970s and 1980s, Norwegians became known as the blue-eyed Arabs of the North – a small population (4.4 million) sitting on lots of oil, and the world's second largest producer after Saudi Arabia. Unlike the true Arabs they have two problems. Firstly, the population is already one of the oldest in Europe, and its pension obligations will rise sharply after 2000. Secondly, output from the offshore sector, which now represents 15% of GDP, will peak early next century and then decline.

Thanks to rising oil output and prices, Norway has transformed a deep Budget deficit in 1993 into a substantial surplus by 1996. To prevent the expected further rise in oil revenue from pushing public expenditure out of control, as happened to Holland after the discovery of the massive Groningen gas field, the outgoing government proposed creaming off this surplus income and investing it abroad as a cushion against the time oil revenues decline. This would also act to smooth economic growth since any fall in the oil price transfers cash from producers to consumers, lowering inflation, raising demand and boosting the stockmarkets of oil importers.

By the end of 1997, the buffer fund could already have reached NKr110–120 billion (£14.5–15.8 billion), equivalent to almost 10% of GDP. Given projections that government oil revenues could rise from NKr70 billion in 1996 to NKr127 billion by 2001, the cumulative cashflow into the fund together with its expected capital appreciation suggests that *within 20 years the fund could reach 130–150% of a projected NKr2000 billion – i.e., around $400 billion. Putting this into context, this is roughly the size of the Swiss or French equity markets in mid-1997, or 12 times that of the Norwegian market at that date.*

The reason for giving such emphasis to the policies of this small economy is that Norway is not alone in building reserves for the future. Indeed it is following in the footsteps of Saudi Arabia and Abu Dhabi who began the process in the 1970s. This approach is not confined to oil producers. Singapore has done the same, and perhaps others will follow. Should the US Administration agree to channel social security cashflow into equities, the impact on world stockmarkets would be dramatic. Not only would it boost markets directly, but would put increasing pressure on other State pension funds to do likewise. As we shall see, demographic trends will transform the countries of South-East Asia from capital importers to capital exporters next century, adding to the funds available for global investment.

By making available equity capital to companies on increasingly favourable terms, such a move could accelerate investment worldwide. While there are undoubted systemic risks to investment at present – for example the severe bad debt problems of China, South-East Asia and South Korea – the build-up of global institutional cashflow early next century provides the backdrop for very exciting stockmarkets worldwide.

Portfolio diversification: 'uncorrelated' is a lovely word

Only those with inside information would put all their investment eggs in one basket, and even then, profits are not assured. The average investor prefers to spread the risk. After all, it's not a good idea to retire the day your entire retirement fund falls out of bed. Mathematicians are in favour of diversification, *provided the different investments are not correlated*. In other words, if all your investments move in the same direction at the same time, then you're kidding yourself that you are spreading the risk – they could *all* melt down together.

Computers enable analysts to check how closely individual markets and stocks follow each other, enabling fund managers to pick 'n' mix their markets to give the best balance of risk and return. In theory, it should be possible to raise the return of a portfolio for a given level of risk (measured by its volatility – how much it moves for a 1% change in the overall market), by investing in a number of uncorrelated markets. Unfortunately for the theorists, recent research seems to cast doubt on this. A study by Michael Hughes, chief economist at BZW, a UK stock-broker, found that the best portfolio for a UK investor in the period 1979–96 (the span covered by the Conservative government) would have had 89–100% invested in UK equities, depending on the preferred risk profile. (Following the collapse of Asian currencies and markets in 1996–7, US researchers have come to the same conclusion – that it is better for US investors to stick at home. This has had a self-feeding effect, driving ratings even higher, until Murphy's Law brings them back to earth.)

There are two explanations for this finding, which may appear to strike at the heart of the diversification argument. The first is that Thatcherism actually worked, and the greater competitiveness that it engendered boosted profits more than in countries that operated on the European social democracy model. The second is based on the fact that only 47% of the sales of the FTSE-100 companies now come from the UK. In effect, one is buying diversification through the back door. Indeed, the trend towards globalisation will lead to further increases in the proportion of these sales coming from outside the UK.

This trend has also been noticed in the USA and in Japan where the proportion of the sales of the multinationals within Japan continues to fall, despite the distorting effects of a strong yen. Between 1990 and 1995, manufacturing production overseas by Japanese multinationals rose from 16.7% to 25.5% of domestic production, while over the same period, employment in their overseas plants doubled to 1.8 million, equivalent to 12% of their domestic employment.

Although the increasing geographic diversification of quoted UK multinationals, and the impact of globalisation on eliminating pockets of unfair advantage within Western Europe may seem to suggest that you can have a quiet life by simply picking a portfolio based solely on the top UK shares, the very dependence of the UK on exports to the EU, where demand growth will be increasingly threatened by poor demographics, suggests that we should cast the net wider. So – it is more prudent to invest in a diversified portfolio, but of what? How do we choose which countries to focus on?

We can put world stockmarkets into context in two ways. First, we can compare their relative sizes. Breaking them into broad blocs, we find the geographical breakdown shown in Table 13.2. 'Other' comprises over 50 stockmarkets, of which around half are represented in the investment universe covered by MSCI, one of the benchmark global indices against which fund managers measure their funds' performance. The MSCI universe does not include *all* the world's stockmarkets, simply those deemed sufficiently large as to be worth the while of fund managers to follow. New markets are emerging all the time; in the past few years, the exchanges of some of the world's leading economies – China, India and Brazil, but not yet Russia – have joined the list, automatically reducing the weightings of the existing components.

Table 13.2 Geographical breakdown of global stockmarkets

Region	%
North America	48
Western Europe	30
Japan	15
Other	7
	100

Readers should remember recent history and resist the temptation to take the simple approach and focus their interest on the top three areas in Table 13.2, ignoring the rest. The table is only a snapshot in time, and gives no hint either of the history of the various markets or of their possible future. For example, in 1990 the Japanese stockmarket was larger than that of the USA – today it is scarcely larger than that of the UK. In US dollar terms, the markets of South-East Asia have fallen by 50–80% in a year, and now hardly appear on the radar screens of global investors. Our screening techniques however show that while Japan should still be avoided, even at these depressed levels, the Asian markets could show strong recovery by the start of the new millennium.

We can also relate the size of markets to that of their underlying economies. Developed countries, with a long history of capitalism have listed the majority of their companies, so market capitalization/GDP ratios are high – over 80% in the USA, over 100% in the UK and 150% in Switzerland. By contrast, countries with markets either newly created, e.g., Russia, or newly opened to foreign investors, such as India, or where institutional factors such as the lack of a strong pension fund sector inhibit their development, have low ratios in this area.

This can however be a pointer to the future, by hinting how large the stockmarket *could* become if adverse factors were eliminated. On this basis, *China* (market capitalization/GDP 20%), *Brazil* (32%), and *India* (38%), have a long way to go, providing that their development is not held back by governments or their taxmen. The tiny East European markets will also become substantially more important in years to come as State assets are privatised and private pension funds set up.

Although it would be relatively simple to mirror the MSCI World Index, and passively accept what the market dictates, there is no reason, therefore, to blindly follow this path. It is possible to apply some intelligence to refine our investment universe. The sections below show how we go about this. It should be emphasised that very different techniques will be used for constructing the initial five-year and the long-term (25–30-year) portfolios. Investments judged unacceptably risky over the short-term (e.g., China or the Philippines) could prove highly attractive to those buying in a few years' time for the long-term. Conversely, some of the most attractive markets for the next five years (e.g., Continental Europe) will prove decidedly less so once adverse demographics kick in by around 2010.

The portfolio to 2005

Screening for risk

Good countries to invest in come in all shapes and sizes, and fund managers apply various filters to select them. A so-called 'top-down' approach would start off with a decision tree which would address (among others) the following basic concerns:

- *What is the risk of investments being expropriated?*
- *If I invest, can I get my money out when I sell?*
- *How financially sound are the local brokers?*

- *What protection exists for foreign shareholders?*
- *Is there a proper custody system?*

The list goes on.

These initial questions relate to the prudential aspect of investment; the first duty of a manager is not to lose his clients' money by taking avoidable risks. Some organisations focus on particular aspects of risk. For example, Transparency International (TI), a non-governmental pressure group publishes an Index of the perceived level of corruption in some 52 countries, based on international surveys of business and public opinion as well as assessment of political risk and international competitiveness. Although this is no guide to stockmarket performance, it at least provides a safety check, especially important if one is not constantly monitoring the market. According to TI, the bottom 10 are ranked as shown in Table 13.3.

Table 13.3 Indices of perceived levels of transparency

Ranking	Country	Score	
		1997	1996
43	Vietnam	2.79	–
44	Venezuela	2.77	2.50
45	India	2.75	2.63
46	Indonesia	2.72	2.65
47	Mexico	2.66	3.30
48	Pakistan	2.53	1.00
49	Russia	2.27	2.58
50	Colombia	2.23	2.73
51	Bolivia	2.05	3.40
52	Nigeria	1.76	0.69

Source: Transparency International.

Certainly none of these, with the possible exception of India, would feature in our portfolio. China, ranked 41, barely escaped the bottom 10, and would similarly fail to make the grade. It is worth noting that Italy ranked 30th, below the Czech Republic, Hungary and Poland, and just above Taiwan, Malaysia and South Africa. Now that Italy has succeeded in joining the single currency, the increase in competitive pressures will ensure reforms take place far faster than in those countries in Table 13.3, and this allows us to consider the country as a candidate for inclusion – at least over the near term.

DRI/McGraw-Hill addresses itself to emerging markets, assessing investment risk over the next five years (*see* Table 13.4). Interestingly, its rankings of the ten largest emerging markets conflict with some in Table 13.3.

Table 13.4 Ranking of emerging market risk

Lowest investment risk	*Highest investment risk*
Argentina	South Africa
Poland	China
Mexico	Indonesia
Turkey	Russia
India	Brazil

Source: DRI/McGraw-Hill.

The organisation measures 50 variables, but is especially concerned with economic policy and the soundness of the banking sector. Their *July 1997 Report* from which the above rankings are taken is particularly apposite, given the subsequent meltdown of South-East Asian markets, since it highlighted the risks inherent in the Chinese banking system, where industry analysts estimate that between 20 and 40% of the $600 billion of outstanding loans could be considered non-performing. Nevertheless, it seems too harsh on Brazil, and not cautious enough on the Tiger economies, in view of their subsequent behaviour.

Transparency, competition and shareholder value

It is still possible to find countries whose economic prospects appear encouraging but whose stockmarkets are less attractive because of slack rules of corporate governance, or because Boards do not consider themselves accountable to investors or are vulnerable to government meddling. This has been a deterrent to investment even in the EU, but a combination of privatisation, globalisation and the need for foreign capital is beginning to bring about an improvement, even in Italy.

The UK has the most developed stockmarket in Europe and one of the most broadly distributed patterns of share ownership. There are relatively few listed family-controlled companies, and because of the openness of the shareholding structure and the high degree of disclosure in the *Annual Reports*, the scope for serious undervaluation amongst listed companies is limited, since this would rapidly lead to a take-over bid. Indeed there has built up such a shortage of new quality public offerings that the conversion of mutual assurance companies into plcs attracted a wave of take-over bids before the listings took place.

At the same time, the pension funds which control a significant proportion of the market are keen to ensure that companies operate efficiently and do not undertake activities that might damage profits, share prices or underlying asset value. Boards are held accountable for their actions through the voting power of their shareholdings, and institutions are becoming increasingly interventionist.

In Continental Europe, traditions are different and the role of the workforce in determining company policy is more established, a factor that may inhibit a company pursuing its best commercial course of action. The equity culture is also a lot shallower – for example, in France, the bulk of life assurance premiums are invested in government securities rather than in equities. Furthermore, the number of French private shareholders has actually fallen from the peak of 6 million reached during the first privatisations that took place in 1986–8 to around 5.5 million today. (By contrast, the proportion of Americans owning shares has doubled to over 40% since 1990.) This means that they hold a smaller proportion of outstanding share capital than in the UK, and their ability to influence companies is further diminished by the passive role they play in AGMs, where their proxy votes are often lodged with the Board. *Annual Reports* can be notoriously opaque.

In much of the Continent, big business is still a cosy club dominated by State-controlled entities whose sphere of action is often circumscribed by government interference. The State appoints directors, and those who tread an independent line get replaced. Too much political patronage is tied up in these companies, and an important benefit of the privatisation programmes forced on governments by Maastricht will be the greater freedom of action that the privatised companies will enjoy. The resignation of Christian Blanc, head of Air France, because of government failure to honour previous commitments to privatise the airline, is to be deplored as a retrograde step in this process.

Companies in all countries are subjected to government influence to a greater or lesser degree. But when this results in State enterprises being run uncommercially, shields them from the scrutiny of outside shareholders, forces them into deals they should not enter and finally demands Brussels sanction bail-outs of those that have failed, to the detriment of their private sector competitors, it is time to look elsewhere for honest investment. This combination of factors has been responsible for the failure of an equity culture to take root in countries such as France and Italy, but there are signs that things are beginning to change.

The French have never felt comfortable with the notion of competition or take-over. Decades ago, the perceived threat was from the USA, whose companies, it was feared, would swallow up smaller European competitors. By the 1980s, the villain had become Japan, intent on invading the Continent through its UK car plants, to the fury of French manufacturers. The lack of local institutional finance has had two opposing consequences. To raise capital, the companies have come to depend increasingly on US and UK pension funds, but to prevent themselves being taken over by foreigners, they frequently protected themselves from outside control by devices for holding a significant proportion of their own equity.

This trend was reinforced by the emergence of four major holding groups, Suez and Paribas in the 1960s, Crédit Lyonnais and UAP in the 1980s, which acquired key stakes in other leading French companies. During the privatisations of the late 1980s and early 1990s they seemed to fulfil two important roles in a country where the equity culture was not well developed. They provided an important part of the funds the government needed, and they gave transitional protection to the newly listed company against foreign take-over.

Fortunately, the system broke down for two reasons. First, the holding companies, the so-called *noyaux durs*, suffered a series of financial misfortunes in the early 1990s, generally linked to the property market, making it difficult to fulfil their former role. Indeed the lack of accountability to outside shareholders of boards protected by these clubby crossholdings may well have contributed to their dismal performance and perceived lack of focus.

Secondly, and in part stemming from a recognition of these shortcomings, and the need to attract new foreign capital to shore up weakened balance sheets, their Boards have been reassessing strategies. Suez, for example, has sold off a range of investments in the financial sector to boost its longstanding investment in Lyonnaise des Eaux and transform itself into a utility company. Similarly, when Axa acquired control of its rival insurance company, UAP, in late 1996, it unravelled a much broader set of relationships. By issuing shares for the acquisition, Axa thereby diluted the control exercised over it by Paribas and a number of mutual insurance companies. Furthermore, Axa has already sold over FFr5 billion of equity stakes held by the combined group to improve the return on shareholders' funds, and even the sale of cross-holdings in Paribas and BNP is not impossible.

The *noyaux* have become a bit less *durs*, but there are those who argue that, deep down little has really changed – the empires remain, they have simply been rearranged. The phrase 'shareholder value' is however creeping into the vocabularies of more and more companies in France and Germany, and some very unGallic hostile take-over bids have taken place in France. A wind of change is blowing through Europe which will ultimately lead to better, more accountable managements, higher profits and happier investors.

Screening for competitiveness

How can we trim the MSCI universe of almost 50 markets to manageable proportions? Eliminating Sri Lanka and Jordan on size grounds, Colombia and Venezuela on perceived high levels of corruption and South Africa, China, Indonesia and Russia as being too high a risk, we are still left with 39 countries. A rough and ready way might be to look at levels of capital investment in a country – particularly *foreign* capital investment. After all, if a foreign manufacturer (who presumably could invest almost anywhere) chooses to set up a factory in, say, Thailand, it is because he expects to make better returns on his investment than elsewhere over a period of perhaps five to ten years, or up to 30 years for a power station. This is the sort of timescale that pension investors should be looking at.

This leads straight on to the matter of competitiveness – not just simply considerations of unit labour costs, but the whole set of ingredients that go to make a country competitive. This is an important point: there are plenty of countries in Africa whose populations are growing at a tremendous rate and where wage rates are low, but which will not be considered suitable for portfolio investment because they do not have the right infrastructure to benefit from it. For example they may lack self-sufficiency in food, an educated workforce, reliable electricity supply, telephone system, efficient deep water port or road network. We need some way of screening these factors to determine whether a particular country has the 'right stuff'. Fortunately, there are institutions that do just that, and on whose hard work we can piggyback.

Some organisations make it their business to monitor *competitiveness*, ranking countries against criteria that range from the strictly objective (inflation rates, budget deficit, etc.) to the more impressionistic (attitude to work, quality of education), since they all have some bearing on whether the country can succeed in the world market.

One of the most authoritative, because of the sheer range of information that it sifts, is the IMD's *World Competitiveness Yearbook*.[1] From our point of view, its great use is in highlighting major deterioration or improvement in competitiveness over a number of years. (Trends in *either* direction are useful – sustained decline may precipitate a crisis which forces the introduction of measures to reverse the trend, if necessary, in the teeth of opposition from large sections of the population.)

When combined with other factors these trends can point to trouble ahead, and they can sometimes be predictive of stockmarket performance. For example, the *Annual Reports* picked up a steady erosion in South Korea's competitive position, and in particular, the weakness in the financial sector since 1991 which ultimately triggered the 1997 currency crisis, the bankruptcy of leading conglomerates and the massive IMF bail-out.

In 1995–6 the markets dramatically underscored the return of the USA to IMD's top competitive slot in 1994. On the other hand, the *Yearbooks* would have failed to alert investors to a deterioration in Japan's overall position before 1994 – well after the market had crashed. The 1997 *Yearbook*, however, signalled a further marked deterioration in Japan's rating, pointing to trouble ahead which has been borne out by events. Further down the table of IMD ratings, China (27th in 1997 *vs* 34th in 1994) and Hungary (36th *vs* 41st), have shown steady progress, while Brazil (33rd *vs* 43rd), Finland (4th *vs* 19th), Norway (5th *vs* 12th), Ireland (15th *vs* 21st) and Canada (10th *vs* 20th) have been spectacular. Russia, however, consistently finds itself on the bottom rung in 46th position for four successive years, 1994–7. Table 13.5 gives the top 12 for 1997, with their 1995 and 1996 ratings.

These ratings can be affected by unforeseen events – e.g., political tensions between neighbours (China/India, or India/Pakistan) which cause withdrawal of foreign funds, forcing up interest rates, weakening the currency and stockmarket – but the more inherently stable a country is, as measured by prior year ratings, the more likely it is to overcome the problem and return to trend. We can write a rough equation:

IMD rating=Risk=Volatility of economy/politics /corporate earnings

This would imply that growing stability creates its own momentum, in the same way that bicycles become easier to ride the faster they go. One

Table 13.5 IMD world competitiveness ratings, 1995–7

Country	1995	1996	1997
USA	1	1	1
Singapore	2	2	2
Hong Kong	3	3	3
Finland	18	15	4
Netherlands	8	7	5
Norway	10	6	6
Denmark	7	5	7
Switzerland	5	9	8
Canada	13	12	9
New Zealand	9	11	10
Japan	4	4	11
UK	15	19	12

Source: IMD, World Competitiveness Yearbook 1997.

can never guarantee that an incoming government will not commit some gross economic blunders in its first few months, usually to honour absurd election pledges, but in an increasingly interdependent world, such good intentions seldom go unpunished. Within Europe, the pressure for economic convergence – even on renegade states such as the UK – is considerable, and this is perhaps reflected in the steady convergence of the ratings of the countries of the EU.

The main drawback of the IMD ranking from a predictive point of view is that it presents historic trends only. While it seems reasonable to expect an improving rating to translate into, say, higher inward investment or rising profit margins in subsequent years, the results are not clear cut because of the wide range of parameters covered, many of which do not impinge directly on companies, and hence indirectly on stockmarket performance.

The Economist Intelligence Unit (EIU) addresses this by focusing specifically on the *business environment* of some 58 countries according to indicators such as market potential, tax and labour market policies, infrastructure, skills and the political environment. Besides assessing this rating over the five-year period 1992–6, the latest review, released in mid-1997, looks forward to the following five years, 1997–2001 (*see* Table 13.6). What is most striking is the expectation that over this period, European and North American countries as a group will move up the pecking order, while emerging economies will show some deterioration, as will Ireland and New Zealand, since the latter are showing signs of overheating and will need corrective action which is likely to lead to slower growth. The excellent performance of the stockmarkets of the former, and the poor performance of those of the latter seems to underscore its value as an investment tool. Re-inforcing this, the same review scored a spectacular hat-trick in downrating Malaysia, Thailand and Indonesia, before the latest crisis, which have certainly led to on-going problems through 1998, and perhaps beyond.

Table 13.6 EIU ranking of country competitiveness (1997)

Country	Current ranking	Ranking 1997–2001	Country	Current ranking	Ranking 1997–2001
Netherlands	3	1	New Zealand	8	13
UK	2	2	Hong Kong	1	14
Canada	5	3	Austria	14	15
Singapore	4	4	Australia	12	16
USA	6	5	Norway	16	17
Denmark	7	6	Ireland	11	18
Germany	10	7	Chile	19	20
France	13	8	Malaysia	20	22
Switzerland	9	9	Taiwan	21	25
Sweden	18	10	Thailand	24	29
Finland	17	11	Israel	27	30
Belgium	15	12	Indonesia	30	33
Italy	29	19			
Spain	22	21			
Japan	25	23			

Source: © The Economist Intelligence Unit Ltd. Reproduced by permission of the Economist Intelligence Unit Ltd.

The reason for the impressive improvement in Europe may partly lie in the currency weakness experienced since late 1996 and in the strenuous efforts to meet Maastricht which are expected to bear fruit in reduced foreign debt/GDP levels and lower interest rates. This could perhaps explain the sharp jump in Italy's rating, while that of Spain was hardly affected, as the latter was sufficiently close to target not to need major reforms. On the other hand, the deterioration in rating of those two countries favoured by economists, New Zealand and Ireland, may suggest that the EIU believes that the benefits of reform are over. For example, New Zealand may find it impossible to introduce a compulsory private pension system; while the Irish economy is showing signs of overheating, and yet the country's central bank will be required to make further cuts in interest rates after monetary union, aggravating the problem.

Interestingly, the IMD's view of France, Germany and Italy is far less upbeat than that of the EIU, recording a fall in their competitiveness since 1995, despite the general weakness of their currencies against the US dollar, ranking Germany 14th in 1997, down from tenth in 1996 and sixth in 1995, France unchanged at 20th and Italy down from 29th to 34th. By contrast, their markets have boomed. Perhaps the explanation for this discrepancy is that while a large range of institutional factors affecting competitiveness have *not* improved (e.g., budget gridlock in Germany), the *companies* have seized the initiative by cutting costs vigorously, and hence boosting profits and share prices.

Picking winners demographically for the long haul

The screening techniques we have used so far only apply to short to medium time frames. Very seldom do these take account of the demographics on anything more than a 2–3 year horizon. Accordingly, they miss the longer-term benefits that such momentum can bring – *once it is properly directed*. The OECD Working Papers mentioned earlier have highlighted the differing demographic pressures on 20 OECD countries over the next 50 years.

Nearly all of them are in the position of people competing to climb to the top of escalators that are going down at different speeds. Some will face far greater problems than others in managing their future debt, and will require of their populations not years but decades of austerity, with rising tax and National Insurance rates, and only limited growth of real wages, after deducting these higher imposts. This will be extremely unpopular to the electorate and could usher in a period of increasing political instability. We can therefore use these Papers to eliminate many major OECD countries that look suspect on demographic grounds in the longer term. But if we do so, where do we invest?

There are plenty of other non-OECD countries out there with stockmarkets worthy of consideration where unfortunately such detailed projections of debt/GDP ratios do not exist. Even here, it is possible for demography to provide another screening tool – the change in the size of the workforce over the period. We have already heard the lament of the Austrians that by 2050 they will not have a workforce large enough to keep their economy operating. So it is with others. In a global economy, falling workforce can mean falling consumption, capital investment, productivity and profit margins. By restricting our universe to those countries which will experience at worst only a minimal decline in the size of the workforce, and preferably an increase, we bring in a number of countries in Asia, Africa and Latin America. *Indeed such screening by demographics clearly implies that over time investors should switch their funds from OECD to non-OECD countries.*

Private pension funds and the markets

So far we have screened out those markets considered too small, too corrupt, too risky, or too demographically challenged, but these are *negative* criteria. How about something that actually *helps* markets? For this, we return to private pension funds, since over time their cashflow can not only sustain but actually boost stockmarkets, as has been the case of Chile. For this to be successful, we need three conditions to apply:

- sound economic policies that keep budget deficits low;
- cashflow into pension funds that is an appreciable proportion of the budget deficit and is growing;
- cashflow that is significant, relative to the capitalisation of the market.

The rationale for these conditions is as follows. Governments satisfy their deficits by issuing bonds. If their deficit is large, they will compel financial institutions to buy large proportions of these bonds. They may even forbid them to commit more than a small part of their cashflow to equities. If, however, the deficit is kept under control, while pension fund in-flow continues to rise, there may come a time when the financial system's cashflow approaches or exceeds the government's need for funds. At this point, restrictions on the pension funds are relaxed, the inflow into equities rises sharply, and the market enjoys a strong rerating. To recall Chile's experience, the pension fund system didn't buy a single equity for the first five years (1981–6), had 11.3% in equities by 1990 and 32.1% by the end of 1994.

Pension funds in countries such as Argentina have learnt from the Chileans, and are already commiting significant sums to domestic equities, and others will follow. At present, the capitalisation of the Latin American markets in which pension funds operate is equivalent to no more than 3% of the MSCI World Index, but by 2005, the ratio could be appreciably higher. We have already noted Salomon Smith Barney's calculations that the amount invested in Latin American pension funds could rise from $135.7 billion in 1997 to $954.2 billion by 2015, of which perhaps some 30% could be invested in equities. At the worst, their cashflow acts as a backstop when prices fall; at best, by raising savings ratios and cutting consumption, they reduce inflation, strengthen the currency and cause a rerating of equity markets.

By 2005, some of the other converts to private pension schemes will be putting in an appearance, and as a result, some markets now too small to be of interest to most private investors will come within our universe. For example, Poland intends to introduce private pensions in 1999, using the proceeds from privatisations to finance the on-going obligations to State pensioners. In other words, the creation of the private pension system is inextricably linked to the rapid expansion of the Polish stockmarket, whose capitalisation has risen from PLN0.16 billion in 1991 to PLN43.61 billion at the end of 1997, and is likely to double again in 1998, thanks to some major privatisations. With a rapidly growing economy restraining the budget deficit, and foreign direct investment keeping down the trade deficit, it seems likely that the new private pension funds will be authorised to invest a significant proportion of their cashflow in equities from an early stage.

Once again the 'private pension fund' filter suggests a move towards developing countries, since these are the ones whose favourable demographics actually allow them to create private pension systems with minimal problems during the transition from public to private funds. As mentioned before, the countries of Continental Europe which are most in need of a switch to funded pensions are least likely to pursue this policy because of the high transitional costs.

Finally, the portfolio . . .

The chart shown in Figure 13.1 is an impressionistic sketch of the relative attractiveness of the major equity market groupings from now to 2050. Encapsulated in it are strong demographic trends, in particular the growth of the workforce – an important ingredient in overall GDP growth – and the population age structure, which affects overall savings rates, and indirectly interest rates and the rating of the stockmarket. The shape of the individual country charts cannot be ascribed entirely to demographics alone. For example, the growth of the private sector pension sector is likely to be a major driver of equity prices in Latin America, while the delay or rejection of private schemes in Germany could ultimately pull the German market to levels far below those likely to be

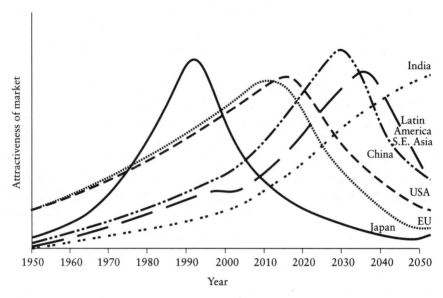

Figure 13.1 Demographic investment waves 1950–2050

reached by, say Argentina. Furthermore, there are short-term inflexions that recognise both the crisis in Asia and the vigorous restructuring of companies in the EU in preparation for the single currency.

(No attempt is made to quantify the impact of the Millennium Bug, however, although it is recognised that the IT sector worldwide has waxed fat on contracts to cure computers and that a marked slowdown of work after 2000 could shake the share prices of many highly rated companies.)

The chart in Figure 13.1 shows a series of waves, peaking at various dates in the future, reflecting the different mixes of the above factors. By catching each wave in turn, like a Bondai Beach surfer, it should be possible to move to new levels of capital appreciation in a different set of markets, depending on your projected retirement date. *In the end, however,* all *the countries and regions on the chart in Figure 13.1 will show a fall as GDP growth slows to levels that make overall profit growth difficult, and that in consumer-based sectors almost impossible.* At that stage, government debt instruments may well prove more rewarding investments . . . but that's another story.

For justification of the prediction of long-term decline for all, it is instructive to look at the experience of the Japanese market – post-war recovery, discovered by UK investors around 1970, rising to a peak in 1990, at which time it was the world's largest stockmarket before shrinking to a market capitalisation below that of the UK by early 1998. Based on the poor demographics alone, more declines are in store. The Lancashire saying, 'Clogs to clogs in three generations,' is being borne out on the other side of the world.

The rest of Asia is generally following suit, with perhaps a lag of 30–40 years, depending on the country, reflecting the later decline in birth rates, the higher TFRs still prevailing and the higher proportion of workforce in the countryside. The steeper the rate of decline in TFRs, the 'peakier' the shape of the 'attractiveness curve'. For example, China becomes a more attractive market earlier, and perhaps reaches higher market ratings than, say the Philippines, but then declines more sharply as a rapidly ageing population's pension and health care needs swallow up an increasing share of national wealth. On the other hand, the economies of Latin America, where birth rates have fallen more gently, and where private sector pension funds are now well established, and countries such as India where the same demographics apply, are likely to show a more gentle and sustained rise, and a more moderate fall thereafter.

It is worth summarising the investment conclusions shown in the curves in Figure 13.1.

- For the first five years, the models favour the **UK** and **parts of Western Europe** over other markets, despite the strong performances their stockmarkets have recorded since 1996. Their short-term demographics remain favourable, the cost of meeting Maastricht will have been overcome, and, in the case of **Germany**, companies are vigorously cutting costs while taxes may actually decline as transfers to East Germany become less necessary, or are forbidden by Brussels. Privatisation will play a major part in reducing public sector debt in **Italy** and **Spain**, and at the same time improve transparency and liquidity of the markets. Spain is also benefiting from changes in labour legislation that are beginning to make inroads into the high levels of unemployment. By contrast, the French government is determined to swim against the tide by increasing taxes on the most mobile part of the economy, the corporate sector, with the result that unemployment will continue to rise, while capital investment falls and companies move out to more rewarding pastures.

- Cashflow into pension funds is likely to drive the US markets higher, but with earnings momentum beginning to flag, and take-overs being done on multiples that leave reality far behind, there is a real risk of a market setback as buyers are drowned in new issues and placements. **It is safer to gain exposure to the USA through UK blue chips, unless the US government routs the tobacco companies, and uses the money from taxing them to underpin Medicare.**

- **It is too early to return to South-East Asia,** to Korea or even Taiwan, despite the massive falls experienced in US$ terms. The position of the banks, finance companies, property, construction and building material companies – in short, a major part of the markets – will continue to deteriorate through 1998. As shown earlier, even the most respectable companies can come unstuck in such circumstances, and there is no way of finding out until it is too late. Why be a hero? Patience *is* a virtue.

- **Latin America** has had a good run in 1997, but there are still deep-seated problems in Brazil, whose market capitalisation represents around 50% of the region. So far, Brazil's reaction to the crisis has been admirably fast and vigorous, and the government has scored some victories over a recalcitrant Congress, but it is too soon to believe that they will be able to keep it up. There have been enough populists and economic illiterates running the country over the past decade not to give any Brazilian government the benefit of the doubt until (i) they have built up a track record, and (ii) there is no risk of the electorate being seduced by other politicians promising the earth at election time. Given the ripple effect when one of the countries in the region encounters difficulties, **it may be better to avoid the entire area for the time being, or participate indirectly through the Spanish market, since Spanish banking and utility groups have invested heavily in the region.**

- By 2000, the expected consolidation resulting from the 1997 property/banking crisis will have run its course in **South-East Asia.** The high savings rates, favourable demographics and a shrunken market capitalisation will encourage a strong rebound and a steady rerating thereafter. Relaxation of the restrictions on foreign ownership should boost investment in-flows, bringing down interest rates and raising corporate profits in Korea and Thailand. **By 2005, some 10% of new** investment should be channelled into the region, including China, providing corporate transparency improves, perhaps rising further as reforms of the banking system and the SOEs yields results. Japan should be avoided, but by 2010, it should be worth committing funds to India – perhaps up to 10% of new investments.

- By 2000 it will also be clear whether Brazil has become a better-governed country. If it has, this is good for the whole region. Cashflow into the pension funds will by then have become significant relative to the size of the equity markets and provide them with a good under-pinning. **Once again, by 2005, perhaps some 10% of the fund could be directed to Latin America.**

- Shortly after 2005, demographics start to deteriorate in much of Western Europe (apart from the UK, Ireland and France) with the result that taxes and social security contributions will be in a new uptrend, economic growth, competitiveness and capital investment will fall and unemployment will rise. The single currency will come under strain because of the different demographic pressures on its members, and could break apart. Investors should begin to reduce their exposure to the region.

- Because of higher TFRs, the US working population will continue to grow, giving the nation a higher GDP growth rate than the EU and Japan. Prospects of a soaring budget deficit will hit interest rates and then the stockmarket. There will be little to look forward to outside the technology stocks where the US has an unassailable lead.

- Further ahead, Figure 13.1 shows clearly how one ought to surf from the cresting European markets and into, progressively, China, the South-East Asian markets, winding up, if you live that long, in India, by then, probably the only game in town, unless they have had a nuclear war with Pakistan in the meantime.

What do I buy?

It is not the purpose of this book to advocate any particular investment vehicle to gain exposure to the required markets. Tax legislation varies from country to country, and what is appropriate in one may not be the case in others. There exists a huge range of broadly-based funds covering practically every country and region imaginable. In recent years, UK investors have done far better in passive indexed funds than in managed funds in major markets, but active managers have generally outperformed in Asia during the recent crisis. So – having laid the groundwork, I will leave it to others to make specific recommendations on PEPs, ISAs and their successors, as well as the best funds to participate in. From now on, you're on your own.

Reference

1 *The World Competitiveness Yearbook, 1997*, IMD International, Lausanne, Switzerland (http://www.imd.ch/wcy.html.).

COUNTRY PROSPECTS

To add a bit of flesh to the criteria used to screen countries for inclusion in the portfolio, the section below reviews their economies on both a medium-term (to 2005) and long-term (to 2050) illustrating their competitive strengths and weaknesses, in particular, the political will of their governments to bring about the reforms necessary to compete in the new millennium and their ability to do so. Also covered are the Asian Tigers, to understand what went wrong in 1997, as well as China, India, and Russia, but not Latin America, where the main driver, pension reform, coupled with fiscal consolidation, has been discussed earlier.

The USA to 2005: taking second place

Nobody loves a killjoy, and the inclination of the US investment community is to shrug off any minatory comments from outsiders. After all, isn't the US the only undisputed world power, with massive military reach, a technological superiority that stretches from stealth bombers to biotech, worldbeating groups such as Microsoft, Intel and Cisco, a budget that is rapidly going into surplus and a booming stockmarket that has made the middle classes very rich? What can go wrong?

Well, for a start, the level of personal debt is soaring, as are bankruptcies, so any upturn in interest rates, or downturn in asset values (shares or properties) could dent personal wealth and compel consumers to rein in their expenditure, hitting the profits of a whole range of companies. Such a rise in rates could come about from a sharp deterioration of the current account in the face of an upsurge of imports from the Asian economies. more importantly, after seven years of expansion, profit margins are so high that further improvement is becoming more difficult. Corporate profit growth is likely to slow down sharply in 1998, whereas it is likely to accelerate in Continental Europe as unemployment begins to fall, and companies vigorously cut costs and increase their operating ratios. The US economy is sounder than for many years, and longer-term budget deficits could well be plugged by a windfall from the tobacco companies. It's just that this is fully recognised in the stockmarket, which is likely to underperform those of the EU over the next few years.

The UK to 2005: still competitive

The Thatcher handbag has done more than skittle the trade unions – it has made Britain competitive. Uneconomic industries such as coal mining have been closed down rather than kept alive by subsidies. British Steel and British Airways have become bywords for efficiency and profitability since privatisation, while the price of gas, electricity and telephone charges have all fallen. The banking and financial sectors are thriving. The tourist industry is seeing record numbers of visitors and GDP has outpaced its continental neighbours in the last few years. Bankruptcies and unemployment levels have fallen while those in Europe continue to rise.

The jobs created are not for hamburger flippers; according to William Waldegrave, then Chief Secretary to the Treasury, two-thirds of the jobs created between the autumn of 1993 and mid-1996 were in industries paying above the average wage for the economy as a whole.

Britain has clawed its way back up the competitiveness league. Between IQ1979 and IVQ1995, productivity rose by 78% and the productivity ratio West Germany/UK has improved from 140% to 117%. Since 1980 Britain has closed the income gap with all its major competitors apart from Japan. During the period, average *per capita* GDP (on a purchasing power parity basis) has risen from 67% to 71% of the US level, while those of France, Germany and Canada have fallen. As a result, between 1985 and 1995 the UK moved up from 19th to 16th in terms of *per capita* GDP. Britain was the only country to raise capital productivity in the business sector.

Much of this turnaround has been due to new management skills brought in by foreign companies. The Japanese have so transformed the car industry that by 1996, Japanese-owned car plants occupied the first, second and fourth places in Europe, in terms of car output per worker. In a statement that would have been inconceivable 15 years ago, the CEO of BMW, Bernd Pischetsrieder, is quoted as saying, 'The UK is the most attractive of all European locations for production of cars.' Heavy investment in the industry by BMW and others boosted 1996 UK car production to its highest level since 1973, almost double the level of 1980, while the quality of auto components has improved dramatically.

In electronics, too, capital investment has increased sharply, and both industries have become more broadly based with the establishment of foreign companies to supply components (e.g., TV monitors, car air-conditioning units, etc.) and provide training and R&D services.

By 1995, only 6 of the UK's 10 top exporters, and only 11 of the top 20 were British,[1] and in the second tier it is generally the UK subsidiaries of Swiss, German, French or Japanese companies (Ciba-Geigy, Siemens, Robert Bosch, Rhone-Poulenc, Michelin and NEC) that are making the

221

running. Unlike the French who have committed untold billions of tax-payers' money in subsidies to tottering national champions, the British are more pragmatic. If Singapore can grow at 8–10% compound by welcoming foreign capital, which regularly comprises 80% of the nation's annual investment in plant and equipment, then the UK is happy to follow its example.

Because the UK economy is out of phase with those of France and Germany, and has shown signs of overheating, interest rates have been raised, with the result that sterling has become dangerously overvalued, export orders are tumbling, profit margins under threat, and growth is slowing sharply. This need not necessarily upset the stockmarket too much, however. For a start, almost half the earnings of the leading UK companies comes from outside the UK, principally from the USA. Secondly, as the UK economy cools while those in Europe accelerate, the UK's interest rate premium will fall, bringing down sterling and boosting the value of overseas earnings. Government projections, moreover, imply that the ratio of government debt to GDP could fall from an estimated 51.9% in 1997/8 to 39.4% by 2002/3 on a Maastricht basis, when many members of the single currency will be straining to hold their own ratios below 60%. Finally, it appears that a new round of mergers is under way, leading to another wave of cost-cutting which will ultimately be reflected in higher profits on which a healthy market depends.

Western Europe to 2005: mergers favour markets

In terms of social philosophy, Europe is a continent divided. The UK has espoused the free market, the rest, or more particularly their electorates, governments and workers, are fighting a losing battle to resist it. Globalisation – and in particular the advent of Monetary Union – will undermine the ability of EU governments not only to keep out the barbarians at their gates but also to control the companies within them. No longer will the investments of pension funds be confined to the home country – they will be able to invest anywhere in the Monetary Union. With this flexibility comes *power* – companies in a country whose stockmarket is not liquid and whose standards of disclosure and corporate governance are poor will find it hard to raise money at the best rates, while investors will put pressure on regulators to ensure transparency, one reason why I am optimistic for the Italian market over this period.

The power of flexibility also applies to *capital investments*. As tariff barriers have fallen, the transport industry deregulated and trade is increasingly carried out via the telephone or the Internet, both industrial and service companies have increasing freedom to flow like water to where costs are lowest. Governments, especially the French, have totally failed to recognise the new-found freedom that this brings, and Jospin's strategy of making the most mobile group of taxpayers – the corporate sector – bear the brunt of the 1997 budget tax increases is bound to end in failure.

Nimble companies can shelter their profits by going overseas, or by threatening that they might, unless government makes concessions. At the same time, tax has to rise as a share of GDP to pay for pensions and health care, so who will bear the brunt of the increase? Obviously the less mobile workforce, either directly or indirectly, and this puts governments in a dilemma. A higher tax burden encourages increasing numbers of workers to drop out of formal employment and join the black economy, with the connivance of employers, as in Italy today. To recapture lost revenue, the most obvious tactic would be to increase sales tax or VAT, on the basis that everyone is a consumer, even if they aren't all paying their income and social security taxes. Such a policy is clearly regressive, disproportionately affecting the poorer members of society, and directly contrary to the instincts of European governments for social justice and the redistribution of wealth.

So, if governments have any sense, they will try to ensure that their own corporate tax rates are not so out of line that it is worth companies to exploit transfer pricing opportunities aggressively or even to run down operations in the country concerned. The same is true for taxes on liquid assets. The more mobile the source of income, the more sensitive a finance minister must be if he is not to produce the opposite of the result intended. After all, nobody is required to so arrange his financial affairs that the Revenue shall put its biggest possible shovel into his store.

For an example of such governmental naivety, one need look no further than Germany, whose decision to levy withholding taxes on interest led to a mass exodus of D-marks in suitcases into Luxemburg, and set back the development of the German financial markets by years. So concerned are the Germans to cover all aspects of the economy that they have created a monster of a tax code, so complex that even accountants cannot understand it, but riddled with loopholes which benefit mainly the rich – again, presumably the complete opposite of what was intended. The conspicuous lack of net foreign investment in Germany is in part due to the regime of high corporate taxes and social costs – something the Jospin government is trying to duplicate in France. With the opening of the Channel Tunnel, there has been an upsurge in the number of companies setting up operations in Kent, exchanging French social costs of 35–48% of wages for a UK figure of 7%.

Industry has become a lot more footloose, moving production from country to country in search of the highest returns. Renault incensed the Jospin government with its announcement of the intended closure of the Villvoorde car plant with the loss of over 3000 jobs, and, almost in the same breath, the expansion of its operations in Spain, where its new plant will benefit from government grants. Despite its huffing and puffing, the French government found itself powerless to intervene – a state of affairs that will become increasingly common in years to come.

Jobs will continue to be exported from France, Germany and Italy until such time as their governments see sense and abandon such nonsense as a 35-hour week for 39 hours' pay, a plan Jospin is pursuing during a period when the currencies of major Asian competitors have fallen by 50–80% in the course of 1997. Foreign direct investment in France declined from FFr118.1 billion in 1995 to FFr112.3 billion the following year, while *French direct investment overseas practically doubled* – FFr155.6 billion *vs* FFr78.6 billion. Net foreign investment into Germany dried up completely in 1996.

This is the comment of Laurence Bossidy, chairman of AlliedSignal, a diversified US manufacturer, who has quintupled his group's market capitalisation since taking charge six years ago. Interviewed by the *Financial Times* in June 1997,[2] he observed:

> If you look at the job migration out of Germany, it's serious. Their business doesn't get any better by taking jobs out of Germany. Their companies might get better, in the sense of being in lower-cost locations, but they don't address the fundamental problem. I don't think the French do either . . . You see French and German businessmen who are clearly as capable as any in the world. It's a question of government: whether they will take the requisite steps to allow their companies to be more competitive.

As we have seen, governments in both countries have failed to drive through the structural reforms to which they pay lip-service, because they are instinctively opposed to any changes to the social contract with labour, and are terrified of confrontation, which would damage economic growth and jeopardise prospects of monetary union.

Because profitability is so low, it is almost impossible to persuade companies to invest unless they receive massive subsidies. These have become so pronounced of late that Germany now accounts for one-third of government subsidies in the entire EU. Brussels, which has been fighting Volkswagen and the State of Lower Saxony for the return of subsidies it deemed illegal, talks acidly about the growing culture of subsidy dependency. Under the definitions of the Finance Ministry, public subsidies doubled from DM31.4 billion in 1970 to DM60.4 billion in 1980 and rose again to DM78.9 billion in 1990.

After reunification, they soared, and are expected to reach DM115.2 billion in 1997, despite the low levels of inflation since 1990.[3] This is not the end of the story, however. According to the Kiel Institute of World Economics, the true level of direct subsidies and tax breaks is nearer to DM300 billion per annum, representing 8.6% of GDP, while including indirect benefits, e.g., guarantees to public sector banks, the total rises to DM400 billion. Small wonder that tax rates in Germany are so high.

Similar considerations apply to France, where a succession of State-owned companies have been bailed out by the taxpayer – Crédit Lyonnais (up to FFr170 billion), Crédit Foncier (FFr22.7 billion), Air France (FFr20 billion), GAN (FFr22.9 billion), Giat (FFr11.8 billion) SNCF (FFr16.6 billion) – to the tune of FFr10 000 per worker.

Employers' federations in both France and Germany are now in open revolt against the policies of their respective governments. The former are furious because of the failure to consult them over the 35-hour week, the latter because of the inability of parliament to pass important tax reforms, to contain social security costs and subsidies and for their attempts to enshrine unfair advantages given to public sector banks in the Amsterdam Treaty, a move thankfully thwarted by Brussels.

Against this background, it might seem strange that Western Europe is seen to provide good equity returns over the period to 2005. There are two reasons for this view:

- *the massive restructuring of European companies*
- *the fall in unemployment beginning early next century, thanks to (you guessed it) demographics.*

The former will cut employment costs and boost profits, the latter may permit a (temporary) easing in taxation levels – an attractive double benefit for investors.

Companies are not standing still, especially in Germany. Squeezed between high social costs and a strong D-mark in 1995, companies began a vigorous cost-cutting programme similar to that undertaken in the UK during the mid-1980s. Unit labour costs fell sharply through 1997 and as the restructuring costs diminish, recorded profits will surge. Complementing this cost-cutting is another corporate imperative whose importance has surged over the past few years – *to expand one's company to a size that will enable it to compete on a continent-wide basis*. The major groups are identifying sectors in which they intend to establish a minimum 10% market share throughout the EU. That means mergers and another wave of cost-cutting.

Bull markets are always good for triggering take-overs and mergers, since it becomes increasingly easy to finance them by issuing shares in rising markets. Over the course of 1997, therefore, M&A activity showed a steady rise before two events moved it into a sharply higher gear. The first, the merger between two major German banks, showed that the fragmented sector could be rationalised (even though political pressure would reduce job losses), raising the likelihood of further take-overs. The second was the realisation that the single currency *was* going ahead, and that the strategy of the major groups had to be Europe-wide. In other words it signalled the need for more cross-border deals. Within weeks, the floodgates burst open with a series of major announcements, including:

- proposed acquisition of BAT's insurance activities by Zurich Group (Switzerland);
- hostile take-over bid for insurance group AGF (France) by Generali (Italy);
- proposed merger between Nordbanken (Sweden) and Merita (Finland) to form the largest bank in Scandinavia;
- proposed merger between Reed Elsevier (UK/NL) with Wolters Kluwer (NL) to form the world's largest scientific and professional publisher;
- hostile takeover bid for Redland (UK) by Lafarge (France).

It is no coincidence that most of the largest deals are in the finance sector. Many of the banks and insurance companies are outgrowing their home markets. Moreover the single currency greatly extends their range of influence by enabling them to market new products across the border through the branch networks of companies acquired. The prospects for the development of the private pension market give a particular incentive to charge into the hole left in the French financial sector by the collapse of Crédit Lyonnais, GAN and others. Fund managers too find it hard to penetrate European markets controlled by banks that are reluctant to distribute financial products they have not developed in-house. At the same time, banks in the smaller countries will be disproportionately affected by the move to the single currency, and are hence keen to find new profit areas abroad.

In Germany, the industrial economy is split into two distinct segments, a small number of large, publicly listed international groups, and a vast number of unlisted fiercely independent family-run firms – the *Mittelstand*. With many owners at or above retirement age and their children evincing little interest in running the business, this sector is ripe for consolidation through take-overs and mergers. The companies which have hitherto relied on bank finance could well tap the equity market and substantially broaden the range of listed securities.

Frankfurt may not be as clubby as Paris, but the leading commercial banks have cemented their relationships with their clients by acquiring equity stakes. These are now showing their disadvantages. Indeed, the very extent of Deutsche Bank's investments in the country's leading companies is debarring the bank from advising them on capital-raising exercises, because of the conflict of interests, leaving the door wide open to US investment banks to steal long-standing clients from under their nose. By weaning these companies off debt financing, these US competitors chip away at the existing profit base of the commercial banks.

On the other hand, the injection of new capital and new management into established companies and a greater level of corporate disclosure will encourage a new wave of foreign investment. *If Germany were to approach the UK market capitalisation/GDP ratio, the capitalisation could rise by US$1.5 trillion.* Clearly this cannot happen overnight, and some major changes will have to be put in place, such as legislation to encourage the establishment of private pension funds, but it shows the potential for investment banks in years to come. *It also shows that German claims that Frankfurt could overtake London in equity trading within a decade must be taken seriously.*

Italy has been the greatest beneficiary in the run-up to the single currency, as interest rates have fallen far more sharply than in the rest of the EU, and the stockmarket has therefore been one of the strongest performers. The members of the *buono salotto*, the inner circle that controls much of Italy's private sector, are still trying to keep all their larger companies in a few hands, with Mediobanco orchestrating the deals in the background, but in an increasingly Continent-wide market, such attempts are ultimately doomed to failure.

As companies such as Generali and Fiat are forced to expand abroad, in order to preserve market share, they will not only have to submit themselves to the scrutiny of the international investment banks but by issuing shares for acquisitions will inevitably dilute the influence of their key shareholders, as in the case of Axa/UAP in France. In worthy contrast to the secrecy of the private sector within Italy, the government at least is embarking on privatisation, selling off Telecom Italia and breaking up the State holding company, Iri. The stock exchange is also attempting to bring in stricter rules of corporate governance.

In all these cases, as in Japan, South Korea and South-East Asia, there is a clear trend towards greater diversity of shareholdings, and greater levels of accountability and transparency, factors that should increase the level of investment interest and boost the rating of the shares.

Mergers mean cost-cutting, and this inevitably means redundancies. The sectors that have hit the headlines in this regard are pharmaceuticals and banking. The aborted Glaxo/Beecham merger would have created the world's largest drug group, and led to the loss of 10 000 jobs worldwide, and probably a substantial number more as other groups felt forced to merge in order to stay in the big league. Similarly, while the UBS/SBC bank merger will result in around 4500 job losses, half in Switzerland, half in the City of London, the threat of aggressive low-cost competitors born of such mergers is galvanising others to examine their own cost bases. In Italy, the merger between Banco Nazionale del Lavoro with Banco di Napoli will lead to the loss of 3000 jobs, and the Italian Banking Association is asking unions to accept a two-year pay freeze if it is to prevent the loss of 60 000 jobs over the next three years. Those countries whose politicians interfere in these corporate decisions because of the impact on employment risk saddling their companies with high costs while those in more pragmatic countries gain a competitive advantage.

This corporate activity will therefore achieve three things:

- a widening and deepening of stockmarkets throughout Europe that will raise their market capitalisations and thereby attract cash from funds that seek to maintain a market weighting on a country basis
- a strong rise in profitability as rationalisation benefits accrue, leading to a rerating of share prices

- a steep rise in redundancies, which will keep unemployment levels high. Since companies are vehemently opposed to work-sharing to create jobs, the onus will be on the politicians to find new solutions to the problem.

Even without new employment initiatives, demographics will gradually eat into the level of unemployment by the year 2005. As Table 14.1 shows, in Germany, the actual workforce could fall by around 1.4 million, and the level of unemployment should show a steady decline, although the impact of restructuring and the heavy dependence of the economy on manufacturing suggests that the decline could be less than that of the workforce. Social security costs will therefore remain high for some years, but could begin to decline significantly after 2000. *By contrast, the rising workforce of France will aggravate the current high levels of unemployment, already threatened by the imposition of a 35-hour week,* although the projected growth of both UK and Irish workforces may act to cool the overheating of their respective economies.

Table 14.1 Change in size of workforce 1995–2005 (000)

Country	Number
Germany	−1426
Italy	−450
Spain	+488
UK	+1204
France	+1052
Ireland	+189

Source: Calculations based on data from World Bank, OECD.

In the case of Germany, there is also scope for some pleasant surprises on the upside, namely:

- some prospect of tax reform which would benefit the corporate sector after the September elections
- Brussels may compel Germany to cut its massive subsidy bill
- transfers to Eastern Germany, which amounted to DM16.5 billion in 1995 should fall substantially.

All three factors will combine to cut taxation levels, stimulating consumption, boosting corporate profits and fuelling the stockmarket.

Ireland – ever seen a green tiger?

Ireland is the new *Wunderkind* on the fringe of Europe. Unlike Sicily, Spain or Portugal, it has not become marginalised by its distance from the main markets of West and Central Europe, nor is it stagnating under high employment and socialist nonsense. Its recent economic achievements would have seemed inconceivable only a decade ago, and provide another example of how proper reforms can transform crisis into opportunity.

During the 1970s and 1980s, the nation recorded annual growth rates averaging 4.9% and 3.1% respectively. Although respectable by European standards, unfortunately it was insufficient to absorb the growth of the labour force, swollen by high historic birth rates and a move off the land into the towns. As late as 1960, some 35% of the total workforce was employed in agriculture. Faced with stubbornly high unemployment, despite the safety valve of significant migration to the UK, successive governments spent lavishly on job creation schemes and raising the quality and quantity of the skilled workforce through education. Unfortunately, the benefits of the policy in terms of higher (taxable) employment, were too long-term to prevent a major deterioration in the government's finances.

By 1987 the country was staring into an abyss, with government debt of 116% of GDP, after a run of budget deficits that put to shame every European country but Italy. Labour participation rates, at 62%, were 10 percentage points below the European average. Unemployment at 17% was the highest in Europe, and the best-educated sought their fortunes overseas. Firm action had to be taken to prevent total loss of credit-worthiness in the eyes of foreign lenders.

Besides reining in the Budget deficit by a remarkably savage reduction in government expenditure, Ireland set out to attract foreign investment, by offering a low-wage workforce whose educational skills were rising rapidly, access to the markets of the EU and generous grants and incentives. Because of the nation's low *per capita* GNP it has also been able to avail itself of substantial EU regional funds to develop infrastructure, etc. The combination of hard graft, grants, golf courses and Guinness has proved irresistible, and direct investment has soared. Overall, some 90 000 jobs have been created by 1000 foreign companies. At the end of 1996, Ireland secured its largest ever foreign investment with a I£350 million factory to make memory chips for IBM. It will create 2850 jobs at a campus in west Dublin and around I£50 million of subcontracting work for local companies.

230

The new companies, although concentrated in a few specialised areas – computers, pharmaceuticals, medical technology, electrical engineering and soft drinks – have transformed the nation's industrial base. For a start, they are far more capital intensive than the traditional part of the economy, and added value per employee is roughly 2.5 times that of the latter. As a result, although this 'modern' part of the economy accounted for only 28% of industrial employment in 1990, it represented 48% of value added and around 60% of gross operating surplus. There has been further growth since.

Capital income share in the business sector has risen from 26.9% in 1990 – the lowest in the OECD apart from Switzerland – to 33.2% by 1996 and a projected 34.9% by 1998. In the period 1979–95, both total factor and labour productivity growth were the highest in the OECD. The OECD expects this momentum to continue, with Ireland rapidly closing the investment gap with the rest of Europe. One consequence of such a concentration of capital intensive industries has been a decline in unit labour costs in five of the last seven years, despite a strong rise in the level of employment and a significant improvement in participation rate, in contrast to the experience of the larger countries in the EU.

GDP is increasingly export driven; indeed exports now represent 70% of GDP – in line with the Asian Tiger economies – and have been growing at twice the rate of GDP. After a respectable 4.5% per annum growth between 1988 and 1993, GDP growth accelerated to 6.4% and 7.7% in 1994 and 1995. Export volumes (+18% in 1995) showed the best performance in the entire OECD after Mexico and the trade surplus surged to $12.4 billion. Furthermore the range of exports has grown to include electronics, chemicals and software (56% of 1995 exports), and Ireland can no longer be dismissed as a mere supplier of meat and livestock to the UK consumer. Indeed, *40% of all packaged software and 60% of business application software sold in Europe is now produced in Ireland.*[4]

Despite a rise in the deficit on investment income (up from $3.2 billion in 1987 to $7.4 billion in 1995) dus to rising royalties and dividends remitted from Ireland, the current account surplus has improved from $100 million to $4.4 billion over the same interval.

Rising employment levels have boosted tax receipts, and transformed the budget from a current deficit to a surplus, and with the strong growth in GDP, gross financial liabilities had fallen to around 80.2% of GDP on Maastricht criteria by the end of 1996. Further improvement should reduce the ratio to 59.5% by the end of 1998, according to the European Commission[5] – certainly a better trend than expected for Italy or even Germany.

In the short-term, the population of working age will continue to increase – by 1.2% per annum between 1995 and 2000, and by 0.8% compound between 2000 and 2005. It is this sheer availability of qualified labour at a time when it will become increasingly hard to find elsewhere in Europe that will distinguish Ireland from the rest, and will sustain high capital in-flows. Some 80% of the 2850 jobs at the new IBM plant will be for graduates.

Given economic growth of 4–5% per annum and labour productivity growth of perhaps 3%, there are grounds for expecting a steady rise in total employment. (This in itself will swell government revenues, underpinning the forecast of declining deficits over the next few years.) Ireland is still an agricultural nation, with around 13% of the workforce employed on the land, in forestry or in fishing, *vs* 3.7% in Germany and 5.1% in France. There remains considerable scope for further migration from the land into industry during the next few years. During the next half-century, when the German workforce could decline be 40%, that of Ireland will rise (conservatively) by 15%, and the number employed in industry at an even faster rate.

Unlike the rest of the EU, however, the population is still comparatively young and the rise in the number of pensionable age will remain manageable for 10–15 years longer than in the case of Germany or Italy. Given the expected increase in participation rates, this is unlikely to pose a problem. Social security taxes should stay well below those in the EU, and indeed, the gap should steadily increase, heightening the country's competitive advantage.

As its novelists point out, the nature of Irish society has been transformed over the past 20 years. The authority of the Catholic Church has been diminished by scandal, and the number called to the priesthood is far outstripped by retirements or the deaths of the incumbents. At the same time, the country has opened up to new influences as its dependence on the UK has declined. While deep pockets of unemployment persist in Cork and Limerick, Dublin is a booming cosmopolitan city that astounds the tourists. Irish politics is becoming less clubby, too, and the politicians who have seen the success of their policies over the past decade are unlikely to throw this away after the latest election.

The Irish Question is not a new one. It has stumped everyone from

King John onwards. Dare we now hope that there can be an economic answer to a political problem? If Ireland continues to grow at its present rate, *per capita* GNP is likely to overtake that of the UK over the next few years, and a labour shortage could emerge. The country is no longer exporting labour but attracting back former emigrants, drawn both by the growing job opportunities and the lifestyle. This might attract back the massive overseas diaspora – some 10 million Americans regard themselves as of pure Irish descent – and this leavening of international culture may further break down the tribalism inherent in Irish society. If, though, there is to be recruitment of workers for Ireland, where better to start than in one's own back yard, Northern Ireland? The prejudices of the Catholic and Protestant hardliners have been reinforced by chronic unemployment. If this could be relieved by emigration from Ulster to Eire, everyone would benefit. The best guarantor of peace for the island of Ireland might turn out to be Eire's continuing success.

Tigernomics – the end of a 12-year spree?

The crisis that started in Thailand in late 1996, and spread like plague through the rest of Asia before leaping across to Australasia, Latin America and Russia, seemed to some to mark the end of a remarkable period of strong economic growth accompanied by rapidly rising living standards but appreciating currencies and low inflation. But when we inquire not only into the aetiology of the crisis but also into that of the preceding period of growth, we can draw altogether different and more optimistic conclusions for the future.

Our story begins with a historic decision in September 1985, known ever after as the Plaza Accord, to let the yen be revalued upwards against the US dollar, in recognition of Japan's impressive and growing trade surplus. Between 1985 and 1988, the yen rose by around 86% against the US dollar, and the consequences electrified South-East Asia. The revaluation catalysed three qualitatively distinct waves of money into the region:

(i) Japanese tourists, whose effective spending power had vastly increased;

(ii) Japanese capital investment from companies seeking to cut costs by buying parts manufactured by affiliates and subcontractors in the region;

(iii) foreign equity funds responding to the upsurge in the profitability of regional companies resulting from (i) and (ii).

The region boomed, and began to increase its already high savings ratios, which became channelled via the banking system into new investments – a virtuous circle, you might think. Unfortunately, the money flowed in faster than it could prudently be on-lent, and furthermore, with the shining exception of Singapore, banking regulations in the region were lax. Money was lent on the basis of name or relationship, or because government ordered funds to be directed to a favoured company. Rigorous credit checks or risk assessment of a project were of lower priority. More worryingly, an increasing proportion of investment was directed not into productive assets but into property.

Banks became dangerously exposed to property loans, either directly to projects or indirectly as collateral for other activities, the risks to which became apparent as the building boom turned into looming over-supply, prices weakened and the cashflow from speculative buyers dried up. This in itself caused growing concern within the banks and finance companies, which was heightened as interest rates began to rise. To find out why this happened, we must return briefly to Japan.

The start of the problems came when falling property prices in Japan began to result in a growing number of collapses in the property and construction sectors, undermining their collateral and making them increasingly unwilling to lend. Their balance sheets were further weakened by the fall in the Nikkei Index, since a proportion of the book profits on their equity investments could be applied to their asset base. Consumer demand weakened, too, bringing down interest rates, and by late 1995, a steady fall in the yen. This in turn triggered a collapse in Japanese tourism to the region, and a revival in Japanese exports.

Japanese direct exports to the USA began to boom again, at the expense not only of affiliates in the USA but also of subcontractors in South-East Asia. Increasing pressure from a more competitive yen coincided not only with depressed demand from the EU, beset with the problems of meeting Maastricht, but also rampant wage inflation that outstripped productivity. Growing competition from Chinese exports, following the devaluation of the renminbi in 1994 and the granting of export incentives, and the collapse in the price structure of memory chips, an important sector of the region's export trade, added to the pressure. Under the circumstances, it is not surprising that exports stagnated, and this, combined with continued strong internal demand for consumer goods, caused a sharp deterioration in the trade balance.

Faced with such a problem, the standard response should be to cut domestic demand through higher taxation or interest rates, or to make imports more expensive and exports more competitive by devaluation, but the Tigers were most reluctant to do either because of the adverse effect on the property market and the balance sheets of major companies heavily borrowed in foreign currencies. Foreign institutions, seeing both Thailand's growing trade deficit and official inaction to deal with it, began to fear for the currency and started selling shares, converting the proceeds into US dollars. The Central Bank belatedly tried to defend the baht by selling dollars from reserves and sharply raising interest rates, but succeeded only in delivering a mortal blow to the property sector and the finance companies that fuelled it, before the currency was washed away by a tidal wave of flight capital. The baht was devalued by an initial 15%.

The government was forced to suspend trading in all financial stocks while plans were worked out to recapitalise ten finance companies, to absorb weaker units facing liquidity problems into stronger banks, and to introduce monitoring and provisions of bad debts throughout the industry. With the precedents of the UK secondary banking crisis in the 1970s, the Mexican banking collapse and the Japanese property bubble in the 1990s, and indeed Thailand's previous pyramid scheme, under Raja Finance, it is disappointing that corrective steps were so late in coming. All emerging markets are allowed one major scandal on the road to maturity, but a second is less easy to forgive.

Once the first domino fell, others followed in quick succession. Either they were seen to have the same problems – a poorly regulated financial system dangerously overexposed to a property sector heading towards a glut – Philippines, Malaysia and Indonesia – or because they would suffer serious collateral damage – e.g., Singapore, heavily dependent on inbound tourism from its neighbours, and whose banks and listed companies were exposed to loans and investments within the region.

Speculative attention then turned to the dominoes still standing, since they were now at a competitive disadvantage to those whose currencies had fallen. Taiwan gave up without much of a struggle, despite its ability to muster massive reserves to support the currency, but Hong Kong mounted a vigorous and successful defence of its fixed exchange rate against the US dollar, although interest rates rose steeply, triggering a

20–30% fall in property prices and defaults by some mainland Chinese companies that had agreed to acquire Hong Kong assets.

The real concern, however, focused on the world's 11th largest economy, Korea, and on Indonesia. In both of these, the leading companies were heavily committed to short-term foreign borrowings, the bulk of which were repayable within a year, and it was also clear that their governments would be unwilling to take politically unpopular action to stabilise their currencies ahead of presidential elections, in December 1997 and March 1998, respectively. As their currencies tumbled, the ability of these companies to repay unhedged foreign debts evaporated, and their credit ratings were downgraded. This in turn increased the anxieties of investors, who renewed the selling of Korean and Indonesian equities and repatriated the proceeds in US dollars, while foreign bankers became unwilling to renew credit lines.

This in its turn provoked a further twist in the downward spiral. Firstly, it greatly increased the pressure on companies that had borrowed heavily in US dollars. In some cases, companies have not matched income against debt servicing – i.e., their main market is domestic, and they are unable to increase the price of their goods in ringgit or baht to completely offset the increased cost of servicing foreign debt. (For example, after the ringgit had fallen from M$2.5=US$1 to M$3=US$1, the capital loss to the Malaysian company, Tenaga, was put by US broker Morgan Stanley Dean Witter, at M$202 million in 1997 and M$435 million in 1998 – massive when compared to 1996 net profits of M$797 million. Since then, the ringgit has fallen a further 20%, and capital losses must have further ballooned.) There is a risk that the huge rise in foreign exchange obligations could imperil their ability to repay both foreign and local banks, hence the particularly sharp fall in the shares of the latter.

Secondly, the fall in share prices triggered margin calls from the banks that had lent money against the security of shares whose value had plummetted. Borrowing to gear up a portfolio works both ways. When shares are rising, it boosts performance, when they fall, net assets fall faster than the market. Consider the case of someone with borrowings of 100, secured against shares valued at 150 – i.e., net assets of 50. If the shares rise by 10%, his net assets rise by 15, or 30%, a gearing of three times. On the other hand, if his shares fall by 33%, his net assets fall to zero. Many shares in many Asian markets have fallen by far more, and it has not always been possible to sell at all, leaving investors with considerable net liabilities. After such an experience, they are unlikely to have either the cash or the inclination to return to the market until well after their finances have been fully restored.

Finally, the behaviour of the Malaysian premier, inveighing against foreign speculators attempting to weaken the country and impose a form of neo-colonialism, and threatening to jail them, alienated the support of the one sector on which Malaysia depends – foreign capital – and triggered a new wave of selling. Refusing to admit his role in the market's collapse, he repeated his views a few weeks later and precipitated a further 6% fall in the ringgit. In the space of three months, the currency fell by 35% against the US dollar. The collapse of the markets, the liquidation of margin accounts and the disappearance of foreign investors has made it almost impossible for local companies to raise money for capital projects or to refinance debt. The wheel has come full circle, 12 years after the historic Plaza Accord meeting.

Only two countries, rich and rocklike, stand out against this dark background – Singapore and Taiwan. Through prudent economic management, each has built up impressive foreign exchange reserves as a means of protecting itself against regional uncertainties, and both are now poised to reap the rewards. Their currencies have fallen by less, their banking systems are intact and their companies strong, at a time when those in the rest of the region are weakened by foreign debt and high interest rates. It is likely that both will use the opportunity to acquire regional assets that may previously been unavailable to foreign investors, and at prices far below pre-crisis levels.

Regional crisis – global impact?

The Asian region is a major consumer of a range of imported goods and services, and the immediate impact of the crisis has been to collapse demand, cause destocking and depress prices in a number of sensitive sectors, with repercussions that stretch from Australia to Mexico. Panglossians may point out that, by cooling global demand it keeps inflation under control and defers the day when Central Banks must raise interest rates and puncture the equity boom, but a quick tour around the affected sectors shows that the problem is serious.

For a start, Asia normally accounts for 25% of world oil consumption, *but 50% of incremental demand*. This year, regional GDP will be negative, as will energy demand. Given that this slowdown coincides with a 10% increase in OPEC quotas and the resumption of Iraq's oil-for-food programme, it is hardly surprising that the Brent 60-day

237

forward oil price slumped from $21 per barrel in late 1997 to a nine-year low of $12.76 per barrel by early March 1998. *This will affect a range of producers, many of which are developing economies needing high oil prices to repay foreign borrowings incurred in previous crises. The list includes Indonesia, Malaysia, Mexico, Brazil, Argentina and – Russia (see pages 253–5).* Already, the Mexican government has had to rein in its expenditure plans in the wake of a sharp fall in oil receipts.

Individuals in Korea and Thailand are also donating gold to their governments to sell for hard currencies, adding to the overhang and pushing the gold price to a 25-year low in real terms, putting pressure on employment in South Africa, and on the level of the rand. The prices of a number of base metals such as copper and zinc, used extensively in the auto industry, have fallen sharply, while kraft pulp, used for making cardboard and packaging, took a nosedive. As with oil, gold, base metals and pulp are global commodities trading at almost the same price world-wide. Falling prices will make mines from Poland to Peru, and pulp producers from Brazil to New Zealand, a lot poorer this year, although there are already signs that destocking is coming to an end and prices are beginning to recover.

The Australasian tourist industry has been devastated – by December 1997, the number of visitors from Korea, which normally provides 6% of Australia's total arrivals, had fallen by 65%, with governments in Korea, Malaysia and Thailand pressing their nationals to take their holidays within their own country. By January, four airlines, including Ansett International and Qantas, had suspended flights between Australia and Korea. The fall in passenger numbers will affect airline profitability worldwide and has already led to the deferment or cancellation of planes on order.

Western economies and markets have already been significantly affected. The US trade deficit is now recording a sharp upturn in imports from the region, and the cancellation of major infrastructure projects throughout the region will also impinge on Western exporters of capital goods, who have become increasingly dependent on the region. Some 30% of US and EU exports (excluding intra-EU trade) go to Asia. Both US and European car manufacturers already fear a renewed onslaught from imports from the region. Japanese steelmakers are cutting output in the wake of falling Asian demand and higher exports from Korea and Taiwan. Countries with port facilities for unloading bulk cement face a surge of imports and sharply lower cement prices in 1998.

How long to recovery?

How long it will take these economies to recover from the deep recession into which they have been plunged depends on a range of factors, chief among which is the determination of the government concerned to force through unpleasant measures demanded by the IMF, and also their appropriateness. There has been criticism that the IMF's prescription for return to financial rectitude was designed to cope with countries running soaring budget deficits, and is not appropriate for those where the problems lie in an overextended private sector. Given the region's growing interdependence, a severe downturn in one country can severely damage the rest, producing further twists in the downward spiral which might ultimately involve the rest of the world.

Even though acceding to many of the IMF's demands will be against the instincts of the governments and the business communities, the rewards may well exceed the pain. Greater compliance results in faster IMF disbursements, improved investor confidence and the return of flight capital. This in turn strengthens the currency, reducing the burden of servicing foreign debts and improving the balance sheets of the major companies, while simultaneously boosting the stockmarket, and making it easier for the listed companies to further restore their solvency through capital issues. In fact, a replay in reverse of the previous collapse – the death spiral transformed into a virtuous circle.

The Year of the Tiger opened with just such a dramatic reversal. Within a week, some markets had risen by 25% in dollar terms, as those funds that had become underweight in the region scrambled to re-establish their positions, and the rating agencies signalled that they were considering upgrading Korea's credit rating. The seeming inability of the Japanese government to reflate its economy, however, soon set the yen skidding again, dragging other regional currencies and stockmarkets down to new lows.

In June the US and Japanese governments mounted a concerted defence of the yen, driving it down from 147 to around 133 against the US dollar, and prompting a rally in those same currencies and markets. While this may establish a level from which recovery can take place, it says little about the *speed* of that recovery. We cannot draw on the experience of other developing countries for this without substantial caveats, since those outside Asia have very different characteristics, but it is tempting to take Argentina as the best example of how to deal with a regional currency crisis – in this case triggered by Mexico.

The Mexican crisis, again the result of overdependence on short-term foreign capital, really began in early 1994 with political problems – insurgency in the state of Chiapas in January, followed by the assassination of a presidential candidate in March – which led to foreign capital leaving the country, and a 15% devaluation that turned into a rout. By March 1995 the currency stood 40–50% below its pre-crisis level, destroying the balance sheets of banks that had borrowed in dollars to on-lend in pesos, and forcing the government to call in the IMF.

When the Mexican shock waves hit the rest of the region, Argentina vigorously defended its currency by a range of measures including raising VAT from 18% to 21%, pressing on with more privatisations and setting up a private pension system to replace the bankrupt State system. These decisive moves convinced the investment community, flight capital returned and Argentina was able to re-enter the international capital markets as early as August 1995 with the successful placing of a DM 1 billion five-year loan. Although the banking system experienced a massive drain on reserves, and construction activity collapsed, the currency held, inflation declined steadily to zero and by 1996 the economy began to revive. By the end of that year, funds under management in the newly formed private pension system had reached $5.4 billion. By 1997, real GDP was rising by 7% and the stock exchange became one of the top performers of 1996–7.

Despite the replacement of the Finance Minister who had masterminded the strategy, foreign investors maintained their faith in the country's economic policies and indeed have greatly increased their investment in the banking sector, whose strength will play a vital part in funding the expansion of the private sector. Argentina has recently been rated by DRI/McGraw-Hill as the least risky of the ten largest emerging markets – something undreamed of only four years ago.

Comparing Asia with Argentina, we can say that, except for one factor, Asia should be better placed to weather a crisis. For a start, both savings ratios and long-term economic growth rates are higher. Moreover, Asia is far more exposed to international trade, and its exports are manufactures rather than oil or agricultural products – i.e., they benefit far more from devaluation. The trade position has already improved substantially in both Korea and Thailand. The exception lies in the health of the corporate sector and the banks; their solvency is a function of the strength of the currency, and ultimately the market's perception of the ability of governments to take vigorous action . . . which is where we came in.

Testing the bottom

Nobody rings a bell to signal either the top or the bottom of any market, but there *are* signs for the observant to read. For example, the day when a record value of US takeovers and mergers is announced must surely rank high on the Richter Scale of Market Tops. At the same time, with Far East markets down by some 70% in US dollar terms in calendar 1997, and in some cases by considerably more since their peak, there is a lot of interest in trying to gauge the market bottom. What is the bear market equivalent of a merger boom? A wave of bankruptcies.

Several previous UK bear markets have bottomed with bankruptcies or financial crises in leading companies such as Rolls-Royce, Burmah Oil and the secondary banks. In November 1985, the Singapore market was similarly shaken by the simultaneous bankruptcy of several leading stockbrokers but the market fall subsequently proved to have been a good buying opportunity. This is the catharsis that the market needs. Even though there may be aftershocks, as a major bankruptcy exposes suppliers, customers or bankers to losses, the point comes when the market sentiment is so depressed that all the bears have sold, so the only way for the market to go is UP. Has Asia yet reached this point?

It is true that bankruptcies have been gathering momentum in both Korea, where six of the top 30 *chaebol* have now filed for bankruptcy, and Japan, where Sanyo, Takugin and Yamaichi Securities have gone under in quick succession. Indeed, the belief that the Japanese authorities were finally grasping the nettle and letting one of the charmed circle of city banks go to the wall was the key factor sparking a sharp rally in the Nikkei. Even within the chaos of the late-November rout, there were some comforting signs. In particular, the Nikkei managed to remain above the critical 16 000 level. Could this be the first swallow of spring? The fact that markets refused to panic when Indonesia effectively declared a moratorium on its foreign debt is another sign that the bottom is near. For now, attention has shifted back to Japan, whose economy dwarfs the rest of the region, and whose government seems incapable of preventing the slide into recession. **The ability of the Japanese to handle this crisis effectively will determine whether Asian recovery begins in 1999 or 2000.**

The survivors

After all the dust has settled, the corporate landscape in the region will resemble a cityscape after the Blitz. The financial sector will be decimated. Deposits will flee from weaker to stronger units. How governments will react, e.g., by bailing out bad banks, letting the weak go to the wall or allowing foreigners to buy into the banking sector, will determine the response of the markets. In Tokyo, for example, the possibility of using taxpayers' money to bail out financial institutions was until late November considered remote because of previous public outrage at the proposed bail-out of the *jusen*, or housing loan companies, some of which were clearly associated with the politicians proposing their rescue. That Y685 billion rescue package, which was blocked by the opposition in parliament, pales in comparison with the funds needed to solve the banking crisis, which have been put at anywhere between Y5000 billion and Y8000 billion. As the Yamaichi bankruptcy brought home to the public the gravity of the situation, popular opinion is turning towards State-funded bail-out of the sector.

Clearly very few of the property and construction companies will survive in their present form anywhere in the region apart from Hong Kong and Singapore, although reform of the bankruptcy laws will at least enable them to repossess properties on which buyers have defaulted. Cement and other building materials companies such as steel producers will be triply squeezed; demand will decline sharply, the cost of production, which is heavily dependent on the price of oil, will soar because of devaluations, but they will be unable to recover this through higher prices, and their customers will default. Exporting will become more profitable, and will depress cement prices as far away as Europe.

Retailing will suffer, and with the combination of high interest rates, restricted credit availability and soaring prices due to the impact of devaluation on imported components such as engines, car sales will collapse. Because travel agencies book rooms a year ahead, international tourism will begin to benefit only in late 1998. In the meantime, regional tourism may hold up, since destinations outside the region will have been made more expensive by the same currency changes.

Telephone companies will benefit from devaluation, since they are net recipients of foreign exchange from international traffic, and they are less likely to suffer from bad debts than other sectors. Power utilities, however, faced with higher oil costs in local currencies may be unable to recoup this in higher prices.

Further ahead

The richer countries get, in *per capita* income terms, the slower they grow – at least a scattergraph of growth against *per capita* income for a range of different countries implies this. The experience of Japan, which started the whole Far East emerging market boom, but is now stagnating, also seems to confirm this. But is this really so? After all, both Singapore and Hong Kong have *per capita* GDPs (on a purchasing power parity basis) greater than that of Japan, but until the current crisis have been growing two to three times as fast. Can we assume that this is a temporary aberration, and that as they become as rich as the EU or USA, they are condemned to slow down to the 2–3% growth experienced by the latter?

Economic growth in any country is an amalgam of labour and capital inputs and productivity gains, the latter being calculated as a residual after deducting labour and capital changes from that of output. It suffers from the same problem of measurement as all residuals – errors are magnified if the other terms in the equation are calculated incorrectly. For example, figures for total factor productivity (TFP), calculated by US economist Alwyn Young[6] for 118 countries over the period 1970–85, seemed to indicate that TFP growth in East Asia was no higher than that of the developed West.

This has prompted another economist, Paul Krugman,[7] to conclude that the so-called Asian miracle is a myth and that the growth is simply due to heavy capital investment and the drift off the land into factories. (Even if this were accepted, and IMF economist Michael Sarel[8] has calculated far higher TFP figures for ASEAN countries – 2–2.5% per annum *vs* 0.3% per annum for the USA – it is no mean feat to marshal such capital investment. Amongst other things it requires the governments concerned to create an environment attractive to suspicious foreign capital, for example a cheap and stable labour force, transparent company law, free capital movement and a reasonable tax structure. Many countries in the West have conspicuously failed to do just that.) What is more interesting here is Krugman's corollary that once the supply of inputs slows down and investment returns converge with Western levels, economic growth will become far more pedestrian. Here, he may well be right.

It must be recognised that, besides the rise in the yen, Tiger economies achieved their spectacular growth as a consequence of two main factors:

- an abundant labour force, with high birth rates reinforced by a move from the land to the cities;
- a growing focus on exports to the West, where consumption levels were so much higher than those of the exporters that even small market penetration made a major impact on their economies.

Both these benefits are now starting to unravel.

What is not in dispute is that one of the inputs, labour, will become increasingly scarce, for three reasons, falling birth rates, the move off the land is substantially over in many countries and rising education. Tightness in domestic labour supply and strong economic growth in South-East Asia has translated into soaring wages (15% per annum in South Korea, aggravated by rigid labour laws) or immigration (Malaysia) and the gradual abandonment of labour intensive industries to the Philippines, Indonesia and Vietnam. It is ironic that UK shipbuilders are now taking back business previously lost to Singapore. In some cases, the size of the population of working age will actually decline (*see* Table 14.2).

Table 14.2 Percentage change in population in 15–64 age group, 1995–2050

Country	1995–2020		2020–2050	
	Total change	% per annum	Total change	% per annum
Philippines	80.0	2.4	31.7	0.9
Malaysia	69.8	2.1	18.6	0.5
India	61.4	1.9	32.3	0.9
Thailand	35.3	1.2	5.3	0.2
China	22.3	0.8	−2.7	−0.1
Taiwan	17.5	0.7	−9.5	−0.3
South Korea	12.7	0.5	−11.2	−0.4
Japan	−13.7	−0.6	−17.0	−0.6

Source: Calculations based on data from World Bank, 1994.

Prospects for labour inputs become increasingly gloomy further down the table; China at least is still a predominantly agrarian society that can transfer labour from fields to factory, but Japan cannot. Furthermore, participation rates in Japan are the highest in all the OECD countries for the over-fifties, so that the scope for 'creating' more workers by bringing more of the elderly back into the workforce is very limited.

The corollary is that countries wanting to maintain their previous real GDP growth rates will have to boost their productivity by 1.0–1.5% per annum over current rates, and this will require substantially increased capital investment. Much of this will come from the West. A recent sign of this encouraging trend was the announcement by the new CEO of ABB, one of the world's leading suppliers of power stations and high-speed trains, that by 2001, around one-half of its workforce (currently 215 000) would be located in developing countries, compared with one-third in 1997, and implying a loss of some 30 000 jobs, mainly in Europe.

On the other hand, import penetration in the West has now reached levels where future growth in imports is likely to converge towards the overall level of economic growth. Furthermore, as population stagnates and then begins to decline in the West and Japan, and spending power comes under pressure from higher taxes, National Insurance contributions and direct payment for services provided by local government, it is hard to see how exports from the Tiger economies to the West can continue to grow at all strongly after the end of the century. There may, of course, be new fields to conquer by then, but spending power in Latin America, Southern Africa or Eastern Europe will take years to come anywhere close to that of the EU or USA. Finally, as mentioned earlier, the resurgence of Japan as an exporter, thanks to the 50% depreciation of the yen from its peak, must concern any competitor in the region, even after their own steep devaluations.

An increasing proportion of regional production will have to be sold within the region, which will pose problems for the manufacturers. In the past, when output was being targeted towards Western markets where domestic production costs were significantly higher, it hardly mattered whether the cost of an imported Korean TV set was 5% higher than one from Singapore or Taiwan, buyers could still be found. If, however these products are to be directed back into the region, where production costs are similar, such price variation could mean the difference between making or losing a sale. Competition will intensify, as will pressure on margins. Prices of goods in Japan are now actually falling.

What, then, of the future? Once the current property-cum-banking difficulties have been overcome, economic growth should resume, but at a lower rate, and the components of growth will be different from previous years. While Singapore has made the transition to higher technologies, neither Malaysia, Indonesia nor Thailand has done likewise, and they may all in the short-term find themselves trapped in labour-intensive medium technologies, lacking the investment in the education of skilled science and engineering graduates to enable them to move higher. The educational systems of Thailand and Indonesia are failing to deliver the increasingly skilled workforces that modern businesses need. As of 1993, under 40% of Thai children in their age group attended secondary school, compared to over 70% for the Philippines. There is a severe shortage of both engineering and science graduates and their quality is in doubt because of the failure of the bureaucracy to adjust to the rapid changes in the global economy. (Contrast this position with that of India, whose engineering institutes attract top quality students, and whose pharmaceutical industry has a growing international reputation.) Indeed, had it not been for the region's massive devaluations, some would have risked being priced out of world markets.

Asian reratings to come, thanks to demography

The shake-out of South-East Asian markets, and the advice to stay away from them until the dust has settled does not mean that the longer-term equity outlook isn't bright. For a start, their labour forces *will* grow, while those of Europe and Japan contract. As a first approximation, we can use Table 14.2 as a gauge of their relative attractiveness – always bearing in mind that rapidly growing population does not *automatically* equate with a buoyant economy unless other ingredients are in place, e.g., prudent government, low corruption, high savings ratios and investment in infrastructure.

Even more important is what is happening to savings rates, thanks to demographic trends. Because of the fall in birth rates, the child dependency ratio, i.e., the number of children aged 0–15 divided by the population of working age (16–59) is also in sharp decline, while the elderly dependency ratio will remain low for decades, because of the comparatively low average age. Furthermore, the average age of the *workforce* is rising, and because older and more experienced people earn more, the overall level of household income will increase, just when a smaller proportion of that income has to be devoted to supporting dependants.

Not all this increase in discretionary income will be spent, although it will help cushion domestic manufacturers faced with a slowdown in export markets and provide comfort to hoteliers worldwide. A lot will be saved, and savings ratios will rise even further from their current high levels. Besides continuing to fuel the domestic stock and property markets, these growing savings should, according to Jeffrey Williamson,

246

a Harvard economist, and Matthew Higgins of the Federal Reserve Bank of New York,[9] turn the region from an importer to an exporter of capital, like Japan before it.

Indeed, Peter S. Heller and Steve Symansky in another IMF Working Paper[10] make it clear just how important the 'Tiger' economies are going to be as a source of global savings next century. Overall savings rates in 'Tiger' economies will begin to fall by 2025, but not to the levels of those in industrialised countries. As a result, *their share of the combined savings of the Tigers' plus those of the industrialised countries is projected to rise to 30% by 2010, almost 50% by 2025 and to over 60% by 2050.*

What is this likely to mean to investors? Japan's rise in savings ratio in the late 1960s onwards was channelled into the domestic stockmarket, leading to a massive expansion of price/earnings multiples. Until the recent crash, the same was becoming true in South-East Asia. While collapsing property values and the cost of bailing out banks will destroy savings in the short-term, the uptrend will resume, and perhaps herald the dawn of higher, if not Japanese-style ratings.

The key to knowing when to begin to put money back into the region for this hoped-for rerating lies in the determination with which the relevant countries put their houses in order. According to Higgins and Williamson, after the perennial money-mill, Singapore, *the most rapid build-up in savings will occur in South Korea and China – two of the countries whose banking systems now give the greatest cause for concern.* If the authorities there can keep the systems afloat for the next three years, perhaps by recapitalising the better banks and allowing in foreign ones, as Thailand with far smaller problems has been forced to do, they could set the scene for a rip-roaring bull market at the start of the new millennium.

Japan

Japan, the world's second-largest stockmarket is likely to remain a disaster area over both the medium- and long-term. Domestic demand is weak, its principal market, South-East Asia, has disintegrated, and government is saddled with a massive bill to bail out the banking sector at a time when it is also under pressure to undertake further reflationary measures (partly to save Asia). Population is ageing rapidly, and the pension bill is set to soar, but as the workforce is already falling, tax rates

247

are bound to increase sharply, further depressing demand. With pedestrian economic growth likely, it is hard to justify high share ratings, while any fall below the 16 000 level would cause severe problems for the financial sector.

India

India has largely escaped the Asian crisis, although the rupee has weakened slightly, and the stockmarket has become, by default one of the largest in Asia. Given the large number of Western-managed funds that invest in the country, the market deserves attention.

Certainly, India is one country where labour inputs are unlikely to pose problems for decades. TFR is declining at a more sedate pace than for the rest of Asia, so the working age population is going to grow for far longer than for many other countries. Furthermore the products of the universities and engineering institutes are of high quality and interested in the rewards of capitalism. Indian expatriates educated overseas are returning home with the skills to make their fortunes. Industry is well-developed, despite the politics of envy acted out by the a Licence Raj that frowned on big business.

Unlike Eastern Europe, which had little in the way of advanced technologies (weaponry excepted), it is expanding rapidly into an area in which it appears to have considerable natural advantages – software development. In an economy where demand for electricity continues to outstrip supply and capital to build major new plants is expensive, but where skilled labour is cheap, a switch from manufacturing to services makes a lot of sense. The Indian software industry directly employs 160 000 in India with perhaps a further 100 000 working on contract overseas. Output grew by over 50% to Rs 63.1 billion in 1996/7 – a fivefold increase in five years – with exports touching $1 billion and forecast to reach $4 billion per annum by the end of the century. (As a sign of the times, in December 1997, a UK software services house, FI Group, agreed to pay £22 million for IIS Infotech, a New Delhi software company.) The two leading private training companies, NIIT and Aptech, claim to provide IT training for around 300 000 students a year, and they are now marketing their educational software and courses overseas.

The pharmaceutical sector, too, is booming. The loss of the system of process patents, which enabled Indian pharma companies to produce and sell drugs developed and still under patent elsewhere without incurring the research and clinical trial costs, has spurred the industry to accelerate its own R&D activities. It would be surprising if this did not lead to the marketing of genuinely new Indian-made products early next century.

India's problem is not demography but *democracy*. In its urge to give parliamentary representation to the entire spectrum of castes, religions, languages and regional identities, the country has saddled itself with a series of coalition governments incapable of taking tough decisions on a range of subjects. Top of the list are reform of *labour laws* which perpetuate overmanning, even if this leads to bankruptcy, of *rent control*, which has led to the decay of some of the finest buildings in Bombay and Calcutta, and of *price control*, which has created an environment of dependency and a crippling subsidy bill for the government.

That being said, economic growth rates have accelerated since the first reforms were introduced and companies given more freedom to operate. Indians are ingenious people. Because of the labour laws, companies are moving into new capital-intensive plants, despite the high cost of finance and the low level of salaries in India, and into new growth sectors, leaving obsolete jute and textile mills to wither on the vine. Moreover, the well-developed nationwide stockmarket has enabled a large number of companies to receive a listing and to tap funds for expansion. A burgeoning middle class, augmented by the new entrepreneurs from the private sector, should provide a rising tax base for the government, if the system is administered efficiently. Within 20–30 years, given sustained economic growth and falling birth rates, one would expect that the cumbersome legislation now in place to preserve jobs will be seen as increasingly irrelevant in the face of growing labour shortages, and that will be the time when Indian productivity will make the Great Leap Forward.

Both Federal and State governments control large portfolios of substantial companies which could be privatised if the political will exists or budget deficits demand. So far, the steps in this direction have been timorous, because of opposition from communists in the coalition and from trade unions. The privatisations that have taken place are so hedged that there is little scope for management to take independent action, but at least they are happening, unlike the case of China. It is however true that the level of foreign direct investment remains well below that of China, clearly signalling that overseas industrialists regard the communist Chinese leadership as more unambiguously capitalist than the Indians.

Tax reform is essential: only 12 million individuals pay tax and there is considerable evasion. Indeed a 1997 tax amnesty revealed hidden net assets of Rs 330 billion – over 3% of GDP – on which government has collected tax of 100 billion, against previous estimates ranging between Rs 20 billion and 60 billion. The scale of the receipts vindicates the view of the finance minister that when tax rates are reduced there is less incentive for evasion. Given tax reforms and improved collection, there is no reason why India should not rack up sustained budget surpluses, like Japan, Taiwan and Germany before it.

In a nation more fissiparous and less *dirigiste* than most of its Asian competitors, it would be surprising if this happened in practice – too many lobby groups want to spend rather than save. If India *did* achieve this, it would bring down inflation and interest rates, leading to lower borrowing costs and higher corporate profits. This in turn would trigger a rerating of the stockmarket enabling companies to greatly accelerate their capital investment programme, and ultimately higher levels of economic growth. Let us hope for a period of good firm government: it could make all the difference.

Meanwhile, the country's exporters have been beached by Asian devaluations, including a 9% devaluation by rival Pakistan. The trade position will deteriorate, and the currency could well come under renewed pressure through 1998. It seems unlikely that expatriate Indians will remit funds at their historic rate until they are confident that the Indian rupee has found a new floor, and nor should we, but the country is certainly one to watch closely this year, despite the impact of international sanctions following its programme of nuclear tests.

China

Since the agricultural reforms of the late 1970s, the economy has been storming along at growth rates of 9–10% a year. Given the marked slowdown in birth rates, the 7–8% annual increase in *per capita* GDP has been far more impressive than that of its Indian neighbour. China has avoided the USSR's approach to reform (which plunged the federation into years of chaos) by keeping strong political control while liberalising the economy and allowing in foreign investment. Between 1985 and 1995, utilised foreign direct investment rose from around $2 billion to $37 billion per annum, and the resultant exports from practically zero to $46 billion per annum where they accounted for 31.5% of total 1995 exports. For a brief period, inflation did get out of hand, but here too a soft landing has been achieved.

There remains much to be done. For a start, the growth in prosperity is not spread uniformly across the country, but concentrated on the coastal fringe. Shenzen, for example, has a *per capita* GDP five times that of the average, while many western provinces remain impoverished. A mass internal migration would be a costly way of solving this imbalance, since it would mean building huge quantities of housing and infrastructure to cope with the incomers. On the other hand, the internal road system is primitive and the railways operating at capacity, greatly increasing both costs and risks to new investors in the more remote regions.

Secondly, agricultural yields are stagnating, but government is unwilling to enable farmers to feed the growing population by giving them title to their land; while this would enable them to make long-term investment plans, it might reduce their dependence on the Party. (Interestingly, some 12 regions of Russia are bringing in laws permitting farmland to be bought and sold. No doubt the Chinese will be monitoring the effects of this closely, and while they remain convinced that the USSR has handled things very badly by bringing in democratic reforms that have led to its dismemberment, they are sufficiently pragmatic to use Russian techniques that are shown to work. After all, it was a Chinese communist leader who remarked that the colour of a cat didn't matter provided that it could catch mice.)

More serious than either of these, however, is the plight of the 305 000 State-owned enterprises (SOEs), inefficient, barely profitable and saddled with debts that they can never repay. These SOEs are in turn in hock to the State-controlled banking system which is similarly inefficient, overmanned and technically insolvent. Outside observers believe that bad debts could represent up to 44% of the banking system's loan portfolio – twice the official government figure. Putting this in context, this represents 35% of GDP; the bad debts of Japanese banks, the legacy of the bubble economy, are around 10% of GDP, while the level of bad debts at the time of the US savings-and-loans crisis reached a mere 2% of US GDP.

There is clearly a crisis looming, and the leadership is prepared to take the next logical step and privatise or close State companies, despite fears that this would cut the roots of their own power base, and that the resulting unemployment would destabilise the country. Thanks to the expansion of foreign investment, private and collectively-owned companies, the State sector's share of industrial output has slumped from around 80% in the late 1970s to around 30% by 1995. *Employment* in the overall State sector, however, has continued to rise from 72 million to over 110 million over the period, and even after a sharp fall in 1996 still accounts for 61% of the urban workforce, so closures must be handled sensitively, and further encouragement given to foreign investors to set up plants that will absorb those made redundant. *Indeed it has been suggested that real GDP must continue to rise by at least 9% compound if severe social unrest is to be avoided.*

Foreign direct investment in China remained at high levels for many years. It accounted for almost 6.5% of GDP by 1994, while that into East Asia represented only 2% of GDP that year and was in steep decline. Indeed, over-investment may have stored up another problem for China and the region. Overexpansion has led to large inventory buildup in Chinese industry, forcing companies to cut production and slash prices to clear stocks.

The recent round of sizeable devaluations and the squeeze on domestic demand in South-East Asia will further aggravate competition for Chinese industry, both within China and in export markets, putting greater pressure on their bankers. It seems that while the momentum was maintained through 1997, with actual foreign investment up by 8% for the first nine months of the year at $31.54 billion, *contracted* investment fell by 38.8% during the same period to $34.92 billion. It is likely that there will be a decline in investment in 1998, further slowing the economy, unless the Authorities take reflationary action. The government response has been a sensible one – accelerated expenditure on infrastructure and a drive to increase home ownership. These will mean a boost for the labour-intensive construction sector and an expansion of bank loans to the more credit-worthy home owners, reducing the dependence of the banks on SOEs. The banks themselves will be recapitalised.

Given both the potential size of the problem, however, and the effect that far less severe crises have had on the markets and economies of Japan and Thailand, it seems unnecessarily bold to invest in Chinese equities at present. The narrowness and lack of choice in the Shanghai and Shenzen markets, the controls exercised over them by government and the lack of strong domestic institutional investment all support the decision to stay away. Only when there is evidence that government is succeeding in tackling the bad debt problem and has sensible plans for coping with redundancies should the position be reviewed.

It is a truism that Hong Kong is a warrant on the Chinese economy, so the troubles of the latter cast a long shadow over the Hong Kong stockmarket to which investors fled to escape the Asian storm. Hong Kong property prices have fallen 20–30% and the support from well-connected mainland Chinese groups buying into Hong Kong assets has evaporated as their bankers can no longer lend them money. Since it is looking increasingly as if China will have a hard landing in 1998, and the fortunes of many listed Hong Kong companies are bound up in China, it may be wise to avoid the Hang Seng Index for some time.

Further ahead, as mentioned earlier, the picture is a lot brighter, and rising Chinese savings could lead to a rerating of markets in both China and Hong Kong.

Russia

Those carpetbaggers who invested in Russian vouchers, treasury bills (GKOs) and equities in 1995 were handsomely rewarded – at least up to late 1997, when the Asian crisis washed over them. Shares have since plummetted, the hot money left in droves and interest rates were hiked to penal levels to protect the currency. When will it be right to return?

At the time they invested, politics were unstable, inflation soaring, the currency plummetting. At the corporate level, there was no management in a Western capitalist sense, reliable information on the financial health of the companies was almost impossible to obtain, the incursions of foreign shareholders were resented and management would often refuse to enter their names as shareholders in the register. The market itself barely existed, there were no rules to prevent practices such as front-running – i.e., executing orders for the broking company ahead of orders from clients – and dealing spreads were as high as 10%.

What lured the buyers, despite all this, was the fact that they could buy into assets (say, a barrel of oil reserves or a kWh of electrical generating capacity) at a fraction of the cost of their equivalent in either developed or emerging markets, and their belief that as the economy became more Westernised, and the level of risk declined, in time, values would converge towards international levels.

In fact, all their sophisticated asset value calculations were based on a mass of assumptions that were wildly unrealistic, for two reasons. First, cash-strapped governments of Russia and Ukraine, and the pipeline companies carrying crude from the oilfields to the West regard the oil companies as fair game for tax and tariff increases, greatly diminishing their profitability and hence the value of oil in the ground. Secondly, because the economy contracted in real terms by 45% between 1989 and 1996, many companies can pay neither their workers nor their suppliers, and have had to resort increasingly to promissory notes or barter. (The government itself is a major cause of this problem: because tax collection has been so poor – tax collectors get shot in Russia – it is unable to pay for the services it receives from the newly privatised companies.) By 1997, barter accounted for almost half of all transactions, and company balance sheets are loaded down with bartered assets whose value it is hard to establish and receivables that may be worthless.

The economy itself is in no better shape. Although it recorded a current account surplus of $11.4 billion for 1996, the reality is far worse due to massive smuggling via Belarus and so-called shuttle goods from Turkey. When the economy finally revives, it will suck in massive quantities of consumer and capital goods. Of 1996 exports 45% were fuels (coal, oil and natural gas) and the price of oil has slumped as Asian demand evaporated and OPEC raised production quotas in late 1997. Capital investment in the Russian oil sector has fallen well below the levels needed to maintain output and the current weakness in the oil price has cut the cashflow of the oil companies, making it even harder for them to do so. Corruption, bureaucracy and the resistance of old-style management have held back foreign investment, and it will take years to restore output after seven years of massive under-investment.

Less than 25% of 1996 Russian exports was in the form of manufactured goods – machinery, chemicals, wood, pulp and paper, and textiles, little of which can be obtained elsewhere. Metals accounted for a further 19%, mostly in the form of scrap or raw metal rather than value-added products. Such a mix hardly gives confidence that Russia can pay its way in the future.

The budget is a mess, with the official 1996 Federal budget deficit of 3.3% of GDP ballooning to an 8.8% General government deficit, once the OECD has adjusted for the sleight-of-hand that kept some major expenditure off the balance sheet.[11] With oil, gold and base metal prices all weak due to the Asian crisis, corporate tax collection will remain a problem, and another difficult year lies ahead.

As with Eastern Europe, the population is in decline, and the trend seems likely to accelerate. On both the medium- and the long-term view, it is hard to believe that Russia will enter our investment universe any time soon. (The possibility of a strong rise in the oil price around 2010 when global production peaks out may appear to benefit Russia, as a major producer of oil and gas. But as Holland, Nigeria, Mexico and Venezuela have shown over the years such oil wealth has to be used responsibly, otherwise it leads to an overvalued currency, overdependence on a single product, massive subsidies and a dependency culture. Only if Russia followed the Norwegian road and placed windfall oil revenues in a trust fund should one be tempted into the market.)

Embarras de richesse?

Buoyant economic growth is rapidly reducing the US budget deficit to zero, while even in the EU, growth is reviving and causing deficits to at least top out and possibly decline in 1998. Japan is pumping up its money supply and interest rates are at record low levels, China and the rest of South-East Asia will be exporting capital and some of the problem countries of Latin America are being brought under control. So – if governments don't need the extra money saved in Asia, what will happen to it?

One of Keynes' recurrent nightmares was of a surplus of investment funds, unable to get the returns their owners required, and therefore idle, precipitating a deep recession. In a sense, this has already happened in Japan, where prime rate is down to 1.65% but investment activity is sluggish because of the huge overcapacity built up in the late 1980s. The problems of the property and financial sectors may mean that Japan is a special case, but Korea, with its high wages, industrial (rather than property) overcapacity and highly geared *chaebol*, seems to be following Japan's example.

On the other hand, it could be argued that the steady decline in global inflation resulting from tighter budgetary policies and the switch to higher savings ratios will reduce both the cost of capital and a company's risk in making a capital investment. This in turn should lead to a decline in the hurdle rate – i.e., the return on investment required if the project is to be authorised. After all, investors may want 40–50% annual returns to compensate for Russian risk, but would settle for 15% in the USA or EU.

The corollary is that existing assets giving returns in excess of this hurdle rate will be bid up in price until the return on purchase cost comes close to the hurdle rate. This will apply whether the asset is a

255

bond, an equity or real estate. In other words, the Keynesian nightmare need not happen. Instead, surplus cash will be attracted to the two lightning conductors that have always earthed it – the stockmarkets and property markets, which will boom, while investors will have to accept lower yields or dividends. As mentioned earlier, this does not mean that the laws of supply and demand have been suspended, merely that the market has been granted a breathing space that could allow it to achieve higher levels before topping out. The important thing is to be positioned to ride the next rerating wave when it occurs.

References

1 *The FT Exporter UK 100*, 1996.

2 *Financial Times*, 3 June 1997.

3 *Financial Times*, 29 August 1997.

4 *Financial Times*, 3 October 1997.

5 *Financial Times*, 26 March 1997.

6 Young, A. 'The Tyranny of numbers: Confronting the Statistical Realities of the East Asian Growth Experience,' *Quarterly Journal of Economics*, Aug. 1995.

7 Krugman, P. 'The Myth of Asia's Miracle,' *Foreign Affairs*, Vol. 73, No. 6, 1994.

8 Sarel, M. 'Growth and Productivity in ASEAN Countries,' IMF Working Paper 97/97, Aug. 1997.

9 Higgins, M. and Williamson, J. G. 'Age Structure Dynamics in Asia and Dependence on Foreign Capital,' *Population and Development Review*, 23 (2): June 1997.

10 Heller, P. S. and Symansky, S. 'Implications for Savings of Aging in the Asian Tigers,' *IMF Working Paper*.

11 *OECD Economic Surveys*, Russia, p. 56, Dec. 1997.

STOCKTAKING

The data presented in this book has a consistent message. Without a marked rise in birth rate, which seems increasingly unlikely, or greatly increased immigration, with all the problems this implies, Europe will begin to die. There will not be sufficient workers to run industry or to tend the sick. Without a radical rethink by government and workers alike, existing State pension schemes will self-destruct because of an unacceptable rise in contribution rates and the growth of the black economy. Tensions between workers and pensioners will increase and will become increasingly bitter at election times. We need a dozen Iron Chancellors throughout Europe to force through the unpalatable reforms necessary to increase the size of the workforce and palliate the looming increases in taxes and/or government debt, otherwise economic growth may not simply slow down – it may vanish completely.

Europe's influence on the world stage will decline, and not only because its population will be falling as those of the Asian Tigers continues to rise. European competitiveness will slip because pensions in emerging economies are increasingly fully funded, and therefore less vulnerable to deteriorating demographics, while those in Europe are not. That is, the social costs funded by employers will rise more rapidly in the EU than elsewhere. This will accelerate the already well-established trend of European companies expanding abroad rather than investing at home.

(*Memo to European Foreign Offices*: The Continent could also become increasingly dependent upon emerging economies to fund government debt. The rapid ageing of workforces in Asia will boost their savings just at the time when the funding needs of European governments take off. There is a risk that financial dependency will bring political dependency. China, with superpower ambitions, may prove a more demanding bank manager than Japan, a country conscious of its military vulnerability and its reliance on the USA for protection.)

There is a small window of opportunity which will remain open until around 2005. Until then, the combination of economic recovery and relatively favourable demographics should enable EU governments to rein in their budget deficits, keeping interest rates low and the environment for equities favourable. Those governments that fail to do so risk storing up possibly unrepayable debts. Individuals saving for their retirement must also make use of this opportunity: after that, deterioration is rapid and continuous for almost a quarter of a century, and could be intensified by a potential upsurge in the oil price from 2010 onwards.

The rate and extent of the deterioration will vary markedly with the country – the demographics and the policy actions of the governments concerned – but what is clear is that those in the weakest position are the least likely to make the necessary reforms. Because of this, economic performance will begin to diverge sharply within Europe, causing strains that could tear the single currency apart early next century. Certainly there can be no prospect of convergent tax rates while the pressures on countries differ so greatly.

Finally, it is hoped that this book has convinced those of you who have read this far of the power of demographics not only to forecast major trends well into the next century but also to enable you to protect yourselves financially in a future that could be far less pleasant than you might have imagined. It even suggests the best place to return to in Europe. See you in Dublin.

GLOSSARY

Demographics

Cohort A group of people sharing a common demographic experience through time, e.g., the female marriage cohort of 1998 would be the women married in that year.

Completed fertility The average number of children born to a cohort of women through their reproductive lives (taken as 15–49).

Net reproduction rate (NRR) The average number of daughters that would theoretically be born alive to a woman during her reproductive lifetime if each childbearing year conformed to the age-specific fertility and mortality rates of a given year. An NRR of 1.0 means that each cohort of women would exactly reproduce itself; in Western countries, this corresponds to a TFR of around 2.1.

Participation rate for a given age group is the ratio of the total (or civilian) labour force to the total population in that age group.

Total fertility rate (TFR) The average number of children that would theoretically be born to a woman during her reproductive lifetime if each childbearing year conformed to the age-specific fertility rate.

Total labour force (or currently active population) comprises all those in employment together with those who are (i) unemployed, (ii) available for work and (iii) are actively seeking work.

Pensions

Benefit rate The ratio of average pension to average economy-wide wage (or covered wage).

Defined benefit A guarantee by the insurer or pension fund that benefits will be paid according to a defined formula.

Defined contributions A pension scheme under which contribution levels are fixed but benefit depends on the level of contributions and investment returns, which are not guaranteed.

Implicit net public pension debt The present value of outstanding pension claims on the public sector less any accumulated reserves.

Old age dependency ratio The ratio of those above retirement age to those of working age.

Pension coverage rate The proportion of the labour force actively contributing to a publicly mandated retirement scheme.

Replacement rate The value of a pension as a proportion of a worker's wage during some base period – e.g., the average of the last few years before retirement.

System dependency The ratio of people receiving benefits from a pension scheme to the number of contributors to the scheme during the same period.

Universal flat benefit Pensions paid solely on the basis of age and citizenship, regardless of prior work or contribution records.

INDEX